THE NEW RULES

An Old Man Held Hostage by the Radical
Right Iowa Legislature and Governor

B. John Burns

DEDICATION
This book is dedicated to Chief Justice Mark Steven Cady, and to the three justices removed in the 2010 purge. All paid a grim price for their courage.

ACKNOWLEDGEMENTS
The author wishes to thank Caitlin Jarzen, Steve Davis, Senator Nate Boulton, Cindy Chooraman and others who helped guide me through the choppy waters of understanding the process of revising the Iowa Rules of Criminal Procedure.

This book recounts, from the perspective of the author, true events. Two fictional characters have been created to play the roles of individuals who are peripheral to the story.

CONTENTS

FOOL ME TWICE

The one thing that might possibly compare to the experience I'm about to relate would be that of carrying a child full-term and checking in to the maternity ward on the blessed date, only to be turned away and told *not today. Come back in a few months and maybe we'll do it then.*

I'm an old man. A few months is a precious commodity for me.

* * *

On Friday, February 17, 2023, the Iowa Supreme Court released a twelve-page written opinion in the case of *Kirk Howsare and Austin Howsare v. Iowa District Court for Polk County*, 986 N.W.2d 114 (Iowa 2023). On August 13, 2021, the Howsares, a father and son business team, were entangled in a dispute with a woman who they believed did not have the necessary paperwork to attend a business meeting in which they were participating. Consequently, they were arrested and charged with simple misdemeanor assault, an offense that in Iowa carries a potential fine of between $105 and $855 and/or a maximum of 30 days in jail.

Pursuant to warrants issued on September 13, the arrests came on the afternoon of Tuesday, November 2, 2021, two and a half months after the incident. The Howsares were detained in the Polk County Jail until the following morning, when they appeared before a district associate court judge. They were released on a $100 bond and orders were issued prohibiting them from having contact with the woman. The following day, crackerjack West Des Moines Defense Attorney Dean Stowers entered his appearance as counsel for both Howsares, along with a plea of not guilty and a jury demand. A week later Stowers filed motions to dismiss charges in both cases.

On various grounds, Attorney Stowers took exception to the September 13 warrants that provided that the Howsares would not be permitted to bond out until they were first brought before a judge. He argued that the no-bond warrants were unreasonable seizures under the Fourth Amendment to the United States Constitution and article 1, section 8 of the Iowa Constitution. There is right under article 1, section 12 of the state constitution to "be bailable, by sufficient sureties." Iowa Code § 804.3 requires a magistrate issuing a warrant for a bailable offense to endorse the warrant with the amount of bail and other necessary conditions of release. Making the two defendants stay in jail overnight, they contended, amounted to unnecessary delay.

Judge Gregory Brandt denied the motion to dismiss on December 1, 2021. On February 2, 2022, the Iowa Supreme Court granted Stowers' motion for a writ of certiorari and agreed to review the legal decisions made by Judge Brandt.

The decision of the Iowa Supreme Court was unanimous, with all seven Justices joining the opinion of Justice Christopher Lee McDonald. In it, the Court ruled against the Howsares on all issues presented. The magistrate made a finding when the warrant was issued that there was probable cause to believe the defendants had committed an offense. A seizure of a person is reasonable under the Fourth Amendment and article 1, section 8 if there is a finding of probable cause. The article 1, section 12 right to bail with sureties does not require "unlimited, unfettered access to bail." There is no right to be released prior to a timely initial appearance before a judge. Necessary conditions of release endorsed on a warrant under § 804.3 may include a requirement that the defendant be held until the initial appearance. Even if there were violations, the proper remedy would not be dismissal. And, because the Howsares were brought before a judge within 24 hours, there was no unnecessary delay.

It's that last one that sparked my interest.

It was twelve days after it was announced that I dug into the *Howsare* opinion. I have to read them all. All the decisions of the Iowa Supreme Court and the United States Supreme Court on cases involving criminal law and procedure. I digest them, summarize them, and work them into my book and my continuing legal education seminar lectures.

I had put this one off a little, because it involved a simple misdemeanor. Minor cases with little significance. Was it even worth my time?

Big things come in small packages.

What grabbed my attention and left me feeling queasy was Justice McDonald's "unnecessary delay" analysis. Under Iowa Rule of Criminal Procedure 2.1(2)(d), unnecessary delay is defined expressly as "any unexcused delay longer than 24 hours (or) a shorter period whenever a magistrate is accessible and available."

Okay, that's right. But there's more, isn't there? *For the love of God, Justice McDonald, please say there's more.*

What Justice McDonald is quoting is the rule. As the rule stands *today*. If I opened up my 2023 Iowa Rules of Court on March 1, that's what I would see. Rule 2.1(2)(d) defined unnecessary delay as "any unexcused delay longer than 24 hours (or) a shorter period whenever a magistrate is accessible and available." But if I accessed the rules digitally, on WestLaw, I would find two versions of Iowa Rule of Criminal Procedure 2.1. There's the version in effect until June 31, 2023, which mirrors the language in the *Howsare* opinion. And there's the "effective July 1, 2023" version, that doesn't mention the 24-hour rule.

What I knew was that post July 1 there was a new Iowa Rule of Criminal Procedure 2.2(2) providing that the defendant must appear "either personally or by interactive audiovisual system as provided by rule 2.27(1)(a) within 24 hours unless no magistrate is available and in all events within 48 hours."

Since Justice McDonald authored an opinion released on February 17, *before* July 1, he was entirely accurate. What's giving me this horrible sinking feeling, however, is that there's no mention at all of the fact that in four and a half months the rules are slated to change. Those Supreme Court opinions are meant to serve as precedent for courts to follow down the line, not just today.

Could this really be happening to me again?

Because as bad as it was for me last year, it would be much worse if they were doing it to me *this* year. Each year, I send the annual revisions to *4A Iowa Practice: Criminal Procedure* to my publisher by December 10. In early February the publisher sends me the proofs for the new edition and gives me two weeks to make corrections and additional updates. The volume is released in April.

Last year, word of the major rules revisions reached me at the same time I received the proofs. I worked like a dog for two weeks to incorporate the new rules into the manual only to learn on the day they were to be submitted that there would be no new rules for the time being. I had to scramble to undo all the new rules revisions, and essentially in the end lost about eighty hours of frantic labor.

But by October it appeared the SNAFU with the new rules had been resolved. After a less desperate but nevertheless labor-intensive push, I managed to work them into my December revisions. The rule changes are *in the proofs.* It was a lot of work for me, and a load of work for the editors, who had gotten them to me on February 21. I had been given until March 7 to make my final revisions.

But then March 1 comes along and I'm reading *Howsare*, the Supreme Court review of a simple misdemeanor case. And there's a discussion of the rules, but *no mention* that the rules are about to change.

Maybe I'm just overthinking this.

So who do I call? I went through this last year. Last year I had friends on the blue-ribbon task force commissioned to revise the rules who had bits and pieces for me. Ultimately, I got the answers I needed from Steve Davis, the communications director for the Iowa Judicial Branch. He was probably my first call this time around, but it went to voice mail. When I feel the blood pressure ramping up like this, I've learned, it's not a wise time to leave a voice mail. My calls to everyone were going to voice mail.

And once again I had no clue what I was dealing with. Or if there was even a problem. It could just be paranoia from living in a world, as Springsteen put it, in which you "end up like a dog that's been beat so much, till you spend all your time just covering up." Maybe I was worrying about absolutely nothing.

Nope.

My former co-worker, Rachele, has had a three-decade career in the Iowa Legislative Services Agency. They help Iowa legislators draft bills. I don't know how much they would know about Supreme Court rules in the Legislative Services Agency but, considering that it was the Legislature that jammed the rake handle in between the spokes of the Court's bicycle last year and sent the whole process careening down the hill, maybe Rachele was worth a call.

Rachele was tied up, but the woman who took the call made one of those *is there something I can do for you* offers. Probably not, I admitted, because this involves the Supreme Court Rules and not the Iowa Code. In a perfect world, the Judicial Branch drafts its own rules and the Legislature passes bills. There *is* a guy in the office who does know quite a bit about the rules, she told me, and put me through to him.

I was bird-dogging so many people that morning that I cannot remember the name of the guy I talked to. But he did understand what I was asking about. And he delivered the bad news. There is a bill in committee in both houses right now that places specific controls on Iowa court procedures. Yes, the new rules will not go into effect until they are amended to be consistent with whatever is passed and signed by the governor. And yes, the new rules, if they are even adopted this year, may be vastly different from what appeared in the October 17 order of the Supreme Court.

I think I'm going to be sick.

Is this even *worth it*? Same question I asked last year. The criminal procedure manual and a small handful of CLE lectures each year are the final vestige of my 38-year law career. My life over the past four years has transitioned from that to a full-time seven-day-a-week diet of songwriting and book-writing. The manual keeps my foot in the door and is my single largest source of earned income. After freeing up those forty or fifty hours formerly spent each week in courthouses, jails, the office and in the car going from one to the other, I have more time to devote to studying the court opinions and making the manual more comprehensive and accurate. But it is a time commitment, and an inordinately major time commitment in 2022 and 2023 as I find myself caught center table in the ping pong match between the Judicial and Legislative (and the Executive) Branches. If I stopped doing the manual, that would signal the end of the law career. I'd burn the license. But I think I'm better now at it than I've ever been, and I think it's especially a benefit to the publisher that it's me doing it last year and this year, because I have the time to make some sense out of the turmoil.

But I can't deny that my resolve on this matter was less firm on March 1 than it is today.

Shortly after my conversation with the gentleman from the Legislative Services Bureau, I received a call from Caitlin Jarzen, an attorney who was the director of intergovernmental affairs for the Judicial Branch. One of my calls to Steve Davis or other officials in the Judicial Branch had been referred to Ms. Jarzen. She updated me on the details of the new legislation.

March 1 falls squarely in the middle of the first "funnel week" of the Iowa Legislature. Any bill that is going to be passed during a 110-day annual session of the Legislature must be approved by a full committee no later Friday, March 3rd. Senate File 204, the fly in the ointment of my manual revisions, had been approved in subcommittee and was coming up this very afternoon for a vote by the Senate Judiciary Committee. Its counterpart in the House of Representatives, House Study Bill

156, was following a similar trajectory. By the second funnel date of March 31, one of them must be approved on the floor of either the House or the Senate and that bill must be approved by a full committee of the other house. There was little doubt but that a bill, in some form, was going to pass.

The Legislature, Ms. Jarzen informed me, was scheduled to adjourn on April 28 which, parenthetically, would be my 67th birthday and the seventh day of my annual nine-day sojourn on the beaches of Waikiki. That's the latest we might have a clear picture of what we're dealing with. She promised to keep me up to date on the progress of the legislation.

It occurred to me after the conversation with Ms. Jarzen that I know someone on the Senate Judiciary Committee. Nate Boulton is a Des Moines attorney and a potential leader of the Iowa Democratic Party. Senator Boulton informed me via a Facebook message that SF204 was coming up for a vote in the committee the following afternoon and contacted me again on Thursday with the heads up that prompted me to watch the proceeding on video. It was over in a matter of minutes.

Senate File 204 was reported out of the committee on Monday, March 6 and renumbered as Senate File 253. House Study Bill 156 was reported out of the House Judiciary Committee on March 7, and renumbered as House File 644. It was amended and passed by the full House on March 22 by a vote of 97-0. On the following day it was attached to SF253.

As this bill was on its way to becoming law, the nagging question was *what the hell do I **do**?* Once passed and signed by the governor, the Supreme Court would have to modify the new rules to match the changes contained within it. Then the new revised rules would be submitted for legislative council review. If the Court didn't play ball, or if the Legislature still balked on approving them, there would be no rules and we'd stay with the old ones until the impasse was resolved. If for some reason the bill *didn't* pass by the end of the session, we might see the same result.

For every piece of legislation on the road to enactment, the legislative services agency must prepare a fiscal note, summarizing the bill and forecasting its impact. The note considers such factors as minority impact, correctional impact and, most importantly, its fiscal impact.

Like the Legislature and the governor, and the Court, what the legislative services agency does *not* consider is the impact a bill like this is going to have on poor John Burns. I was caught in the damned crossfire. I was in limbo.

As of mid-March, what my publisher had was a proof version of the 2023 manual which incorporated the rules as they would have looked after the previous October, when the Supreme Court released what I was comfortable believing was the final version of the newly revised Iowa Rules of Criminal Procedure that would go into effect on July 1, 2023. To meet the March 17 deadline for final revisions, the publisher also had my post-December updates and my corrections to the proof version. The manual was ready to go, as it had been every year for two decades, in April.

But no matter what happened in the next one to two months with the Legislature, the governor and the Court, the manual in its present form was inaccurate. It could only be accurate if the Legislature stepped in and said, "Never mind. We're going to leave things the way they were after October. Sorry for the inconvenience."

That was unlikely.

The difference between the status quo and what would come out after Governor Kim Reynolds signed the bill into law might be relatively minimal. That didn't make my work any easier. The inevitable slight change in a rule number or the addition or deletion of a few phrases would send me burrowing through a 1200-page manuscript line-by-line to ensure that what is in my book accurately reflects what is in the rules.

And if the impasse festered on, and the Court didn't amend the rules to the satisfaction of the Legislature, then the old rules would remain in effect. I'd have to go through the proof manuscript and *remove* the hundreds and hundreds of revisions I submitted in November. That would be worse even than last year, when I had to set aside hundreds and hundreds of revisions before they went to the publisher. The same would be true in the unlikely occurrence that no bill was passed.

On top of this all is the increased potential for human error. Mistakes by *me*. I'm looking at revisions to revisions to revisions. When the Court first proposed the new rules, it attached summaries of how they differed from the previous ones. When it released the October 2022 revisions, it explained how they differed from the original proposed rules. Now there's another round coming. As I reviewed my final product, I'd be holding the changes up in comparison not to the original rules but to the rules as they would have existed after October, because that's how they appear in the proofs. Does that sound confusing?

My point exactly.

HOW I GOT THIS GIG

To be completely honest, I'd never put myself high on any list of the great legal minds one might expect to see authoring a legal treatise on criminal procedure.

It's not that I'm necessarily stupid. I did, after all, manage to graduate *Phi Beta Kappa*, for whatever that's worth. And, once I started taking it seriously after returning from my four-year hiatus as a failed rock star, I found ways to finish at the top of each of my undergraduate classes. I was selected as the 1982 Outstanding Senior in the University of Iowa College of Journalism, so there obviously was some potential as a writer.

I was very impressed with myself.

My boyhood career aspiration had been to become a lawyer, but any taste for that faded the first time, as a high school senior, I played one of my songs to an appreciative audience. I knew I couldn't make the grades to get into law school.

I was a different person when I came back.

Early in my junior year of college after the rock dream had flared out, I was on the phone with Paul Goldsmith, a high school classmate now in his second year of law school.

"How'd you do on your LSATs?" he asked me. Actually, it hadn't occurred to me to sit for the Law School Admission Test. That ambition had left me six years earlier. But Paul brought it up, so I took the test. I really didn't have any other plans after graduation.

I was accepted into the law school of my choice.

I figured I would *breeze* through law school.

Law School

The first thing you discover in law school, however, is that from day one you are surrounded by men and women who, without exception, were at the tops of every class *they* were in. And some of them had taken the intense science and math classes, yet *still* maintained their 4.0 grade point averages. The strategic course selection and politicking augmented with a modicum of bribery and intimidation, all of which had gotten me through the door, had little utility once inside. I'd have to earn whatever I got here.

And the gospel truth is that the author of a manual in criminal procedure that has been used by defense attorneys, some judges and even prosecutors in a new edition released every year for nearly a quarter century received his *lowest grade in law school* in criminal procedure. When I was there at least, they didn't issue letter grades in law school. But my final grade of 66, from the conventional wisdom of the time about the relationship between the 0 to100 scores that were given out and A through F letter grades, was a solid D. The instructor in that course, along with an evidence course the same semester in which I did just slightly better, was a visiting professor who, for the class text, sold us draft manuscripts of a casebook he was in the process of writing. He and I didn't gel on any level.

I did somewhat better in other courses. With a different professor I scored an 87 in criminal law, close to what was considered an A. My best grades, ironically, were in tax classes. There was one called taxation of gratuitous transfers in which I brought in my best grade in law school. Not only did I come in at the top of that class; my score was the highest any student had ever attained on one of that professor's multiple-choice finals.

Passing in the hallway just days after course grades were posted, the professor, a well-regarded expert in his field, pulled me aside for the only conversation we would ever have outside of one of his classes.

"Was that you?" he asked.

"It was."

"I don't understand it."

"I don't, either."

That was it. What is funny about that whole chain of circumstances was that, even after earning the highest grade any student ever attained in that study of taxation of gratuitous transfers, I couldn't tell you what the phrase "taxation of gratuitous transfers" *meant*. Just recently, 40 years later, I have deconstructed the phrase and now figure it must have had something to do with gift taxes.

I can't escape the feeling that my failure to thrive in law school as well as I did as an undergraduate had to have something to do with my abysmal handwriting. That's something I inherited from my father who, in turn, inherited it from his father. I can't decipher my own writing at times.

But the final grade in every class in law school was based exclusively upon a final examination consisting of a handful of essay questions. Students were assigned small booklets into which they were expected to scribble their answers in pencil. I didn't have a fighting chance. The only exception I recall, notably, was the multiple-choice examination for taxation of gratuitous transfers.

I didn't complain. I didn't kill myself jockeying for a spot at the top of my class. Because I had been out of school for four years after my freshman undergraduate year, and because my father was helping me out with tuition and expenses, I did what I could to get in and out of law school as painlessly as possible. The University of Iowa, at least in 1982, had an accelerated program. You entered in the summer rather than in the fall. There is a summer semester of classes in lieu of the three months others take off to regroup and to attain some practical work experience. It was possible for a summer entrant to complete law school in two years and three months rather than the conventional three years.

My undergraduate commencement, which should have been a joyous celebration, was consequently one of the most depressing days of my early life. I walked the plank for my diploma on Saturday morning, ate lunch with my family, then spent the afternoon buried in law books preparing for my first law school class on Monday.

But one unique facet of the program was that most of the summer entrants were people like me, who'd had other careers or were primarily interested in augmenting an ongoing professional career with a law degree. We were older students with more practical life experience than the fall entrants, and with a little acquired wisdom. There was more to life, for us, than doing battle with the budding young barristers for class rank and order of the coif. We worked hard, but we made the time for other pursuits.

I did all right. I battled back quite a bit in the final year. While many of my classmates were consumed with job searches and internships, I buckled down and reverted to the trusted undergraduate strategy of signing up for the less complex electives to boost my GPA. Ultimately, I graduated with distinction, which means simply that I graduated in the top *half* of my class. Considering that every one of my classmates was at the top of his or her class as an undergraduate, I'll take that.

Clinic

Salvation for me was the clinic. The entire direction of my career as a lawyer was charted when I signed up for the University of Iowa Prisoner Assistance Clinic. There is this perception of me that I was destined from the start to be a criminal defense attorney, especially since my exit from the music business and return to college was precipitated by a near miss with the criminal justice system. The truth is that, well into my final semesters, I still had no idea what direction I was headed with my law degree. I'd worked at the bank the last eight months before returning to college and during the summers after my sophomore and junior years. Considering that together with my success in law school tax classes, I'd toyed with the prospect of pursuing a job as a trust officer in a bank. A D in criminal procedure didn't bode well for a career in criminal defense.

But I spent my final two semesters immersed in providing a panoply of legal services to inmates of the Iowa State Penitentiary at Fort Madison and of what was then the Iowa Men's Reformatory in Anamosa. We did not represent defendants in their pending criminal cases. Much time in clinic was focused upon responding to correspondence from inmates, providing answers where answers were readily available. I compiled three years of tax returns for a lifer who was suing the state after being injured while working in prison industries.

The clinic was involved in monitoring the performance of a settlement of long-term ongoing litigation concerning conditions in the maximum security units at the penitentiary. For that, there were three 180-mile round trips to Fort Madison, at the time the oldest prison facility west of the Mississippi River, for meetings between a council of violent offenders, two or three students from the clinic and our faculty advisor.

Many of my clinical hours went into the case of a University of Iowa football player who had been convicted nine years earlier of the 1973 murder of a nursing student in her dormitory room, the first murder ever on the Iowa campus. The second-degree murder conviction had been vacated in May of 1984 based upon misconduct by law enforcement during the original investigation. I spent the summer of '84 reviewing voluminous police reports, scientific reports, trial transcripts and depositions, all in preparation for the impending retrial. During the final week of August, however, the case was brought before the grand jury, which declined to indict the defendant, and the case was dismissed.

During the fall semester leading to my graduation, the University of Iowa murder case now concluded, I dug into *Fryer v. Nix*, the case that opened the door to a 34-year seven-month criminal defense career.

On a late evening just over a decade earlier, five teenagers encircled a campfire at Gitchie Manatou State

Park in Lyon County, Iowa, playing guitars and smoking marijuana. The four boys and one girl, ranging in age from 13 to 18, were unaware that they were being observed by three brothers, Allen, David and James Fryer. Thinking they could purloin the marijuana for themselves, the Fryers retrieved shotguns from their pickup truck. Allen and David Fryer took positions on a ridge and opened fire, killing one of the boys instantly and wounding another. They ordered the others to come out of hiding and, when they emerged, Allen shot and injured another of the boys. The brothers identified themselves to the youths during the siege as police officers.

Allen tied the hands of the one girl, 13-year-old Sandra Cheskey, behind her back. Later, he untied her and drove away with her in the pickup truck. It would be the last time she saw her friends alive. As they drove around the area Allen told Sandra that, in his capacity as a police officer, he was trying to keep her out of trouble and that she was too young to be arrested for the marijuana. After they met up with the other Fryers on the road, James accompanied them to an abandoned farmhouse, where he sexually abused Sandra. Though he promised his brothers he was going to kill her, Allen then drove Sandra home. All four of the boys died that night.

For days, law enforcement was perplexed. In the absence of any useful leads as to who committed the heinous offense, investigators drove Sandra over the country roads she believed she had traveled with Allen on November 17, 1973, and to the old farmhouse where she was raped by Allen's brother. The break in the case came one afternoon as she sat in the police vehicle, and suddenly observed a passing pickup truck that she recognized as the Fryers' vehicle. Allen was driving. The pieces of the puzzle all fell into place after that.

It was Allen's case that I worked on during my final semester in law school.

Allen was convicted of four counts of murder in the first degree on August 13, 1974. He appealed his conviction, but his lawyer could find no appealable issues in his case and his appeal was dismissed as frivolous on March 19, 1975. Allen's petition for writ of habeas corpus in federal court was dismissed because he had not yet pursued the remedy of postconviction relief in state court after the dismissal of his state appeal. A postconviction relief application filed in 1977 was dismissed by the state district court on the ground that Allen had not met time deadlines set by the court in that case. The dismissal was overruled on April 25, 1979 and Allen was given permission to move ahead with his postconviction action.

This, I believe, was where the prisoner assistance clinic at the Iowa Law School began working on the case. In his renewed postconviction relief petition, Allen raised nine separate claims as to why his conviction violated the law. The district court rejected each of them, and the case went up to the Iowa Supreme Court. Allen was represented at that level by Professor Michael D. Green of the Iowa Law School and three legal interns from the prisoner assistance clinic. In a unanimous five-justice majority opinion authored by Justice Arthur McGiverin and released on October 27, 1982, the Supreme Court ruled against Mr. Fryer on all issues.

A term of a student in the prisoner assistance clinic is one semester, about three months, although a student is welcome to serve more than one term. I served two, the summer and fall semesters of 1984. Several cases handled by the clinic, such as Mr. Fryer's, progress over a period of years. They consequently involve a progression of legal interns akin to a long-distance relay race. The constants are the faculty advisors like Professor Green. One intern or team of interns gets the ball rolling, and others pick up where the previous ones left off.

After the Iowa Supreme Court, a team of interns prepared the elaborate petition for habeas corpus to be filed in the United States District Court. By May 11, 1983, when it was filed, I was halfway through law school but not yet involved in clinic. I had no idea at the time that this was occurring. The issues set out in the habeas corpus petition generally paralleled those in the state proceeding. With rare exceptions, the federal court will consider only the issues that have been "fully exhausted" in state court, so they say. United States District Court Judge William Stuart denied the petition in full and the case was brought up on review to the Eighth Circuit Court of Appeals, the last stop before the United States Supreme Court.

When I entered the picture, the Eighth Circuit brief had already been written by Professor Green and the prisoner assistance clinic interns who preceded me on the case. The brief is the written argument to the Court and the centerpiece of a party's representation in an appeal. It sets out, in detail, the history of procedures that have taken place in the case to date, the factual evidence that was brought out in the district court, and the issues – the legal reasons why the district court did not correctly follow the law in reaching the decision that is now on appeal. The argument on each issue is supported by *precedent*, the appellate courts' decisions in other cases in which the same or similar issues were raised and the reasoning behind them. The appeals court generally will consider only the arguments raised in the brief. By necessity, the issues argued at the federal level mirrored those raised by the clinic in the state postconviction proceeding.

Although my recollection has faded somewhat after 39 years, I believe the *Fryer* brief was about sixty pages long. It was not something that I, at that stage of my career, could have written. It was typographically and grammatically immaculate (having come out of a lucrative private practice, Professor Green was a stickler for perfection in everything that bore his signature, right down to letters to our clients) and the issues were thoroughly researched and argued. It seems I had a role in finalizing the brief before filing it. Primarily, I was there to present the case if it was set for argument during my term in the clinic.

The Bar Exam

Aside from the fact that nearly four decades have passed since my clinic days, there's a reason why my recollection of much of that experience is rather dim. As much time as I put into it, clinic wasn't my driving preoccupation during those two final semesters. Commencement from the Iowa College of Law would take place on Saturday, December 15, 1984. Thirty-seven days later I would sit for the three-day Iowa bar exam.

The bar exam is not something you prepare for in five weeks. It is the most consequential and stress-filled ordeal in the lives of most lawyers. That's exactly what it is. An ordeal. In the classic sense.

One of the two things you don't discover until you become a licensed, practicing attorney (at least in my day) is that law school prepares you for one thing, and it's *not* taking the bar exam. Law school is the basic training you undergo to acquire the tools that help you "think like a lawyer." It trains you to find the law and then to analyze it. They teach you very little law in law school. You're expected to accept the tools with which you are equipped and use them to go out and find the law yourself. That's important, because the law is a dynamic organism. It is always changing. If I take a course on federal taxation during my second semester of law school, it is possible that by the time I graduate and sit for the bar a measurable amount of what I was taught in that course has already become obsolete. What was the "law" in 1982 may, by 1985, have been ameliorated by rule changes, new statutes and the decisions of appellate courts that analyze the law as it applies to the cases before them and consequently to all cases that follow.

But the bar exam is all about the law. It's about the law as it exists on the day you take the exam. It may be different today with the more uniform multi-state examination, but in my day the exam consisted of five three-hour sessions – two on Monday, two on Tuesday and one on Wednesday. In each, they threw five hypothetical stories at you, and you were required to choose three to which to respond with an essay. After reading the meandering fact pattern, the first task was to determine what area of the law is evoked by it. This, you write, is a contract question, or a constitutional question, or a question relating to conflicts of law. This can be the hardest step in the process and often the one most crucial to divining an accurate answer. The issue may be buried deeply in a morass of irrelevant details. It's not unlike your first meeting with a prospective client a week later, if you pass the test. She feeds you the story of her life, and you have to sort through the intricate details to determine where you step in as her counselor and advocate.

Once you've ascertained the area of law controlling the fact pattern, you articulate the issue and formulate your best answer.

To be able to pull this off over that two-and-a-half-day odyssey, therefore, the prospective lawyer must be fluent in at least fifteen areas of the law, even if she elected to focus on one or two in her selection of elective courses during law school. If you are fully prepared, you will know more about the law on the day you take your bar exam than at any point in your life before or after that.

And it's not an easy test. In some jurisdictions, it is common for an applicant to take the exam multiple times before earning his or her license. From what I knew, Iowa historically had a near universal passage rate. But the July 1984 bar examination, the one coming before mine, was a harsh wake-up call. The failure rate on that one was about thirty percent. Failing the bar can be devastating to someone who has lined up employment after graduation. You can't be a lawyer until you have the license, and you have to wait six months to take the exam again. There seemed to be no rhyme or reason as to who did and didn't pass in July. Several who were unsuccessful were ranked near the top of their class, and a couple had landed prestigious jobs as clerks for judges.

Going into 1985, it didn't appear I had that to worry about. There was no plan in place for me following graduation.

Nevertheless, I wasn't going to put myself twice through that ringer. During the two semesters I was in clinic, I made bar preparation my full-time job. Between graduation and the test there were several weeks of review sessions. During the preceding summer I purchased a six-volume collection of outlines covering every area of law that would be covered on the exam. While it had taken me about half of my career as a law student to develop a system for internalizing what was being thrown at me in my classes, the strategies that served me well through my undergraduate years were well-suited for bar review. I thoroughly read through each of the outlines twice, then read through them again with a highlight pen. After that, I studied the highlighted portions. I took copious notes in the review classes, then followed the same process for studying my notes.

I wasn't going to take the bar exam twice.

Into the Fire . . .

Midway through my final semester the word came down from the Eighth Circuit administrator that the *Fryer* case was set for oral argument in the Court of Appeals on Monday, January 28, 1985. And because the appeal had been handled by interns in the Iowa prisoner assistance clinic, the argument would not be held in St. Louis or St. Paul, where the Court customarily sits. The oral argument in *Fryer v. Nix* would take place in the large lecture hall at the University of Iowa College of Law. Because I was the last man standing in the clinic working on the *Fryer* appeal, Professor Green extended to me the opportunity to appear with him as co-counsel and to argue several of the issues before the Court.

I said yes.

A better answer may have been *no*. Thank you for the offer. *Five days* after taking the bar exam. An hour-long oral argument before a three-judge panel of a *federal court of appeals*. That's one heartbeat down from the United States Supreme Court. And they're doing it in front of the *whole Iowa law school.* What could possibly go wrong with that? And, like those judicial clerks who had taken the test in July, I now had to pass the damned bar. Had the argument been set before December 15, I could appear under the auspices of the student practice rule. From then on, I'd have to be a lawyer with a license.

On top of all that, I was perilously clueless as to what I was expected to do in the argument.

The other thing they don't teach you in law school, besides the law, is how to be a lawyer. There were, at least in my day, a few several-hour seminars on real-world practice. But the bulk of your education in that direction comes from getting out and doing it. Clinic was good for much of that. But, prior to *Fryer*, there hadn't been any meaningful appellate practice. Early in law school there was something called Appellate Advocacy (A.A.) appended to Professor Sam Fahr's property course like a barnacle on the hull of a schooner. They hand you a collection of pre-fab briefs arguing both sides of a relatively simple property issue, and assign you to a partner. An L3 (third-year law student) advisor sits down with you and guides you through the process. Over the course of my life post-law school, I have always introduced my appellate advocacy advisor, Kim West, as my "AA sponsor." The A.A. activity culminates in a simulated oral argument on a Wednesday evening between your team and a duo of your classmates. Professor Fahr and his two research assistants acted as judges, interrupting our prepared remarks with questions as real-world appellate judges are wont to do. The whole thing is over in a half-hour, and I was able to draw on my high school debate experience for survival in A.A.

I had a strong sense that an Eighth Circuit argument in front of the entire Iowa Law student body less than a week after finishing the bar exam might be somewhat more challenging than standing up and front of Sam Fahr and his two students for five minutes and answering their questions. I had read through the entire record and all the briefs in *Fryer* multiple times, and felt conversant in their contents. But these three Judges were likely to bring up other cases as precedent or raise hypotheticals not contained in the briefs. What the hell would I do then? I was comfortable responding to questions that were answered by the students who had composed the arguments in the first place. How far outside the box I could venture without putting my inexperience on display and torpedoing my case was a serious question.

Then suddenly, on the Friday afternoon just before the bar exam, there was another development. I received a job offer. And it was *Fryer v. Nix* that put me in contention for the position.

The offer came from the Iowa State Appellate Defender, the office that handles the appeals of criminal convictions and postconviction relief actions in state court. Charlie Harrington, who had worked in the office since its inception and was now its chief, was interested in me because he had handled a postconviction relief challenge to the murder convictions of one of Allen Fryer's brothers. He was also impressed that my first court appearance as a licensed attorney (with the help of God) would be an argument in the Eighth Circuit Court of Appeals. Our interview focused more on the details of *Fryer* than upon my very limited education and experience. But what I was doing in clinic was right down the line of what I would be expected to do with the appellate defender, so I was a good fit. The most enduring memory of my interview with Charlie was the massive cramp in one of my legs that I did my best to conceal as we bantered about the details of that bloody night at Gitchie Manitou State Park. I think Charlie interpreted my sweating, blushing countenance as signs of empathy, a healthy attribute for a career public defender.

So I launched into the January 1985 bar exam with that one additional layer of pressure and stress. There was now a job I would lose if I failed the test.

My friend Matt, who lives in Cedar Rapids, came down and stayed with me at my parents' house beginning on Sunday afternoon. That was a mixed blessing. My personal rule for preparing for the test was that I would work my butt off right up until the afternoon before the exam, and then cut off studying completely. I'd play the piano for a while. Maybe I'd go to a movie. I wanted to rest my brain for the onslaught coming on Monday morning.

Matt had other ideas. Matt wanted to cram. Matt wanted to spend Sunday night and all the interstitial movements between test sessions pelting me with questions about the subject matter he was afraid he would encounter on the exam. Do you understand *this*? Can you explain *this* to me?

It wasn't just Matt. Matt was a symptom of my entire law school experience. I swear it was something I did nothing to foster. I didn't want it. But all through law school I'd acquired an undeserved reputation in some quarters as being this towering intellect who had answers to all the questions. People would come to me regularly to explain things I could barely comprehend myself. Maybe I was just that good of a bullshit artist.

On the afternoon following our law school graduation just a month before the bar exam, Jim Larew organized a reception at his grandfather's house on Woolf Avenue. My family was with me. During that get together my brother-in-law approached Eleanor, my girlfriend. Eleanor had transferred in from Case Western University Law School in Cleveland during the spring semester of 1983, and she and I connected almost from the beginning. One of the reasons I extended my law school career at Iowa for the extra semester in clinic was to enable us to graduate together. By now, however, we were already experiencing what the pilot might characterize as "some slight turbulence." What I truly didn't need to hear in that place in time was what came next.

"John tells me you don't have any self-confidence," Hal blurted out to Eleanor, within earshot of everyone in the room. "He thinks you don't think you're good enough."

What the fuck is he talking about?

"I *never* said anything like that," I protested vigorously. Over and above the nimbus clouds of tension already developing between Eleanor and me, there was enough pressure from the impending bar exam that I certainly didn't need to hear Hal poison the water with shit like that. I couldn't *believe* what I was hearing. Why would he even say that? But Hal doesn't make things up. He doesn't lie. But I certainly didn't say anything like *that*. Jesus Christ.

Despite my denials, I didn't anticipate that Hal's comment would simply roll off Eleanor's back and be forgotten. It didn't.

That haunted me for decades.

Then just recently, nearly forty years later, it dawned on me. It occurred to me exactly what Hal was talking about.

This past spring I submitted to an two-hour radio interview with Jim Larew for a series he does regularly on an Iowa City radio station. At the outset of our show, Jim repeated the myth about me being one of the brightest students in our class to whom all the classmates turned for advice. Once again, I felt compelled to explain that it *was* just a myth. People would run to me in a panic under the impression that I held some level of knowledge that they didn't. The punch line always was that when the test scores came back theirs invariably were higher than mine.

That's what Hal had heard me say about Eleanor. He was absolutely right. Eleanor was one of those people. It wasn't just her.

Matt was another one. And Matt stuck to me like glue over those four days in January during which we took the test.

The weather exacerbated the drama. On the Sunday before the bar exam commenced, the day Matt drove in from Cedar Rapids, temperatures in Des Moines dropped to 20 below zero, making it the coldest day of the winter of '84-85. The morning low on Monday rose to a balmy two degrees above zero. And by the end of the exam on Wednesday it nearly reached the freezing point.

All said and done, I felt relatively good about the test. One of the questions the future author of Iowa's criminal procedure manual elected *not* to answer, however, was the criminal procedure question. It was the only non-essay question, consisting of a list of about two dozen stages of a criminal proceeding. The applicant was asked to identify the ones at which jeopardy attaches for Fifth Amendment purposes and the ones at which it doesn't.

I do have to say that there was a property law question that eerily paralleled a hypothetical that Matt had tossed out to me for my input just before the final morning of the exam. As cranky as I'm sure I was when he did that to me, formulating an answer to Matt's query undoubtedly equipped me to respond to that question when it popped up on Wednesday morning.

In modern times, there is a six-week wait after the bar exam before the results are posted. In my day, you finished the exam at noon on Wednesday and results were posted by late afternoon on Thursday. New lawyers were sworn during a formal breakfast on Friday morning.

Once the test was concluded for me, however, I hightailed it to Iowa City to begin preparing for the argument the following Monday, under the wishful assumption that I would be a licensed attorney by then.

The news on Thursday was good. A list was posted in the hallway of the law school with the test numbers of applicants who passed, and the test numbers of the applicants who had not. The success rate for the January bar had risen back to the near 100 percent level.

Years later, my friend Matt confided in me that a partner in his firm had gotten his hands on a list of the results of the January 1985 bar exam. I'll never know if he was bullshitting me about it but, according to the partner, Matt's score was the second highest of anyone taking that test.

"I don't even want to *know* that," I berated him. "I just want to assume that if you came in second on the test I must have come in first."

Because I wouldn't be driving back to Des Moines for the swearing in on Friday, I went to work with the law school clinical staff to find the nearest Supreme Court justice available to do the honors for me. Justice Louis Schultz had an office in Iowa City, so on January 25, 1985 I trudged downtown to the Paul-Helen Building and took the oath that would bind me for 38 years and counting. We would be seeing a lot of each other soon, because the appellate defender practices exclusively before the Iowa Supreme Court and the Iowa Court of Appeals. Justice Schultz' prediction that my stay at the appellate defender would be very temporary, and that I would soon move on to another area of practice, was belied by the fact that I remained with the office for nine years. Many years after I had moved on, my mother and father came home from one of their winters in either the Florida panhandle or the beaches of Alabama with the news that they had played cards regularly down there with some judge from Iowa City.

From Thursday through Sunday, I worked and reworked through an outline of my argument to the Court on the issues assigned to me by Professor Green, knowing that the flow of my presentation was likely to be broken by questions from the Judges. Again and again, I read the briefs and reviewed the record, and looked up some of the cases cited in both parties' briefs, hoping that enough of the details would stick in my mind to enable me to articulate some persuasive responses to the interrogation.

The issues raised in the briefs were numerous and, for me, complex. The evidence at trial, we argued, wasn't sufficient for the case to even go to the jury. The conventional wisdom, I know now, is that sufficiency issues are rarely successful. It's the jury, not the judge, that decides whether the evidence is persuasive. Especially not judges on appeal. The prosecution knew of evidence that might assist the defense but that it didn't disclose in discovery. That's an issue. Law enforcement obtained admissions from Mr. Fryer that should have been excluded. The jury instructions were written in such a way that a jury might convict Mr. Fryer on less than a unanimous decision. And more. And I had to be conversant, not only in the ones assigned to me by Professor Green, but in all of them. There's no rule that the Court can't ask me questions about the other issues.

On Thursday afternoon, we did a practice argument with members of the law school faculty standing in for the court of appeals judges. One question from Professor Barbara Schwarz laid bare the undeniable truth that I had a long, long way to go before I was ready to argue a case before the United States Court of Appeals. Or any appellate court for that matter.

"What's the standard of review?" she asked, almost as an aside.

It was like she was speaking to me in a foreign language. I had never heard that phrase before. Standard of review. I couldn't even bullshit an answer. I hemmed and I hawed and I gave her one of those *I'll get back to you on that one* type responses. If that had happened to me during the actual *Fryer* argument, or during oral argument in any case for the duration of my appellate career, it would have figured prominently on the highlight reel of my most embarrassing moments in the profession. It was embarrassing that day, but more so now looking back on it with my acquired knowledge and experience.

It was actually five years later, after *five years* of appellate practice, that I fully came to realize the import of what Professor Schwarz was asking. Four of us from the appellate defender's office were sent down to New Orleans in April 1990 for a week-long seminar in appellate practice. An aged Supreme Court justice from one of the southern states finally beat into my thick skull the central role of the standard of review in resolving an appeal.

The standard of review is the polestar of appellate practice. It controls where the appellate court's authority lies in upholding or reversing a decision of the lower court. There are many decisions that the lower court are allowed to make, that are within its discretion to do so. They are the decisions a court makes to ensure that a trial or another proceeding is conducted smoothly and fairly. How much leeway is given to the lawyers during jury selection, the control of witnesses and the parties, the admission of evidence, and the selection of an appropriate sentence are a few examples of matters left mostly to the trial court's discretion. The district court is in the best position to observe the proceedings, and the appeals court will not second guess its decisions except where the trial court abuses its discretion by acting arbitrarily, capriciously or unreasonably.

Some decisions, on the other hand, are guided by the law. They include questions of whether a defendant's speedy trial right has been violated, whether some evidentiary privilege applies and whether certain jury instructions are permitted or even required under the law. For these issues the appellate court will look at the facts of the case, the controlling statute, rule or case precedent, and the ruling of the district court to determine whether there was error in its legal interpretation.

Finally, for certain types of issues like those involving a defendant's rights under the state or federal constitutions, there is *de novo* review. The reviewing court will look at the facts, often giving weight to the factual findings of the district court, but will make its own independent decision as to whether the constitution has been violated.

I didn't know any of this when Professor Schwarz asked the question. A better man would have locked himself in the law library and spent the weekend scouring every text he could find exploring and explaining the concept of an appellate court's standard of review. Not me, I'm sorry to say. I probably worked up some answer that would pass during the argument on Monday. But it took years to appreciate that ascertaining the correct standard of review is the first step towards deciding whether you've even got an issue to advance and, if so, how to structure your argument.

In Monday's Eighth Circuit argument in *Fryer v. Nix*, the State of Iowa was represented by 34-year-old Deputy Iowa Attorney General Brent Appel. After earning bachelor's and master's degrees in history at Stanford, Mr. Appel attended law school at the University of California at Berkely, where he was an editor of the *California Law Review*. He was now the resident gunslinger for Attorney General Tom Miller and had been up to the United States Supreme Court four times arguing celebrated cases that included *Nix v. Williams* and *Nix v. Whiteside.*

Just as the argument was about to commence, we encountered another hurdle. For three days I had been an attorney licensed to practice in the Iowa state courts. But the Court of Appeals is federal, and one needs a specific license to practice before the Eight Circuit Court of Appeals. It was no problem, the clerk told us. He handed me a one-page application for admission, which I filled out and returned to him with my check for $32. On the faculty of the Iowa College of Law there was no dearth of attorneys licensed to practice in the Eighth Circuit who could vouch for my application. Apparently my signature on the $32 check wasn't sufficiently visible because a week or so after the argument it was returned to me along with my application, with instructions to sign it more legibly and return it. It was one of those things that sat in my to-do bin for months. I don't know that I ever got around to it. When I did find myself back before the Court of Appeals several years later, I filled out a new application.

The presiding judge on the panel was Chief Judge Don Lay, a 58-year-old Iowa Law School graduate who was appointed to the Court of Appeals in 1966 by President Lyndon Johnson. Judge George Fagg was a Drake University graduate appointed by President Reagan in 1982 after ten years on the state bench. The most recently appointed panelist, and the one with no Iowa ties, was Judge Pasco Bowman. A graduate of New York University Law School, Judge Bowman had taught at several law schools before being brought on board by President Reagan in 1983. Later in his judicial career, Judge Bowman was on President Reagan's short list to replace United Supreme Court Justice Lewis Powell, but that seat went to Justice Anthony Kennedy.

The Court was congenial and polite and asked very few questions. Mercifully, none of the Justices quizzed me about the appropriate standard of review. The argument was uneventful and seemed to go quickly.

The most remarkable aspect of the *Fryer* argument for me was the contrast between my performance and that of my adversary, Brent Appel. With maybe one exception, this was probably the first time I had been inside a courtroom, with an opportunity to witness an actual lawyer practicing law. Here we were, playing to an audience of several dozen law students and faculty. I'm sure my delivery was stilted, canned and over-rehearsed. The deputy attorney general, on the other hand, strolled calmly to the podium and drew upon a large loose-leaf notebook containing all the documents he felt were relevant to his argument. Confident and relaxed, he spoke to the panel as if they were sitting across from each other at the dining room table, all the while flipping through the notebook to portions he deemed relevant. He wasn't a tall man, but was gifted with the movie star good looks to accompany his authoritative eloquence.

It was the only time I was ever involved in a court proceeding with Brent Appel. But there's more to say about him later.

Nearly nine months later we lost *Fryer v. Nix*. Judge Bowman wrote the opinion in what was a unanimous decision.

You can read it at *Fryer v. Nix*, 775 F.2nd 979 (8th Cir. 1985).

The Appellate Defender

When the sun set on January 28, 1985 I was an attorney licensed in Iowa and specializing in criminal appellate practice. My sole in-court experience was an oral argument in the United States Court of Appeals. That Friday, February 1, was the first day of what would be a nine-year stint with the Iowa Appellate Defender.

With the Appellate Defender I would be doing all the things I did in the *Fryer* case, only in state court. Over the years since '85 I've had large doses of both appellate practice and trial practice. I once heard an appellate defender complain that the trial attorneys cannot fathom how much more stressful it is to practice in the appellate courts than in the state courts. That person, I knew immediately, has never practiced at the trial court level.

Appellate practice is cerebral, structured and antiseptic. There is no rushing to the courthouse first thing in the morning for an unanticipated initial appearance. There are no arraignments, detention hearings, suppression hearings, sentencings and one, two, three, four weeks or more tied up in jury trials. The only court appearances in appellate cases are the oral arguments in which each lawyer is allotted ten or fifteen minutes to speak, with perhaps a five-minute rebuttal. In the trial court, on the other hand, you prepare vigorously for your district court hearings, and you're often required to speak off the cuff for an hour or more. Occasionally you hear from a client and his or her family once or twice during an appeal, but it's not the daily contact you have when you're representing a defendant in the district court.

Appellate practice is a thinking man's game. You read printed transcripts of every word spoken by the attorneys, the judge, the defendant and the witnesses at the trial and at all the hearings before and after the trial. You study the rulings of the court on all motions and objections made while the case is in the district court. You familiarize yourself with appellate court opinions in cases in which issues like yours have been raised and ruled upon. That's the way the law is made and refined. You write briefs, sometimes asking the court to make new law that will apply to other cases in the future. That's the job. But I can't say I fully "got it" before that seminar in New Orleans in 1990 when I was schooled in the central importance of knowing the court's standard of review on every issue that comes before it.

Few people who aren't in the field understand what an appeals court does. When the jury comes down the wrong way in the movies, you see the lawyer whispering confidently into the client's ear, "We'll get it back in the appeal." That's usually not how it works. If you've got a winnable case, you're much better off winning it at trial and not counting on the appeal. If you win your appeal, all you get in most cases is another trial.

The most appropriate analog for an appeal, I always say, is the instant replay feature in the NFL. In football, the presiding official reviews the video of the previous play to see if the referee made the correct call. The referee's decision is overruled only when there is "indisputable visual evidence" that the call was incorrect. An appeal isn't a second bite from the apple. It's not an opportunity to be found not guilty after the jury has found you guilty. It generally doesn't involve a weighing of the evidence to prove one's factual innocence.

The appeals court reviews, not the decision of the jury on the facts, but the rulings of the trial judge on motions filed and objections made at the trial court level, to determine whether they are legally sound. Most issues will not be considered by the appeals court if they were not first presented to the trial court in a motion or an objection. The Supreme Court cannot gauge the propriety of the district court's decisions if the district court was not first invited to make them. There is an occasional exception to this preservation rule in cases where the trial lawyer didn't object because his or her representation of the defendant was so egregiously ineffective that the defendant in the eyes of the law was denied the right to counsel under the Sixth Amendment.

The "standard of review" that I came to appreciate in New Orleans five years after the *Fryer* argument tells the appeals court how much deference the rulings of the trial court must be accorded. Decisions subject to abuse of discretion review are rarely appealable. The trial court makes them and they're final. If the standard is a review of errors of law, the appeals court holds the trial record and the court's ruling up to the light – the law provided in the Code, the court rules, the Constitution, and prior decisions of appellate courts in the same jurisdiction that interpret the Code, the rules and the Constitution.

And then there is *Marbury v. Madison*, 5 U.S. 137 (1803). This is the one that gets people's blood boiling, even people who have never heard it mentioned by name. The power of judicial review. If it wasn't clear in the language of Article III of the United States Constitution, *Marbury* makes it clear that the unelected Supreme Court is a check on the power of the two elected branches. In the criminal courts, if the defendant is convicted of an offense that criminalizes behavior that is protected by the Constitution, the appellate court has the authority to declare that the statute that creates the offense is unconstitutional. If the defendant is convicted in a proceeding in which he or she is denied a right guaranteed under the Constitution, the appeals court may reverse the conviction and send the case back for a new trial.

There are some violations that are of a nature that the case may not be remanded for retrial and the conviction is simply vacated once and for all. A finding on appeal that no substantial evidence was admitted at trial that would support even putting the case to the jury, because one or more of the "essential elements" of the charge was entirely unproven, is the equivalent of an acquittal. A retrial in such a case would violate the double jeopardy clause of the Fifth Amendment.

Judicial review of statutes or of the constitutionality of procedures followed in the trial court is *de novo*. The appeals court takes a fresh look at the evidence and, regardless of how the trial court came down on them, makes its own determination as to how the Constitution must be interpreted in this case and in cases to follow.

A case like that was assigned to me late in my first year with the Appellate Defender.

State v. Coy.

Coy

In August that year, two 13-year–old girls pitched a tent in the back yard of the home in which one of them lived. In the dead of the night, a strange man entered the tent and assaulted them. At the time they had no idea who the man was, but the girls and the father of one of them suspected that it may have been a man who lived nearby. The father had seen the neighbor, subsequently identified as a musician named John Coy, leaving his house with a suitcase shortly after the assault. After Coy was taken into custody on a traffic warrant, the girl's father and another individual conducted a private search of the residence and observed a yellow plastic cup matching cups the girls had brought with them for their campout.

Being "pleasantly pleased" with what the two men had discovered, the local investigator obtained a warrant to search Coy's home. The search yielded the plastic cup along with a flashlight and flashlight batteries consistent with what the girls reported were used in the invasion and assault.

At Mr. Coy's jury trial, the judge utilized a brand-new statute, Iowa Code § 910A.3(1), which authorized the court to allow the girls to testify from behind a screen that precluded them from seeing him and that precluded Coy from seeing them. John Coy was convicted of two counts of lascivious acts with a child.

In my brief and in my argument to the Supreme Court I raised three issues, all raised at trial by Clinton, Iowa attorney Jack Wolfe and all of which involved violations of the United States Constitution, making them susceptible to *de novo* review by the Court.

My first argument, and the one about which I was most fervid, involved what I perceived to be a violation of Mr. Coy's Fourth Amendment rights in the search of his house. Absent some exigent circumstances, the police are not entitled to search a person's house without a warrant based on probable cause to believe a crime has been committed and that evidence of the crime will be found therein. Private individuals like the girl's father and the other man are not subject to the Fourth Amendment. They may be sued for trespass, or even charged criminally with trespass or burglary in the unlikely occurrence that law enforcement chooses to do so, but the exclusionary rule that precludes admission at trial of evidence obtained in violation of the Constitution does not apply to private searches. However, I argued, when they do it at the behest of the police they *become* the police. The men had encountered investigators before going in and were told what police were searching for. Though they did not expressly instruct them to enter Coy's house, law enforcement encouraged the men to walk the grounds around the neighborhood residences in search of useful evidence. I cried foul on that one.

The other two arguments arose from the use of the screen during the girls' testimony. Criminal defendants enjoy a Sixth Amendment right of confrontation. When a witness testifies against you he or she ought to see who they are accusing, and you ought to be able to see your accuser doing it. But constitutional analysis often involves a balancing of competing interests. I recognize now as I did in 1986 when I wrote the *Coy* brief that, while John Coy had a protected interest under the Sixth Amendment, the state also had an interest in shielding the young girls from the trauma of being revictimized by having to see the face of their assailant while they testify. But § 910A.3(1) did not require the trial court to balance any competing interests before using the screen, and no such balancing was done at Mr. Coy's trial.

My second challenge to the screen was on due process grounds. The Fifth Amendment, which applies to the federal government, provides that a person may not "be deprived of life, liberty, or property, without due process of law." To this, the post-Civil War Fourteenth Amendment added, "nor shall any State deprive any person of life, liberty, or property, without due process of law." Historically, the courts have found that the use of some procedures during trial are so prejudicial to the defendant that they engender in the minds of the jury an inference that the defendant is guilty, and thus violate due process under the Fourteenth Amendment. Having the defendant appear in front of the jury in handcuffs and shackles, or dressed in prison garb, are impermissible indicia of guilt.

Mr. Coy's argument was that the spectacle of a huge screen placed between him and the witnesses was as much an indicia of guilt as parading him in front of the jury in handcuffs, shackles and jail clothes. Once again, the strength of this issue might be reduced substantially by a trial court finding that the trauma to the particular victims in the case outweighed Mr. Coy's Fourteenth Amendment deprivation. But no such balancing was done.

I lost that one on December 17, 1986. The two men were not agents of police, Chief Justice Ward Reynoldson concluded in his unanimous opinion. Though they were asked to canvass the neighborhood grounds in search of useful evidence, they were not told to enter the house and, according to officers' testimony, they were not aware that the men did so. Being "pleasantly surprised" after the fact did not amount to deputizing the civilians to act as agents of the investigators.

The confrontation clause ruling was, for me, the least unexpected. I was familiar with language in at least one prior Iowa case citing dicta in a United States Supreme Court case explaining that the right of confrontation in the Sixth Amendment is "not [guaranteed] for the idle purpose of [allowing a defendant to] gaze . . . upon the witness or of being gazed upon by [her]." Confrontation is served by placing the witness before the judge and the jury, enabling them to observe the witness's deportment during questioning and by permitting the defendant, through counsel, to cross examine the witness. Chief Justice Reynoldson did not veer from these thin strands of precedent in rejecting our Sixth Amendment claim.

We also lost on the Fourteenth Amendment ground. In the Court's view, the screen wasn't prejudicial. It was only used during the testimony of the girls. The jury was told that it was standard procedure in a case of this nature. It did not "brand" Mr. Coy as being guilty.

You can read it yourself at *State v. Coy*, 397 N.W.2d 730 (Iowa 1986).

I was furious all day on the Wednesday the *Coy* opinion was announced. That furor was focused on the Fourth Amendment search and seizure argument. During the pendency of the appeal, the Iowa Attorney General had made a specific request that the case be resolved as expediently as possible to minimize the trauma to the child witnesses. It didn't strike me as an unreasonable request. I don't procrastinate, and I was easily able to perform all of my duties in the case within the set time guidelines, without requesting extensions. Subsequently, however, it was brought to my attention that the girl's father who had trespassed in Mr. Coy's house was a licensed attorney with a possible personal connection to the Iowa attorney general. Being full-blooded Irish (with a touch of English), my anger did not subside as Wednesday progressed. It grew.

In the late afternoon, I burst into the office of Dr. Roxann Ryan, the deputy attorney general who handled the Coy appeal for the state and who, on any other day, was my close personal friend, and unleashed a profane tirade of frustration over how this flagrant violation of the Fourth Amendment had gone unpunished. It would have been nice, I steamed, if there would have at least been some dicta in the Court's opinion saying that we don't endorse the brand of vigilante justice that went down in Clinton, Iowa during the Coy investigation. She just listened calmly and waited for me to bark myself out.

"Fine," I hollered. "I'll just go right to the attorney general and confront him."

"Knock yourself out. I doubt you're going to get any response from Tom."

Roxann was right. I stalked into Tom Miller's office and reprised my performance, *sans* some of the expletives. I tried to call him out on his close relationship with the licensed attorney who'd gone into my client's house at the behest of law enforcement. And why was it so important to resolve *this* case so rapidly? But Tom and his immedicable poker face just gazed back upon this young lawyer whom he had never met before, and said absolutely nothing.

So I stewed some more. Things don't die down with me. They fester. On Friday I called Professor Paul Papak at the University of Iowa law school, who had been the clinical advisor on a few of the major cases I'd worked in the prisoner assistance clinic, including the class action settlement involving prison conditions at the Penitentiary and the second-degree murder prosecution of the Iowa Hawkeye football player. I told him the whole story. Most of my diatribe centered on the illegal search issue. They also put up a screen between my client and the girl witnesses, I added almost as an aside.

One of the conditions to obtain a license to appear in the United States Supreme Court, at least at that time, was three years of practice as a licensed attorney. As of December 1986, I was coming up on two. Down inside me, I think I also recognized that I wasn't equipped at the time to take a case into the United States Supreme Court. The issues in *Coy* were straight forward. While there were a lot of aspects of the law that I still "didn't get," I had a reasonably strong grasp on what was involved in a Fourth Amendment challenge. But I've come to realize over the years since then that attorneys who practice frequently and effectively in the United States Supreme Court speak a language entirely different from that employed by us mere mortals. The most prudent move for me would be to bring in someone with the resources and the experience to take *State v. Coy* to that level.

Send me what you've got, Paul advised, and I'll let you know.

Paul was back in touch within the week. He was highly interested in *Coy*. It wasn't really the search and seizure issue that garnered his attention, he told me. The new provision of the Iowa Code, allowing the trial court to put up the screen -- *there's* an issue. Those things have been cropping up around the country, and nobody's gotten a confrontation clause challenge to the screen procedure before the Supreme Court.

It was possible at that time to do a direct appeal of a state conviction to the United States Supreme Court. That ended in 1987, and since then the Supreme Court will only review a state conviction if it grants permission to bring the case up *via* what is called a writ of certiorari. Even then, it was up to the Court whether or not to hear an appeal. The two times a direct appeal was appropriate were (1) when a state court found that a federal law was unconstitutional, and (2) when a state court found that its own law was *constitutional*. It was a logical guideline, because it enabled the federal court to provide the ultimate interpretation of the federal Constitution. Because the Iowa Supreme Court had found Iowa Code § 910A.3(1) to be valid under the Sixth Amendment, *Coy* was ripe for Supreme Court review.

Paul took the ball and ran with it. With the assistance of clinical interns at the law school, he prepared the documents to initiate the appeal. He sent everything that would be filed to me first for my review and held the door open for any level of participation I wanted to provide. But the more I read what was coming out of him and his team, the more I realized that I had nothing meaningful to contribute. It was way over my head. My only suggestion from time to time was that he consider adding the Fourth Amendment issue. The search issue is fact-dependent, he explained, and doesn't hinge on a novel interpretation of the law. For that reason, it's not likely to be reviewed by the Supreme Court. He didn't want to dilute the issue of first impression that had some chance of bearing fruit.

I wasn't about to look that gift horse in the mouth. Paul knew what he was doing.

And the Supreme Court accepted the appeal for review. From what I can see, *Coy v. Iowa* may have been the last state case, or at least the final published case, to go up to the Supreme Court on direct appeal.

As the appeal progressed, Paul continued to send me all the briefs for my review. Once again, there was little I could say. He had taken what I had done in state court and built upon it a well-written, well-researched, persuasive argument suitable for filing in the highest court of the land.

My grandmother turned 90 in October 1987 in Worcester, Massachusetts. There was a huge weekend-long family reunion in Worcester to celebrate the occasion, to which I brought my new girlfriend, Pam (who three years later would be my wife). It was the first time anyone in my family had met Pam. We left after work on Thursday and drove all night and all day Friday to make the event. We came through upstate New York on Interstate 90.

After lunch on Sunday we began the trip back, this time taking Interstate 80 through southern Pennsylvania. It was very late when we stopped for the first night at a roadside hotel, probably a Holiday Inn, in Clarion. As I checked in, I glanced down at a handwritten monthly calendar of October events at the hotel. Guests at the hotel on the previous Tuesday had been treated to "John Coy sings and plays his guitar in our hotel lounge."

"Oh, my God," I gasped. *It was him.*

John Coy was from Shippenville, Pennsylvania. He had moved to Clinton, Iowa to be with a girlfriend. After the arrest and conviction, he posted an appeal bond to remain at liberty until the conclusion of his appeal and made his way back to Pennsylvania. The Iowa Supreme Court allowed him to remain out on bond while the case wound its way through the United States Supreme Court. Shippenville is five and a half miles from Clarion. I knew that John Coy was a musician. Now, there it was. John Coy had played in *this hotel* just four days earlier. I wouldn't know him if I saw him. I'd spoken to him on the phone a few times, but he was out of Iowa before I ever got the case. But it was *him*. There was no doubt.

The desk clerk observed my reaction and chuckled.

"Yeah, that's what everybody says."

"Really. What does everybody say?"

"What *big names* we bring into our lounge."

She doesn't know. I wonder if she and others in Clarion ever drew the connection when the decision came down.

Paul Papak was back in touch with me in late 1987 to tell me that *Coy* had been set for oral argument before the Supreme Court on January 13, 1988. Though I had contributed absolutely nothing to the appeal, Paul invited me to sit with him at counsel table during the argument. Our third attorney would be Barbara Schwartz, the clinical professor who three years earlier had functionally derailed my practice argument in *Fryer* with the question about the standard of review.

A week or so before the oral argument, I went to Iowa City

to watch a practice argument in which Paul presented his case before a panel of Iowa faculty members playing the roles of the Supreme Court justices. Practice arguments were probably also held at other locations. The questioning from the panel was fierce, and Paul held his own. Paul was prepared. Once again, I had nothing to add to what he already knew.

I had just one suggestion.

Paul had an entire argument written out. You could do that in my job at the time, appearing before the Iowa Supreme Court, because that Court in 1987 and 1988 wasn't asking questions. But in a "hot" court like the United States Supreme Court, in which all the justices participate actively in questioning the advocates, a written argument would almost instantly go out the window. Paul opened his with "In the small town of Clinton, Iowa . . ."

I approached him after it was over. His performance was beyond reproach – certainly head and shoulders above what I could muster. The only thing I would suggest is that he steer clear of the flowery language, like "in the small town of Clinton." Don't give them something that's going to draw them off unnecessarily. Paul wasn't concerned, and indicated he would go with what he'd written. That was fine with me. It's his prerogative. It's his day.

The Show

My spot was reserved at counsel table. There was a seat in the gallery for Pam. She'd had some business in Davenport the day before the argument. We drove together to Davenport, where I dropped her off and continued on to Washington. For our three days in D.C., I stayed at the apartment of my cousin and her fiancé in a Washington suburb. Once she finished in Davenport, Pam would ride the Amtrak to Washington, arriving at Union Station over the noon hour. It's a 12-minute walk from there to the Supreme Court Building, where *Coy* was scheduled for argument at 1 p.m. Still living in an era when there were no cell phones, I don't know that I ever considered how dangerously close I was cutting it.

To get the lay of the land, Paul and I arrived first thing in the morning at the Supreme Court Building to watch the argument in the case on the docket before *Coy*. Before that, we ate breakfast in the Court's cafeteria, where I learned something I didn't know about the Court. I don't know if Paul was aware of this.

At a taekwondo class several weeks after the argument, in a discussion with another black belt who had argued before the Court not long before *Coy*, she asked me, "Did you get to hear Justice Blackmun talking about your case with his law clerks?"

Well, yes. As a matter of fact, I did.

Every weekday morning that the Court was in session, I discovered, Justice Harry Blackmun would join his clerks for breakfast in the cafeteria. On January 13, they were situated just one table over from where Paul and I were sitting. I think Paul was actively tuned in to their conversation, while I did what I could to avoid the appearance of eavesdropping. But then I realized they were talking about *Coy*.

"Whoever argued this case in the state court," Justice Blackmun noted, "apparently didn't argue the due process issue very forcefully."

What a minute.

He's talking about *me. I argued the case in the state court. And I **focused** on the due process issue, that the presence of the screen in the courtroom was a prejudicial indicia of Mr. Coy's guilt.* I thought the confrontation clause angle was foreclosed by the dicta in other cases that face-to-face confrontation isn't required.

I think Paul could sense from my flushed visage and perhaps the tiny vein pulsating on the side of my neck that I was coiling to spring into action.

"Let's go," he instructed, and we made our way to the seats in the Court's chambers. The United States of America was a party in the case before ours, and was represented by an attorney in the solicitor general's office. Until now-Justice Elena

Kagan served as solicitor general it was the practice of attorneys in the office to appear before the Court wearing morning coats. So this young character with his dirty blond hair pulled back into a short ponytail argued his case sporting a morning coat that was about two sizes too large. But he was very articulate, and the Justices seemed to know him.

When the first case was submitted and the Court took its noon recess I made the mad dash for Union Station, making the misguided command decision to drive over there rather than to walk. Pam could store her suitcases in the car during the argument. Circumstances there took a fortunate turn in that I found a nearby parking spot. Predictably, the train was late. But there was ample time to spirit Pam off to the car, to find a spot near the Court building, and to get through security and into chambers in time for the *Coy* argument.

I imagine that any attorney who has had one case come before the Supreme Court will characterize that day as the highlight of his or her professional career. I now had two years and 353 days under my belt since that snowy day Justice Louis Schultz administered the oath to me in his Iowa City office. My tenure as a practicing attorney spanned five months short of 35 years, and in it there was never another day for me like January 13, 1988.

The Supreme Court in person is not what you would expect. The Justices aren't seated at a high bench towering over the room, like you see in other Courts. They don't have to be. I don't know if they're elevated at all. You sit at counsel table and there they are, just a few feet in front of you looking you directly in the eye. It's like being seated on a scaffold at eye level at Mount Rushmore. These are *giants*. These people make history, every day. If you're in the room with them, then *you're* making history.

I am sitting across the room from *Thurgood Marshall*, the first African American Supreme Court Justice, and Sandra Day O'Connor, the first woman. The other great liberal Justice in the room, William Brennan, had been appointed by Dwight Eisenhower. Justice Byron "Whizzer" White, had earned two bronze stars in the Navy during the Second World War, then came back and was the lead rusher in the NFL for two seasons with the Detroit Lions.

The newest addition on the Rehnquist Court was Justice Antonin Scalia, a Reagan appointee who had served just under 15 months at the time of the *Coy* argument and who brandished unabashedly a reputation for being an arch-conservative.

They all filed in and took their seats, and Chief Justice Rehnquist invited Paul to make his argument.

"On November 13, 1985 in the small town of Clinton, Iowa," Paul began, "twelve members of a criminal jury witnessed an extraordinary and unprecedented event. Following opening statements by the county prosecutor and defense counsel, the court ordered the bailiff to turn off the courtroom lights and to close the window blinds. And with that courtroom thrust into near total darkness –"

This is where Paul was first interrupted by, I believe, Justice White.

"How large a town is Clinton?" the Justice asked.

"Thirty-some thousand, your Honor."

"Small town?"

"Relatively small town."

"Relatively small *city*," a different Justice chided.

Paul was then able to steer the argument back on track. I may have been the weakest link on the team as far as the law went. But my instincts had been right about the "small town in Iowa" allusion. Even if the Court ruled against us on the merits, I would have at least that to take home with me.

From then on, Paul handled himself admirably. There were no questions that hadn't come out more forcefully during the practice arguments. Paul Papak, the Princeton University graduate who earned his Juris Doctorate at the University of Wisconsin, was characteristically calm, unflappable and articulate. It wasn't a cakewalk. There were tough questions. But Paul rode it out. And they *did* discuss the due process claim.

What was getting my attention during Paul's remarks

was that Justice O'Connor seemed to be staring at me from the far side of the bench during the entire argument. The top button of my shirt was buttoned, my necktie was taut around my neck and there were no foreign objects of which I was aware that were noticeable on my person or clothing. A few years afterwards, I discovered that there is a dress code for attorneys appearing in front of the Court. I wore a solid gray suit that had been dry cleaned and pressed. Litigants are not required to follow the lead of the solicitor general and wear morning coats during arguments (although they are free to do so if they choose), but they must wear solid white dress shirts. My button-down dress shirt was white with blue pinstripes. Under her suit, Professor Schwartz wore a loud purple blouse. Maybe that was it.

Paul finished his opening, reserving some time for rebuttal. Gordon Allen took the podium on behalf of the State of Iowa. The Court was hard on Gordy. A lot harder than I expected. I guess down inside I saw the *Coy* argument as a trip to Washington with front-row seats to a Supreme Court argument. To be honest, I don't know that I believed we were actually going to *win* the case. Then Justice Scalia started asking his confrontation clause questions, with Gordy providing the stock response that confrontation means putting the witnesses in front of the judge and giving defense counsel an opportunity to cross examine.

I've lived through one sizable earthquake in my life. About thirty years ago Pam and I flew out to San Diego for a week with my sister at her house on the rim of Miramar Canyon. The plane arrived very late and we went right to the house and went to bed. At about 6:30 the following morning I had a dream that I was still on the plane, and that we were experiencing turbulence. I woke up from the dream, and the turbulence was still going on. It seemed to go on for a full minute.

But during that quake I didn't sense the rupture going right to the core of the planet that I felt during Justice Scalia's questioning of Gordy.

The Sixth Amendment, Justice Scalia read, "says in all

criminal prosecutions the accused shall enjoy the right to be confronted with the witnesses against him. I find confront means, according to an 1828 dictionary, to stand face to face in full view. Now what has changed since then? I mean, did people not know about the tenderness of children when the Bill of Rights was adopted and we've suddenly discovered it now?"

Gordy did not believe "that the confrontation usage of that word in the Sixth Amendment means eye to eye."

"That's what confront *means*."

"These children did stand face to face with the Defendant in front of the jury so that the jury could in fact view their demeanor while –"

"The whole purpose of it was to prevent them from having to look him in the eye. Now one of the things that could happen from that is that they'll be traumatized or terrorized and for that reason won't tell the truth. But another thing that can happen is that they'll be shamed into telling the truth rather than lying. That's certainly the theory of the confrontation clause."

"It's one theory."

"It's why they use the word confront. They could have said right to cross examine if that's all they meant. They believed there was something valuable in being able to confront your accuser, and you're telling us that the state can simply say, well, we've decided that you don't have to do that when it's a child offense. You can go to jail just as well for a child offense, it's just as much a criminal prosecution. I don't see –"

"This Court has historically said that confrontation includes the right to have an oath, the right to be in front of a jury, the right to know the demeanor, and the right to have unlimited cross examination."

"Those were *hard* cases. That's extending the meaning of the word confront. The easy cases confront means confronting."

"All of which this Defendant had. Plus the Defendant had the opportunity to view the witnesses. The Defendant did get the opportunity to face his accusers."

"And dimly see them according to the way the judge described it when he looked through the screen."

"But nevertheless see them."

"No. It is to stand face to face. It's not just that he see them, it's that they see him. You know the saying, look me in the eye and say that. You've heard people say that. It means, you know, you're lying and you won't say it to me face. That's the whole purpose of that clause, and you're saying here, we can simply say you don't need it when there is a juvenile witness."

Over the course of his service to Court, you would always hear people who do what I did for a living saying bad things about Justice Scalia. But in the 28 years and one month that he remained alive and on the bench after the *Coy* argument, I would never be one of them. You couldn't know that day if the views expressed in his questioning were shared by other members of the Court. Justice Scalia may have been an outlier. He was often an outlier. There was also the possibility that he was simply playing devil's advocate in his questioning. Appellate judges will do that, and you can't predict with certainty from their questioning how they will vote in the end.

But he sure seemed to get it that day. Gordy wasn't necessarily wrong in his argument. The Court had never come out and said that the Sixth Amendment requires face to face confrontation. But following Justice Scalia's January 13 reasoning, why would it? It was obvious. It was the easy case. At least that's what I thought. What does confrontation *mean* if it's not face to face? But what is obvious to John Burns is not the law (at least until I wrote the Criminal Procedure manual and started quoting *myself* during Eighth Circuit Court of Appeals arguments, which was a source of amusement to the judges). What is self-evident in the minds of the average man or woman on the street is not the law. The law is what the courts say it is, and there is a multitude of rules of construction that allow appellate courts to proclaim that one plus one, in their jurisdictions, equals three. And in no written decision had any court ever come out and stated the obvious – that the Sixth

Amendment entitles you to have your accuser look you in the eye. The dicta, in fact, strongly suggested that it didn't.

We'd have to wait and see.

It was an afternoon of dignified celebration following the argument. We hung out for a while with Gordy and Roxann Ryan, who had litigated the case against me before the Iowa Supreme Court and was the passive onlooker during my verbal assault on the attorney general the afternoon *State v. Coy* was announced thirteen months earlier. Like me, she was permitted to sit quietly at counsel table during the argument.

Then we dispersed. Pam and I returned to my cousin's apartment in the suburbs for dinner and would spend a few days sightseeing. I had been born in Arlington. My father was stationed in the Pentagon during the Korean War and remained there for about four years after the war ended. When my mother became pregnant with my little sister eight months after my arrival we returned to our ancestral home of Worcester, Massachusetts. Other than one night at the Washington Hilton on the bus trip from Nashville to New York City in 1975, the *Coy* argument was my first opportunity to visit my birthplace.

I was, of course, still buzzing from the afternoon's experience when we bid goodbye to the other attorneys and Pam and I made our way to my 1985 Renault Alliance. My excitement wasn't something Pam could fully share, as the subtleties and the significance of what had transpired between Justice Scalia and Gordy Allen were clearly apparent only to a lawyer or to a student of constitutional history. As we had been dating only five months, however, Pam played along.

Pam definitely would have exhibited far less tolerance for what happened next had it gone down after five years of marriage.

In the hustle to meet up at Union Station and make the mad dash back for the argument, I was fortunate to have scored an open parking space in a residential neighborhood within three blocks of the Supreme Court building. It wasn't much closer than the train station itself, but picking her up with the car presented the opportunity to lock Pam's luggage in the trunk. She would not have been permitted to bring it into the Court building. The alternative, I suppose, would have been to store the luggage in a locker in the station and return to retrieve it after the argument. This worked out better.

Finding the Court from the street had not been difficult. You can *see* the Supreme Court building from the residential neighborhood. And one block beyond the Court building was the United States Capitol. You can see *that* all the way across Washington. Getting to the argument, like I say, was a cake walk.

Getting back to the car was not so easy. The hour before the argument was one of those classic *get me to the Court on time, Jesus, and I promise I'll never cuss again* moments. We got there. That's all that mattered. And then there was the oral argument which, like I say, was instantly the crown jewel of a 35-year legal career. When the smoke had cleared, only vague memories remained of the events of the day before Chief Justice Rehnquist called Paul Papak to the podium.

Things like *where did I park the damn car*?

It shouldn't be hard, you'd think. The Court is just east of the Capitol, and the residential neighborhoods begin just east of the Court. And it was about three blocks from the car to the Court. But we didn't leave a trail of breadcrumbs from the car. The cars are parked bumper to bumper in the street. All the houses look alike. There were no recognizable landmarks. And on January 13 the sun goes down at 5:08 p.m. in Washington. It was already starting to get dark.

First, we took the direct route. Walk three blocks from the Court building toward the east. Stop and look all around. Nothing. Walk up and down 4th Street. Nothing. 5th Street. Nope. Couldn't have been as far as 6th, but to be on the safe side we checked 6th. Then we came back and walked Miller's Court and even 3rd street, which seemed awfully close. Maybe we should have walked further up and down each of those streets.

There was one possibility that didn't even creep into our naive midwestern minds. In the hours we were cloistered in that big white stone building making historic inroads into the interpretation of the Sixth Amendment to the United States Constitution, perhaps some young opportunist had decided to bring home a three-year-old Renault with Iowa plates, of all things. We kept looking.

Feeling that we'd covered the neighborhood and considering that it was now quite dark and maybe not totally safe to be wandering the streets of Washington like lost tourists, we hailed a cab. Though it's no longer the case today, in 1988 taxis in Washington had a zone system. There were no meters that based fares on time and mileage. If you stayed within your zone you paid a fixed rate. There were higher fixed rates for traveling to other specific zones. I wondered how the zone system would work in a case like ours, where we weren't traveling directly from point A to point B. In our case, we would be driving repetitively up and down streets within a three-block radius. Maybe the driver would put us back out on the street, being that we had no set destination.

He didn't do that. Our driver was congenial and empathetic. It was he who first suggested the possibility we couldn't locate the Renault because it had been stolen. But patiently he took us on the circle tour of the neighborhood as he asked us questions about life in Iowa and threw out a few tips about visiting the Capital City. I don't know how long we were out there. But it was at least twenty minutes before I spotted my car nestled between two older vehicles. I thanked the driver for his patient assistance and braced for what the fare would be.

No charge, he told me. It was an honor to meet someone who was in town making history with the Supreme Court.

How much history was made that day remained to be seen.

The Verdict

The Supreme Court's annual term begins on the first Monday in October each year and ends the last week in June. The big decisions, the blockbusters, are often announced on the final day of the term, or at least during the final week. The end of June 1988 was approaching, and there was no word from the Supreme Court about *Coy v. Iowa*.

On the final day of the 1987 Session, the Court announced the denial of a petition for writ of certiorari in *Nicks v. Alabama*, a challenge to the petitioner's death sentence. Joined by Justice Brennan, Justice Marshall wrote a dissent repeating his oft-articulated position that the death penalty was cruel and unusual punishment in all cases, and thus violates the Eighth Amendment.

The day before that, Wednesday, June 29, 1988, was for all practical purposes the final one of the session. Nine decisions were announced that day. I think the news came to me from Sue Mason, a reporter at local CBS affiliate KCCI Television in Des Moines, that one of them was *Coy v. Iowa*. These were the days long before I was able to switch on a computer and read a court opinion that had been issued that very morning. But Sue Mason had a copy, and wanted my comments.

It was good news for us.

It was a 6-2 decision. Justice Anthony Kennedy had joined the bench after the oral argument and did not participate. Justice Harry Blackmun, who had dissed me over breakfast the morning of the argument, wrote the dissenting opinion that was joined by Chief Justice Rehnquist.

The majority opinion was written by none other than Justice Antonin Scalia, who gave us more than we'd asked for. His opinion in *Coy v. Iowa*, 487 U.S. 1012 (1988) is eight pages long. But he summarized the law as it existed after *Coy* in his June 29 pronouncement of the decision:

The right to face-to-face confrontation has ancient roots although our opinions have discussed it less frequently than other more complicated aspects of the Confrontation Clause, such as the admissibility of out-of-courts statements.   But both ancient and modern sources suggest that a face-to-face encounter as the words of the clause suggest is an important element of a fair trial which serves the goal of assuring the integrity of the fact-finding process. Today, we reaffirmed the core meaning of the Confrontation Clause. It is difficult to imagine a more obvious or damaging violation of the confrontation right than the screen in this case, which was specifically designed to prevent the witnesses from seeing the appellant. We do not decide whether exceptions to the right exist since any exception would require more than the legislatively imposed presumption of trauma that was the sole justification for use of the screen here. There was no individualized finding that these witnesses needed special protection.

It was exactly what he was saying during the argument. Notwithstanding the dicta upon which Gordy Allen and the Iowa Supreme Court had hung their hats, the "core meaning" of the confrontation clause requires face-to-face confrontation. We would have been happy with the standard constitutional balancing test. Does the potential trauma to the victim outweigh the defendant's interests under the Sixth Amendment? We're not saying either way, was today's holding. Joined by Justice White, Justice O'Connor stressed in her concurring opinion that she would consider limitations on face-to-face confrontation to address some showing of an important governmental interest, which hadn't been done here. Two years later she implemented a balancing test in *Maryland v. Craig*, 110 S.Ct. 3157 (1990) over Justice Scalia's dissent (joined by Justice Marshall and Justice Brennan).

I was chosen by Sue Mason to do the interview on the 29th because Paul Papak was on vacation in Europe. I perused the opinion beforehand but didn't study it carefully. KCCI wanted a 20-second sound bite, not a scholarly dissertation. If I took the time to digest it, she'd miss her deadline. I knew what I wanted to say about it.

"It's a landmark decision," I pontificated. "The Supreme Court has never before said you have a right to look your accuser in the eye. Now you do."

I was basking in it. Once again, the lawyer who didn't write a word of the Supreme Court briefs or open his mouth during the oral argument was dancing in the limelight.

It just kept getting better. Later that day, on the CBS evening news with Dan Rather, a major headline was the Supreme Court closing out its 1987 session with some major decisions. When mention was made of *Coy v. Iowa*, my face filled the screen as I characterized the case as "a landmark decision. The Supreme Court has never before said you have a right to look your accuser in the eye. Now you do." It was the only time in my life I appeared in front of a national television audience until Court TV came to town in 1999 to broadcast the potato gun trial.

After the news, I went to my taekwondo class. My master instructor, Eric Heintz, himself a former prosecutor for the Iowa attorney general's office who several years earlier had sent my boss to prison, had seen the story on both the local and national news. He congratulated me for it in front of the entire class.

That was my victory lap.

Street Cred

Whether or not it was deserved, my street cred went through the roof after *Coy*. Some of it you get for just being in the appellate defender's office. You read the cases. You make the cases. You research the law. You're the experts on the law called upon by other practitioners when they face what to them is a novel issue. I hadn't gotten so much of that in my first three years. The folks out in the trenches hadn't really heard my name, and I was surrounded by the heavy hitters. There were lawyers in the office like John Messina, Ray Rogers and Charlie Harrington who truly had the goods. They could rattle off the case names, and often the case cites, with ease. I couldn't do that. They were the scholars. I was the playboy. Hell, I hadn't yet come to grips with the concept of the courts' standard of review.

In 1992, a book was published entitled *In Our Defense: The Bill of Rights in Action*, written by Caroline Kennedy, a Columbia Law graduate who today serves as the United States Ambassador to Australia but who is best known as the only daughter of President John Fitzgerald Kennedy, along with a woman by the name of Ellen Alderman. Her book is a very interesting study for both lawyers and laypersons. For each of the rights enumerated in the first ten amendments to the United States Constitution, the book examines the development of the right in history and in the common law. For each, there is a detailed discussion of one or two celebrated cases that illustrate how the right is put into play in practice. For the Sixth Amendment right of confrontation, Caroline discusses *Coy v. Iowa*. No mention of B. John Burns, however.

After *Coy* the calls started coming. My standard practice when I fielded a question that was over my head, as most of them were, was to get a number and promise to call them back. Then I'd go find Ray or Messina for an answer before I returned the call. Increasingly, I was surrounded during the cocktail hours following CLE seminars by the trial court foot soldiers who would regale me with the fact patterns of the cases they were handling.

"What do you think?" they'd ask.

At the outset of 1989 the public defender offices across Iowa, previously organized and financed by the counties in which they were located, all became part of a state public defender system. The chief defender for the state, former Waterloo Public Defender Bill Wegman, would tout me as an example of the expertise that could be found in the Iowa defender community. He would bring up *Coy* without mentioning, or probably even realizing, that I was little more than a spectator when that case went up the ladder.

My bromance with Bill came screeching to a halt two years later when I was elected president of the Iowa Public Defenders Association, a quasi-union which soon made an unfortunate shift in course to becoming a body that was adversarial to management. The tension was exacerbated by the monthly publication (by me) of a very primitive *PDA Update* that was intended to share information about the goings on in the individual defender offices and about developments in the law. But no *PDA Update* was ever complete without some cheap shot at Bill or at state government, or both.

But the reputation, which still amounted to a gross exaggeration of my skills and prowess as an attorney, was beginning to stick. It was time, I decided, for me to follow the example of the true scholars in the office, and to begin reading and summarizing the published opinions in all of the criminal cases decided by the Iowa Supreme Court and the United States Supreme Court, and not just those that came down in my own cases.

It was harder than it looked. Some of them are very long, upwards of 100 pages, and not necessarily compelling reads. I would do it as I did in law school. After reading through an opinion I would jot down, on a legal pad, a brief summary of the relevant facts followed by a concise summary of the issues raised and the courts' holdings. It was an exercise that helped me to visualize the connections between cases resolving related classes of issues. Increasingly, the guiding principles would come into view.

Then came the April 1990 seminar in New Orleans, my road to Damascus as an attorney, where the scales finally fell from my eyes to illuminate the concept of the appellate courts' standards of review. Knowing the correct standard of review does more than assist you in evaluating the strength of your appellate case. It also enhances the predictive quality of your reading of precedent. If the Supreme Court holds that the trial court did not abuse its discretion in submitting a particular instruction of law to the jury, it does not follow that the next court is required to give the same instruction. The same level of deference that enabled the first court to provide the instruction also permits the second court to deny it. But if the Court finds the tried court committed *error* in giving the instruction, it would be error for the second court to follow suit.

Just being able to say things like that made me sound, and feel, smarter than I had been before.

Then I started giving continuing legal education lectures. Every lawyer in Iowa is required to attend at least 15 hours of approved classes each year to maintain his or her law license. Except for a few ethics hours, the Supreme Court doesn't care what classes you take. You can be a criminal lawyer and attend corporate tax lectures. And you can be a corporate tax attorney and attend lectures dealing with criminal law and procedure. But efforts are made to organize seminars with a high concentration of presentations relevant to one's area of practice. The reason for the CLE requirement, of course, is to make the attendee a competent practitioner in his or her field. To this end, there are several associations that endeavor to organize seminars that benefit criminal defense attorneys.

Criminal law and procedure are broad fields, and CLE seminars plow a wide-ranging swarth of subject matter. I've attended seminars that break down, over two or three days, the secrets to selecting a favorable jury for a criminal case, to cross examining a witness you know is lying, and to how to carry oneself and to dress for success at trial. But every seminar I've ever attended included a criminal caselaw update. Charlie was doing it when I first started. Then it was Jim Whalen.

Jim Whalen joined the appellate defender's office not long after I did. He'd had a frenzied private trial practice in Waterloo, and then decided to take it down a notch for at least a while. Jim was one of those guys who seemed to be in love with the law. He loved talking about it and exchanging volleys of ideas on new directions that might be taken with the Court. He brought it home with him.

He was a natural for the caselaw update. To do one, the speaker customarily prepares an outline containing summaries of the consequential recent decisions of the Iowa appellate courts and the United States Supreme Court. For some, the oral presentation simply follows the outline and the speaker tries, as much as possible, to say something about each case mentioned in the written materials. Jim has a very dry, occasionally scatological, sense of humor. But any objectionable comments soar over the heads of all but the few who are paying close attention.

In late 1990, the Iowa Trial Lawyers Association invited me to speak at their annual criminal law seminar in Iowa City. As Jim was doing the caselaw update for that one, the request was for me to do a presentation on Fourth Amendment decisions, on cases involving search and seizure. It was an opportunity for me to organize some of the case summaries I'd prepared into an outline I could use as the springboard for a one-hour presentation.

By the early 90s Jim decided that he'd sat out long enough and was eager to get back into the game. He was able to make a lateral transfer into the Des Moines Public Defender office, a move less like going from the frying pan to the fire than it was like going from the refrigerator crisper bin into the fire. Fully aware of the tidal wave in which he would soon be awash, Jim hung up the cleats and stepped aside for someone else to handle the caselaw updates he was presenting for various groups.

Those calls started coming to me.

Every year since then I've done it from two to seven or eight times, depending on who wants to hear me. All the cases would go in my outline. The United States Supreme Court decisions. The published Iowa Supreme Court decisions, and many of the published decisions of the Iowa Court of Appeals. I lay off the unpublished ones. There are certain circumstances under which it's appropriate to mention an unpublished decision in one's advocacy. But they are not authority and shouldn't be cited as such. That's my view.

Not everyone agrees with me on this one, but there are good reasons to let the unpublished decisions remain obscure. Rendering an unpublished decision is an opportunity for the court to *do the right thing*. When you've got really ugly facts, but have the law on your side, the attitude of the appeals court may be that *this monster's getting out of prison over my dead body*. With an unpublished decision, the appeals court can reach a decision that runs counter to precedent, one that would set bad precedent if it was published. On the other hand, if you've got a sympathetic client who's dead in the water on the law, you can ignore the unhelpful precedent and do the right thing for the poor bastard.

I've never once heard anyone on the inside track even speculate that this actually happens. But the rule says that unpublished cases aren't precedent, so I don't read them (at least for my CLE presentations) and don't include them in my outlines. But all the others are there. A standard organization for my outlines has evolved over the years. Each includes summaries of cases going back anywhere from a year to sixteen months. I generally start a fresh one each June for the Iowa Public Defender Seminar and add onto it until the Iowa Association of Criminal Lawyers Seminar in November. By the end of the cycle, my outlines have between 60 and 100 pages.

Even in my own practice, the caselaw update outlines I've prepared for CLE seminars have been a helpful starting point for research. By the mid-90s, it struck me that I had put so much work into them that I should compile them into a general outline incorporating all the cases I've summarized over the course of the decade. A comprehensive outline of my research, following my organization, is more user friendly for me than even the electronic research that was now becoming available. In whatever spare time I had, I began that process. As a work in progress, the combined outline was growing to three or four hundred pages in length.

The process became more arduous for me in May 1994

when I followed Jim's lead and transferred from the appellate defender to the Des Moines public defender. I actually took Jim's place in that office, as he and Nick Drees were departing to join the newly established federal public defender for the Southern District of Iowa. After nine years of being paid to do quiet reflection, I was conscious of the reality that moving from appellate practice to trial practice would be a trembling shock to the system.

Jim Whalen, I already knew, was a much smarter attorney than I was. Clear evidence of that had been his wise decision to step away from the responsibility of doing the caselaw update when he moved from appellate practice to trial practice. The latter is sufficiently labor intensive without the additional task of constantly reading and summarizing appellate decisions and stepping away from a daunting caseload several times a year to do the song and dance at CLE seminars.

But I was relishing the experience of being the big fish in the small pond that came from doing those lectures. To be honest, my oral presentations at the seminars were packed with less useful practical information than those of most other speakers. The outlines were comprehensive. An attorney wanting to review the most recent developments could easily go to the outline for that. In my lectures, I would pinpoint ten or eleven decisions I deemed worthy of mention and go to town on them. That would fill maybe twenty minutes of a sixty-minute presentation. The remainder of my time went into humorous anecdotes and irreverent digs against our mutual enemies – the governor, the state public defender, the conservative (from my perspective at the time) courts and, it goes without saying, prosecutors. It held their attention and got them laughing. Most of them. It was like doing standup. I loved it.

I was, consequently, acquiring a reputation. Maybe because I was able to treat the often dark and tedious subject matter with such levity, the notion began to circulate that I was this great legal mind. An oracle. But it wasn't universal. Word was getting back to me that the humor in my seminar presentations, as well as the humor in my monthly *PDA Update*, was not settling well with the state public defender and with certain members of the Supreme Court. I was called out and excoriated on a number of occasions by Bill Wegman, and each confrontation found its way into the following month's *PDA Update*. That added fuel to the fire. The battle would continue for as long as Bill remained the state public defender and I remained president of the PDA.

On one occasion early in my presidential administration, I was summoned to answer for a cartoon I had drawn for the front page of the *Update*. Each summer I purchased a block of tickets to a Friday evening home game of the Iowa Cubs, the Chicago Cubs' Triple A affiliate in Des Moines, and dubbed it "PDA Night at Sec Taylor Stadium." To promote one of them I sketched a cartoon in which the pitcher, who bore some resemblance to me, struck the batter on the side of the face with an errant pitch. The home plate umpire, however, called it a strike. There was a perception by some that the injured batter in my cartoon looked a lot like Governor Terry Branstad, and that the renegade umpire may be Bill Wegman.

"The chief justice called me in," Bill reported, "wondering about the ethics of an attorney drawing a picture of himself assassinating the governor with a baseball."

"Well, that's just silly," I responded.

"I know," said Bill. "I told him it was just tongue in cheek."

I would learn several years later from someone who at the time was close to the Court that Bill's account wasn't quite accurate. The chief justice hadn't called Bill in. Rather, it was Bill who showed up in the chief's office with the cartoon, only to be told that the Court wasn't interested in getting in the middle of our internal squabbles.

That's not to say I was always in the chief justice's good graces. A story once reached me that the chief justice considered lodging an ethical complaint for language in a petition for rehearing asserting that "[i]n this case, the chief justice of the Iowa Supreme Court stepped down off the bench and donned the mantle of advocacy." Admittedly, I crossed the line with that one.

While none of these stunts made me a better attorney, they contributed to the folklore. As people like John Messina, Ray Rogers and Jim Whalen cycled out of the system, I found myself being characterized as the brain of the public defender system. The reputation facilitated my move from the appellate defender to the Des Moines trial office.

Trial Attorney

The Des Moines office was considered at the time to be a garden spot for trial practitioners, due in large part to the prestige of its managing attorney. As a 17-year-old Roosevelt High School wrestler, John Wellman was seriously injured in a hunting accident that left him totally blind. He nevertheless went to college and to Drake Law School, and became one of the most talented trial attorneys in Iowa. During jury selection in any case, John would commit to memory the names and biographical information for each of the forty potential jury panelists, along with their locations in the room. He would address them without notes. He was sharp and forceful and good on his feet, and was a known slavedriver to the attorneys who worked under him.

The decision to make the jump came as I approached the Grand Canyon by car in the Sonoran Desert. We'd buried my grandmother in Worcester on St. Patrick's Day. I was back in Des Moines the following morning to embark on a spring break road trip to the Grand Canyon and Las Vegas. It was an opportunity for some deep thought. It wasn't that I was unhappy being an appellate defender. But, with the openings created by the departures of Jim and Nick, there was this nagging feeling that if I didn't move on now I would be an appellate defender for the remainder of my professional life. Home again a week later, I called Wellman to see if he was interested in having me.

John was in Cedar Rapids that week trying a major murder case that had been moved there on a change of venue.

He returned my call when the trial was adjourned for the day. He was elated. My call, he said, was the one bright spot of that day. I'd probably had a total of two conversations with John before that, but this reputation I'd acquired infused him with the feeling that he'd just signed Michael Jordan.

I worked for John for five years until 1999, when I followed Jim and Nick into the federal public defender's office. The benefits from that move were tangible. My salary nearly doubled from what I was earning in state court. The number of cases in my file was a fraction of what I'd been assigned by John Wellman, though each was a major felony. The available trial resources seemed boundless compared to what we had in state court.

Federal defenders across the country enjoy some well-deserved prestige in the criminal law sector. Paul Papak, who represented John Coy in the Supreme Court at my behest, had left academia in 1994 to become the senior litigator in the Cedar Rapids Office of the federal defender. By 1996 he was the chief federal defender for the State of Iowa. I came aboard when Paul left Iowa to become an assistant with the federal defender in Oregon. Five years later, he was appointed as a federal magistrate in that district, where he remains today. Nick Drees, a Harvard College graduate who earned his law degree at the University of Illinois, succeeded Paul as managing attorney in Iowa. It was Nick who hired me. When Nick succumbed, twelve years later, to the very rare and virtually incurable anaplastic thyroid cancer, Jim Whalen stepped into the managing attorney role for what would be the remainder of my legal career.

A coworker in our Cedar Rapids office, Jane Kelly, was appointed in 2013 by President Barack Obama, her Harvard Law classmate, to serve as a judge on the Eighth Circuit Court of Appeals, making her the first federal defender employee in history to move directly from that position into a seat on a federal court of appeals bench. In 2016, Judge Kelly reportedly was on President Obama's short list to replace Justice Antonin Scalia on the Supreme Court. Fortunately for her, the President instead nominated Merrick Garland. Judge Garland's nomination was never put to a vote in the Republican-dominated Senate, which instead confirmed President Donald Trump's nomination of Neil Gorsuch after the 2016 election.

In 2022, Ketanji Brown Jackson became the first former federal defender attorney to sit on the United States Supreme Court when she succeeded Justice Steven Breyer on the Court. If Justice Brown attended the annual national federal defender training seminar in 2005, 2006 and 2007, the years she served in the office, I probably saw her there. But hundreds of federal defender attorneys attend those seminars, and I came to know only a handful personally.

That was the company I was now keeping.

For me, one of the real selling points of moving to the federal defender was the potential for a hybrid practice. In the Des Moines trial office, there was little opportunity to flex the appellate muscles that had carried me through my nine years with the appellate defender. Although the federal defender employed one or two appellate attorneys during my years there, the trial attorneys are permitted to handle their own appeals. The appeals are before the Eighth Circuit Court of Appeals, the arena for my first appearance as a licensed attorney four days after passing the bar. Most oral arguments are held in St. Paul and St. Louis. A trip to the latter meant at least two nights in the luxurious Ballpark Hilton overlooking Busch Stadium. I caught a game or two over the years. If I ever managed to land the right case with the right issue, there was the possibility that I could once again find myself taking that next step after the Eighth Circuit appeal.

Another trip to Washington and the United States Supreme Court.

Calls from Professor Rigg

During the transition of 1999, I received a phone call from Professor Robert Rigg. For as long as I could remember, Bob had been one of Wellman's crew at the Des Moines adult public defender. When I joined the office we worked side by side for a year or two until he landed a position as a clinical professor at Drake University Law School, where he has remained ever since.

In 1997 Bob was in touch to tell me he was forming an R&B band. I wasn't aware until then that Bob owned an impressive collection of Fender and Gibson guitars, and that he was a decent blues guitarist. I don't know if he had seen the movie *The Commitments*, like I had, and fell in love with the idea. But that's what he wanted to do. A lawyer band. We learned that Jamie Bowers, a much-feared drug prosecutor with the Polk County Attorney's Office, was a renaissance man at the core. He was a master gardener, a former champion high school wrestler, and an accomplished bass player. The singer would be Mary Pat Gunderson, also a prosecutor though not as feared as Jamie, who would one day do a stint as a district court judge. I knew already that in her formative years Mary Pat had been part of the Up With People music ensemble. So I knew she could sing. The only non-lawyer in the original group, mortgage banker Craig Hatler, kept the beat. Bob wanted me to play keyboards.

We called ourselves "Goodnight, Dallas," based upon the historic photograph of Lee Harvey Oswald taking the bullet in the stomach from Jack Ruby, photoshopped to replace the handgun with a Fender stratocaster, to put Oswald behind a microphone and to station the sheriff to his right behind a pair of Roland D-20 keyboards. The caption of the meme was "Thank you, Dallas. Good night!"

Others passed in and out of Goodnight Dallas over the course of its seven-year stretch. Clarence Key, Jr., a former assistant state ombudsman who one Thursday in the 80s made it possible for me to visit my clients in their cells inside the walls of the Iowa State Penitentiary and who was now the executive director of the Iowa Board of Parole, succeeded Mary Pat as our singer. Private attorney Tom Schlapkohl played the B-3 organ. We had a procession of bass players. Jamie Bowers made the jump to federal court the same time I did. Only he went to Sioux City, 197 miles away. After a few years there, he accepted United

States Attorney positions in Guam, and then in Saipan. We found a guy to replace him who was very accomplished on the instrument but unable to overcome a narcotics addiction that ultimately would claim his life. Then there was Mac Stanfield, a lawyer who had amassed a respectable playing resume with popular bands like Scruffy the Cat. For a while, his wife Jodi joined us as our singer. I think Donny Guisinger was with us at the end of our run. Rather than giving away pens and calendars to prized customers like other mortgage bankers do, Craig rewarded his by making them part of Goodnight Dallas. I once had a dream during that period that we were playing a gig in a dark smokey bar and I noticed two people gyrating on the stage.

"Who are they?" I asked one of my bandmates.

"They're background dancers. Craig brought them in."

"I swear to God," I muttered. "If those people are getting a share of the fee I'm going to unplug and quit the band right now."

Then I woke up.

Bob's call in 1999 had to do with something besides "making a little noise," as he always called our playing.

Bob was calling about Volume 4 of West Publishing's Iowa Practice Series, entitled *Criminal Law and Procedure.* Founded in St. Paul in 1872 by brothers John and Horatio West, West Publishing was the Coca Cola of law book publishers. West was acquired in the 1990s by The Thomson Corporation, originally a newspaper publishing operation founded in Canada. In 2008 Thomson joined with the Reuters Group PLC to form Thomson Reuters. Publications that once bore the West name are now Thomson Reuters. They are everywhere and publish reference materials in every area of the law. In Iowa and other jurisdictions, treatises authored by practitioners are grouped into Practice Series. In recent years they have been published in digital format to aid in computer research.

Criminal Law and Procedure, written by Drake Law Professor John J. Yeager and Washington University Law

Professor Ronald L. Carlson was published in 1978. The impetus for releasing the treatise at that time was the adoption a year earlier of the new Iowa Criminal Code, that restructured both criminal law and procedure in the state. The process had been ongoing for eight years, with Professor Yeager acting as a legislative consultant on criminal law and sentencing, and Professor Carlson similarly consulting on matters relating to criminal procedure. The duties of writing Volume 4 were split down those same lines.

The practice manual, which for two decades was the Bible for criminal practitioners, was a hard-bound volume. Not unexpectedly, changes in the law come often and come very quickly. The way changes in the law were handled in legal publishing was through the use of a "pocket part," a supplemental booklet that slides into a pocket in the back inside cover of the volume, containing all the cumulative changes that have arisen since the book's original publication. After 20 years, the pocket part for Volume 4 had grown to be very hefty. The time had come to replace the original publication. By 1999, however, Professors Yeager and Carlson had both retired.

Now a professor himself, Bob had been invited by a representative from West to meet about attacking the project, following the same approach employed by Yeager and Carlson in 1978. If Bob agreed to write the criminal law section of the new book, could he identify a suitable author for the section on procedure?

I don't know if I was Bob's first candidate, but I was the one who said yes.

The West representative took us to dinner at the 801 Chophouse. The upscale steakhouse on the second floor of Iowa's tallest building had been open for six years, but this was the first time I'd had any reason to venture inside. Over filet mignon and lobster mashed potatoes, the rep laid out the deal.

For the next three years, Bob and I would be responsible for the pocket parts for Yeager and Carlson. Then, in 2002, we would publish the brand spanking new *4 Iowa Practice*: *Criminal*

Law and Procedure. It would not be a mere revision of Yeager and Carlson. It would be our project from the ground up. The rep had contracts to sign. I would have signed them just for those lobster mashed potatoes, but there was money involved as well.

Published Author

I don't know that what I'd agreed to fully sunk in until I was well on my way to writing the book. This was an *immense* project, to say the least. It was a project I took on just as I was starting the new job with the federal defender office. The federal defender gig alone is a full-time job and a half. Even before the West guy showed up, I'd wondered if I'd be able to maintain the outlines and continue doing the caselaw updates for the CLEs. The job responsibilities of the federal defender include educating other members of the bar about criminal defense, but it was questionable how much value my review of developments in state criminal law held for a practice that was exclusively federal. Nick Drees would justify it with the observation that it was good to have someone in the office who was conversant in Iowa state law. But *writing a book* about state law was something entirely different.

The first thing Bob and I were asked to do was to submit outlines for our portions of the book. That was the easy part for me. I had an outline in place for the caselaw updates I had now been doing for nearly a decade. I dug out the compilation I'd worked on sporadically and winnowed it down to a skeletal outline. I moved the section on constitutional law from the front of the outline to the back and removed all sections relating to the criminal law and specific sentences. Bob would be writing on those matters.

That was the birth of my book. West was happy with my outline.

I did three things in 1999. I started a new job. I built a new house (with the windfall derived from the new job). And I started writing a treatise on criminal procedure.

It's a backbreaking process.

It isn't that I hadn't written a book before. In 1996, I managed to write the first draft of *Baby Pictures*, a memoir of my experiences on the road in the mid-70s playing the Holiday Inn circuit with Baby Lester and the Buggybumpers. Then, earlier in 1999, I wrote a first draft of *Dead Horses*, all my stories that didn't make it into *Baby Pictures*.

This clearly would be different. *Baby Pictures*, when finally published, came in at about 350 pages. *Dead Horses* was around 450 pages. This would be longer. It would be more detailed, and I would have to strive for accuracy in every paragraph on every page. There was a home office in the new house, and the tower computer was set up at the desk in that small dark room, facing the wall. The next three years held the prospect of hours and hours of slogging away at that desk.

It may have been my first ever purchase online, later in 1999, when I dropped $200 on a used Dell laptop computer. Although the 'a' key was detached, the new investment enabled me to work on the manual in varied and more comfortable settings. I don't know if I otherwise would have been able to complete my volume confined in that little office facing the wall.

But even so it was still damned difficult. It was a book that was not going to write itself. From 1999 until 2002 every night, every weekend and all my vacation time went into the manual.

I approached the construction of the manual like waves of infantry in a battle. The first wave consisted of the outlines from my CLE caselaw updates. I wanted them to be the heart and soul of the project because they comprised a decade of my personal research. I had read and summarized each of the cases discussed in the outlines, and my impressions from doing that shaped my understanding of Iowa criminal practice. It was what would make this *my* book. I welcomed the new book as a vehicle for my desire to compile all the work I'd done over the years into an accessible format that was useful as much to myself as it was to others.

The next wave involved sifting through all the statutes and court rules relating to criminal procedure. You learn in law school that the law derives from two sources. The common law essentially flows from the decisions of the appellate courts, each of which is a small particle in the mosaic that is the big picture. That's what I kept in my caselaw updates. The second source are the laws that are actually written out, enacted and enforced. The Ten Commandments. The Constitution. The Iowa Constitution. The Iowa Code. The Iowa Rules of Criminal Procedure. The Iowa Rules of Evidence. The Iowa Rules of Appellate Procedure. The Iowa Rules of Civil Procedure. The City of Johnston, Iowa Code of Ordinances. There are many sources of statutory law. If Congress or the Iowa Legislature puts something into the Code, or if the Supreme Court puts something into the rules, it overrides the common law as expressed in court decisions. A major exception to that is where the appellate court, exercising its judicial review authority, finds that the statute or rule violates a provision of the constitution. So I pored through what I hoped was every statute and rule governing criminal procedure and applied them to what I had written during the first wave.

The final step of the process for me was to read carefully through pages 161 to 388 of Yeager and Carlson, the first *4 Iowa Practice: Criminal Law and Procedure*. This was Professor Carlson's discussion of procedure. I put this last on my list not to slight Professor Carlson and his work. With a law degree from Northwestern University, an LL.M. from Georgetown and at least 16 books on evidence and trial practice under his belt, Professor Carlson is far more qualified than I was to author a procedural treatise. But this new book was not going to be a revision of his 1978 work. It would be my original work. One hundred percent. The original purpose of the 1978 manual was to explain the massive changes in law and procedure brought about with the new Code in 1977, and to provide practitioners with a roadmap for applying them. With the release of my book a quarter century later, it was less an issue of how the new Code would be applied and more one of how it *has been* applied since its passage. While the new versions written by Bob and me have been in print now for over twenty years, some of the language of Yeager and Carlson is still cited by practitioners and by the courts today.

Which is the reason why I did not ignore Yeager and Carlson in writing the new manual in 1999 through 2002. Having in hand what functionally was a completed first draft, the last booth on the tollway was the 1978 manual. Did I leave anything out of mine that was in Yeager and Carlson? Are there inconsistencies between the two that might indicate some flaw in what I had written? Is there anything in Yeager and Carlson that I should cite that would make my book more understandable or useful?

If anything, my review of their book assuaged any concerns I may have held about whether my book was sufficiently comprehensive. But I will add that the Yeager and Carlson volume is cited as authority at least seven times in my book.

At the end of three years of hard labor, the seven floppy disks and the hard copy of the manuscript that I mailed to West on December 26, 2001 comprised the single most intensive project of my life. More than law school. More than the bar exam. I had come up with 703 pages, 611 without the appendices. Bob was coming in with the same number of pages. With all the tables, etc., Yeager and Carlson totaled 779 pages. Professor Carlson had written 227 pages on procedure. After Bob and I submitted our manuscripts, the publisher made the decision that what we had was not one book, but two separate volumes.

So Prof. Robert R. Rigg published *4 Iowa Practice*: *Criminal Law*. And in May 2002, West Publishing released Burns, *4A Iowa Practice*: *Criminal Procedure*.

That's how I got this gig.

REVISING THE MANUAL

I have never given birth, and I never will. I'm too old, among other things. So I'm in no position to pontificate about the experience. I don't think it's a stretch, however, to imagine that gestation is one of the hard parts. The waiting. Those nine miserable months.

Expecting.

Then the little fella pops out and things settle down. The worst is over. It's happily ever after from that point forward. Smooth sailing.

I *know* that's not true. I've played at least a peripheral role in raising some children, and it can get pretty hairy. It's expensive. It's time-consuming. Things come up that you don't expect, didn't plan for, and didn't include in the budget.

And believe me – it *doesn't* end when they turn 18. But you already know that.

My friend Joe was the coauthor of an Iowa Practice Manual covering a different area of the law, and of its annual updates. When I was putting the final touches on my original volume in 2002 Joe advised me, "You don't get rich on the publication of one of these books. But you do quite well over time with the updates."

Some truth rang in Joe's advice.

I spent three years of hard labor putting together *4A Iowa Practice: Criminal Procedure 2002-03*. Nearly all my nights, weekends, holidays and vacation time went into that book. What came out at the end of *that* gestation period was different in a major respect from the previous Yeager and Carlson volume. It wasn't a hard cover book. It was a paperback. A hard cover edition would be nice, I thought, after all that work.

Furthermore, I noticed in some of the sales materials that West was referring to it as a "pamphlet." A pamphlet? In my world, a pamphlet is a 30-page guide they hand you when you visit the zoo that tells you where the animals are located and how you can donate to the Zoo Foundation. In other sales materials they call it a "treatise." I like that better. You see, I've written a *treatise* on Iowa criminal procedure. Yeah.

Under either label, it's definitely a "law book." As the years went on, parenthetically, having this book in my name would serve me well in my practice over and above the smiles elicited from the judges on the Eighth Circuit Court of Appeals when I cited myself as authority during oral argument. My meetings with clients would often include discussion of the status of the law that might support defenses in their cases or, on the other hand, might blow us completely out of the water.

Some of them would disagree, often vehemently, with my interpretation of the law. Occasionally there would be spirited arguments, with cuss words hurled in both directions. One thing I learned very early on as a lawyer was *don't discount what the client is telling you about the law or the facts. He (or she) may be right.* You're the lawyer. They're not. The advice in which they *do* place some credence often comes from other inmates who are not lawyers themselves. The thing about taking advice from other inmates, I tell them, is that some inmates actually know what they're talking about and some don't. And you can't determine which is which based on how confident they sound dispensing the advice (the same, by the way, can be said about some attorneys).

The other thing some clients don't realize is that when I argue back, when I come down hard on what they're trying to tell me, sometimes what I'm doing with them is what we lawyers do habitually in the privacy of our conference rooms. I'm "testing the mettle" of their arguments. Before some prosecutor, trial judge or appellate court has an opportunity to punch holes in our position I'm going to do it first here, to see how it holds up.

The client doesn't always lose those debates. It's his case and his life and, while ethically most decisions about legal strategy are left in the hands of the attorney, the client ought to have meaningful input. More than a few times I carried a banner into battle that was first handed to me by the client, sometimes taking it right up to the Court of Appeals.

But the waters from which you'd best steer clear if you're my client are the truths derived from something you read in "the law books." I've met individuals who have spent nearly the entirety of their adult lives incarcerated who are as accomplished as researchers in the law as any Ivy League academic. They've memorized the titles and citations of relevant cases and can quote treatises and the decennial digests chapter, page and verse. When they've got a point to make, they can direct me right to the source.

But then there are others . . .

"I know what I'm talking about. I read it in the law book."

"What law book did you read it in?"

"Which law book?"

"Yeah. There's thousands and thousands of law books. Which one have you read?"

No answer. So I dig into the stack of books and files I carried with me into the jail, and whip out the latest volume of *4A Iowa Practice: Criminal Procedure* and slap it down on the table.

"Now *here's* a law book," I tell him. "Is *this* the book you're talking about?"

"Maybe. I don't think so."

"Well, look how big it is. It talks about pretrial motions, trial procedure, constitutional law. Everything you want to know about criminal procedure. Let's see what it says about your point."

I flip open the manual and leaf right to the page that

addresses the client's contention. I read to him the language that torpedoes his claim.

"Oh," he mutters.

"Now different law books reach different conclusions on an issue, so this law book could be wrong. I don't think it is. But I want you to see something."

I close the book and show him the front cover.

"Look who wrote this," I instruct him. "Do you know who that is?"

That nearly always brings them around. There was one time, however, that I did that with a client.

"Do you know who that is?" I asked the client as I pointed to the author's name.

"Your father?" he asked.

So for two decades there has never been a hard cover volume of *4A Iowa Practice: Criminal Procedure.* It's always been a paperback "pamphlet." The utility of doing it this way soon became apparent. Unlike Yeager and Carlson, there would be no pocket parts for this manual. Instead, a new paperback edition would be published each year. The practitioner would no longer be relegated to having to first search the body of the hard cover manual for the answer to a legal question, and then to pore through page after page of small type in the pocket parts to ascertain how the law had developed over a quarter century. If I did it carefully, I could now work the changes into the original text, resulting in a single unified, comprehensive volume.

One drawback will arise when the time arrives for me to turn over the revision process to another writer, as Professors Yeager and Carlson had done when Bob and I came on board. Under the 1999 contract with West, all my parental rights will be terminated. Proceeds of sales of the work will go to the new writer and, in a more damaging blow to my ego, the name on the cover will go as well. The new guy may add 25 pages each year to the 1300 pages I'd written over a period of a quarter century but, in the eyes of the reader, it's the new guy's book. It will also be the new guy's prerogative, of course, to go line by line and do a complete rewrite, as Bob and I had done. I think I'd almost prefer that.

But the new process reaped immediate benefits for me and my book.

One thing into which I hadn't looked deeply as I was writing the first volume was how involved West Publishing would be in the process of copyediting. I sent them the manuscript. Several months later the proofs came in the mail. They looked fine, so I gave them the thumbs up. In May 2002 the publishing stork visited the Burns house.

There is no feeling more gratifying than holding in your hands a published book that you have authored, especially a big fat one like this. And I guess I'm one of those parents who don't spot the flaws in their own children. I didn't spot them the two or three times I read through the manuscript before sending it in. I didn't spot them when I approved the proofs. And I didn't spot them as I proudly toted my newborn everywhere I went.

Then the honeymoon comes to an end, and the blemishes become noticeable. There are *typos* in this book. I'm sitting on an airplane, paging through *my book* and hoping a passenger in an adjoining seat will take an interest and ask me about it. But there's a typographical error on this page. There's another two pages later. Soon I'm counting them. I find 125 typos in all.

It's a hard lesson I'm forced to confront about myself, that I'm so enamored with seeing my book in print that the flaws are invisible to me. It still holds true today, though hopefully my awareness makes me better at proofreading my own work than I was in 2001.

Had I been Professor Yeager or Professor Carlson, the problem would have been a more substantial one than it was for me. I am sure that, in the late 1970s, their book was set the old-fashioned way. Once it was out, the authors would be hard-pressed to secure another edition to correct a misplaced apostrophe or an improperly italicized case cite.

With the annually revised paperback volume, all my sins were forgiven in April 2003 when the new edition came out. Not only could I add analysis gleaned from the new Supreme Court decisions issued in the intervening year, I was able to purge all the embarrassing typographical errors. If there were some I missed, I could address them the following year.

So that's the process, the annual cycle. The Supreme Courts of Iowa and the United States release their decisions between October and June. When a few hours open up, I read through them and summarize them. I organize the summaries into an outline for my caselaw update lectures at CLE seminars throughout the year. Beginning in September or October, I meld the summaries into the appropriate pages of *4A Iowa Practice: Criminal Procedure*. Do they change the law? Do they reinforce and add to what the Court has said in earlier cases? Do they provide more clarity and detail in how defense attorneys (and prosecutors and even judges) should apply the law in their practice?

Along with the new cases, I peruse all of the legislation passed by the Iowa House of Representatives and Senate and signed by the governor. Criminal procedure in Iowa must comport with the Iowa Code as much as it does with the rules and the Constitution. I scour the orders issued by the Supreme Court for any changes in the court rules.

On or before December 10 each year, I compile it all into a set of revisions, a list of instructions to the editors at West, now Thomson Reuters, for specific changes to be made to the language of my book. It is no longer necessary to send in the mail a packet of floppy disks and a hard copy. I simply email a digital file to the publisher. Then I sit back and enjoy the holidays.

In February I receive an email from the publisher with the proofs, for my review. The proofs are a copy of how the new edition of my book will appear with the changes I have made. I have two weeks to look them over, make corrections and to add any new content based upon court decisions and rule changes since December. The obvious objective is a volume that is fully up to date when it is published.

In April the postal service drops a box on my doorstep with my six copies of the newest manifestation of *4A Iowa Practice: Criminal Procedure.*

Over the years, my boy has grown. It varies from year to year how many pages are added to the previous edition. Much of it depends upon the number and complexity of the published criminal opinions released by the appellate courts during the year. While the 2002-03 edition had 611 pages of substantive text, not counting tables and indices, the 2022 volume was 1159 pages long. From the beginning my book has been organized into seven parts covering (1) the initiation of a case, (2) pretrial practice, (3) trial practice, (4) evidence and witnesses in criminal cases, (5) appellate and postconviction remedies, (6) constitutional issues, and (7) prison law.

In some years, revision of the manual is a very smooth, seamless process. There is little for me to do besides simply reading the cases and sending in the revisions. In others, it's been a challenge.

Some jarring bumps in the road have cropped up on the eves of deadlines. The most formidable of them prior to 2022 came just as I was preparing to submit the final manuscript for the very first edition.

It was one of those fortuitous circumstances that I managed to spot an order from the Supreme Court announcing that, effective in February 2002, all of the rules of court in Iowa would be renumbered to add one-digit prefixes identifying the sets of rules in which they were included. The rules of criminal procedure, for example, were given the prefix 2, while the rules of evidence were 5. The highly litigated rule about the admissibility into evidence of a person's prior bad acts thus went from being Rule of Evidence 404(b) to being Rule of Evidence 5.404(b). Rule of Criminal Procedure 33(2), setting speedy trial deadlines, became Rule of Criminal Procedure 2.33(2).

Few, if any, were substantive changes. But this book, coming out in May, now contained about 1200 incorrect citations spread out over its pages. It had to be fixed. There was only one thing I could do.

Although he'd graduated from Drake Law School first in his class and Order of the Coif, Chief Justice Louis Lavorato had sat for seven years on the Polk County trial court bench before being appointed to the Supreme Court by Governor Branstad in 1986. So I viewed him more as a streetfighter like myself than as a closed-door academic. In at least one of the stories that filtered back to me about the preceding chief justice going on the warpath over some of my rhetoric, it was Justice Lavorato who had come to my defense. I felt comfortable calling him on the telephone to vent.

"What are you guys trying to do to me?" I scolded.

"What did we do to *you*?"

"Do you know what I've been doing for the last three years?"

Of course, the chief justice had no idea what I'd been working on.

"I'm rewriting Yeager and Carlson ground up, day and night. Three solid years, and I finally get it to where it's ready. Then *you guys* come along and change all the rule numbers. I've got to go back through the whole thing."

The chief justice agreed that it was thoughtless of the Court to drop this on John Burns' shoulders as he's coming up to the deadline. The rules, he promised, would stay the way they were.

That wasn't *really* going to happen. I went right to work on it, toiling away all weekend and into the following week to change all the Rule 19(5)s to Rule 2.19(5) and all the Rule 813s to Rule 5.813. But I got it done.

As I've said, I strive for accuracy in the manual. In 2021, I emailed my final February revisions to the publisher on February 21. On March 19, the Supreme Court decided *State v. Hillery*, 956 N.W.2d 492 (Iowa 2021). On the evening before *Hillery* was announced, I read through the parties' briefs in that case to get an idea of the issues expected to be resolved by the Court's decision. I was pleased, as I always am, to see that the appellate defender had quoted *4A Iowa Practice: Criminal Procedure* in support of a search and seizure argument.

"Despite hints in the dicta," I had written in the manual, "the Supreme Court has never expressly held that the odor of burnt marijuana alone constitutes sufficient probable cause for a warrantless search, although it has been considered in combination with other factors."

The quoted language had been in the manual from the outset in 2002. The issue in *Hillery* was slightly different, relating to the warrantless arrest of a defendant rather than a search. In the *Hillery* opinion, Justice Thomas Waterman noted first that the arrest was valid even without resolving the marijuana odor question, but felt it was important to articulate an answer for cases in which it might arise in the future. He seized on language in the Court's 2011 decision in *State v. Watts*, 801 N.W.2d 845 (Iowa 2011) that "a trained officer's detection of a sufficiently distinctive odor [of marijuana], by itself or when accompanied by other facts, may establish probable cause."

Justice Waterman didn't mention the manual, or me, expressly in the *Hillery* opinion. But the fact that he reached out to make the point in dicta was a strong suggestion that the *Watts* language concerning probable cause for an arrest applied equally to questions of probable cause for a search. If it mattered enough to the Court to make that statement, it was important enough to not leave potentially misleading information hanging out there for 13 months until the 2022 edition was published.

I contacted the editor. Is there still time to get four more revisions into the book for 2021? It could be done. The presses were stopped.

That was stressful – for an old man.

But then 2022 happened. . .

THE ACTIVIST (ALBEIT REPUBLICAN) COURT

Iowa became a state on December 28, 1846.

It was the 29th to be admitted to the United States of America. The earliest evidence of indigenous inhabitants in the area stretches back to the 11th or 12th Centuries B.C. The first Europeans, led by Jacques Marquette and Louis Jolliet, made their appearances in 1673. Congress made Iowa a United States territory on the Fourth of July 1838. A three-justice Supreme Court was established nearly five months later, on November 28 – six days after Thanksgiving.

Blazing the Trails

Iowa's first three justices were Charles Mason, Joseph Williams and Thomas S. Wilson. The Court issued its first opinion on July 4, 1839. A case titled *in re matter of Ralph*.

Eighteen years after *Ralph*, the United States Supreme Court addressed a similar issue in *Dred Scott v. Sanford*, 60 U.S. 347 (1857). Born into slavery in 1799, Dred Scott had moved from state to state for the first 46 years of his life. Several of the states in which he lived, including at one point Iowa, were free states.

Living in the slave state of Missouri, Scott and his wife first sued for their freedom in 1846 pursuant to two state statutes, one of which provided that a slave who had resided in a free state was a free person who could no longer be enslaved in a slave state. They were successful at one point in the lower Missouri state courts but were re-enslaved when the Missouri

Supreme Court reversed the favorable decision in 1852. After similarly being unsuccessful in the United States district court, Scott took his case to the Supreme Court in 1854.

Chief Justice Roger Taney's opinion ruling against Dred Scott was one of the factors that would ignite the Civil War. Slaves and their descendants are not citizens, he held, and thus may not take refuge in the federal courts. They are property, and their owners are protected by the Fifth Amendment. To the extent that the Missouri Compromise of 1820 operated to free slaves within United States territories, it was unconstitutional.

The Iowa Supreme Court reached a different conclusion in *Ralph*.

Rafe Nelson was born a slave in Virginia in 1795, the property of William Montgomery. In 1830, he was one of five slaves sold by Montgomery to his son Jordan of Lincoln County, Kentucky for a total of $820. It is possible that two of the others, 80-year-old Ben and 60-year-old Celia, were his parents. Listed as Ralph on the bill of sale, he became Ralph Montgomery. When he was 39 years old, he signed an agreement with Jordan that would allow him to travel from their home in Palmyra, Missouri to Dubuque, Iowa. Ralph worked in the lead mines in Dubuque, and the arrangement was that he could buy his freedom for $550 plus interest (or, according to a different account, for $500 which included interest). After five years with little success as a miner Ralph was unable to earn the agreed-upon amount. Jordan meanwhile was falling upon hard times and paid two bounty hunters $100 to travel the 232 miles to Dubuque to return Ralph to Missouri. A local magistrate in Dubuque gave the bounty hunters permission to capture Ralph, then handcuff him and return him to Missouri.

Ralph's closest friend Alexander Butterworth witnessed the abduction and brought it to the attention of Judge Thomas S. Wilson who, just weeks earlier at the age of 25, had been appointed as one of the first three justices of the fledgling Iowa Territorial Supreme Court. Justice Wilson issued a hastily prepared writ of habeas corpus ordering the return of Ralph, who had just been placed aboard a riverboat bound for Missouri. Having already departed at the Jackson County town of Bellevue, the vessel returned with Ralph.

Apparently by agreement of the parties, the case was heard on July 4, 1839 by the territorial Supreme Court. Ralph was represented in the proceeding by David Rorer, a Virginia native who had owned seven slaves as a judge in Arkansas but whose evolving anti-slavery sentiment brought him to reside in Wisconsin and ultimately Iowa, where it is believed that he built the first house in the territory that was constructed of brick.

Represented by J.D. Learned, Jordan Montgomery invoked the provisions of the Fugitive Slave Act to support Ralph's return to Missouri. Rorer responded that, since he had resided in the free territory of Iowa, Ralph was a free man and could not be returned. He also relied on a common law principle that, having lived in a free territory, Ralph could not forcibly be returned to a slave state. He did not deny owing the $550 debt under the contract with Jordan Montgomery.

The Court's ruling was announced that day. Because he had issued the writ, Justice Wilson did not participate in the decision. Chief Justice George Mason found that Jordan Montgomery had allowed Ralph to live in Iowa, a free territory, and by doing so gave Ralph his freedom. Under the Ordinance of 1787, governing the Northwest Territory which included what would become Iowa, "no man shall be deprived of his liberty... but by the law of the land . . . [T]here shall be neither slavery nor involuntary servitude." Similarly, the Missouri Compromise of 1820 abolished slavery and involuntary servitude, except as criminal punishment. A construction of those acts that authorized the return of Ralph to slavery, Mason wrote, would "introduce almost unqualified slavery into all the free states." The $550 is "a debt which he ought to pay, but for the non-payment of which no man in this territory can be reduced to slavery." It might have been a different story had Montgomery sent Ralph into Iowa on a brief errand, or if Ralph had escaped as they traveled together through the state. The Fugitive Slave Act might apply. But by being allowed to live unfettered in Iowa for several years, Ralph had been given unconditional freedom.

The bottom line of the decision in the first case decided by the Iowa Supreme Court is that Ralph Montgomery was not property to be returned to its rightful owner.

"Property, in the slave, cannot exist without the existence of slavery; the prohibition of the later annihilates the former, and, thus being destroyed, he becomes free."

"Old Rafe," as he was called in his *Chicago Tribune* obituary printed five days after his June 23, 1870 passing from smallpox, lived the rest of his life mining lead in Dubuque. It is said that in 1840 he showed up at the home of Justice Thomas Wilson to work in his garden. It was not intended as remuneration for the writ of habeas corpus that brought his case into the Supreme Court and secured his freedom, but rather as a reminder "that I never forget."

In its very first decision, the Iowa Supreme Court got it right on an issue that was taken up eighteen years later by the United States Supreme Court, which didn't. That was an error corrected only by a bloody Civil War that cost the lives of 660,000 soldiers and 50,000 civilians.

A monument to the *Ralph* case, and particularly to the courage of Alexander Butterworth, who took action when he saw his friend being abducted by bounty hunters, is a 30-foot-tall sculpture constructed of Dubuque limestone and stainless steel. Called *Shattering the Silence*, it stands outside the Iowa Judicial Building in Des Moines and celebrates, not just the one case, but Iowa's occasionally progressive civil rights history. *Ralph* wasn't the only time in its history that the Iowa Supreme Court stood at the forefront.

It is due, perhaps, to the fact that our state Supreme Court enforces a constitution that, from the outset in 1857, has recognized in section 1 of its first article that "[a]ll men are, by nature, free and equal."

In 1868, the Supreme Court decided *Clark v. The Board of Directors*, 24 Iowa 266 (1868). Susan B. Clark was a 12-year-old girl who was denied admission to Grammar School No. 2 in her neighborhood in Muscatine on the ground that she was African American. She had previously attended a separate "school for colored children, in a comfortable building, with proper furniture and provided with a competent teacher" located in a different district. She was instructed to enroll there, and she sued. The district court granted mandamus ordering the district to admit her to Grammar School No. 2.

The Supreme Court affirmed the mandamus. Earlier manifestations of Iowa law had in fact provided for the creation of separate schools for students of African descent. As late as 1860, Iowa law permitted African American students to attend white schools only with the "unanimous consent" of all the students enrolled there. But the 1857 Constitution provided for "the education of *all the youths of the State*, through a system of common schools," (emphasis supplied) with no mention of separate schools for African American students. Similar language appeared in legislation adopted in 1860, 1862 and 1865. While local school boards are vested with discretion on many matters relating to the construction and operation of schools, there is no discretion to construct separate schools for African American students. This would be no different from requiring students of Irish-American or German-American descent, or students who were Catholic or Protestant, or who were more shabbily dressed, to attend separate schools.

Justice Chester C. Cole reached this decision over the dissent of Justice George Grover Wright, who argued that the "principle of equal rights to all does not demand that all the children of the district should be taught in the same building, nor by the same teacher; nor that a colored child shall be transferred from one school to another, nor that this should be done for a white child. The true inquiry is: Have all equal school privileges? And, if so, being all children alike, and alike equal before the law, but no more, this equality is preserved by adopting the same rule as to all."

With this in mind, the import of *Clark v. The Board of*

Directors is that by 1857 the Iowa Supreme Court had reached the watershed point of enlightenment that education is not sufficient under law where it is separate but equal. Eighty-six years would pass before the United States Supreme Court would catch up, in *Brown v. Board of Education*, 347 U.S. 483 (1954).

One peripheral aside to *Clark* is that Justice Cole, who wrote the majority opinion, and Justice Wright, who authored the dissent, joined forces in 1865 to establish in Des Moines the first law school west of the Mississippi River. It would become, in time, the University of Iowa College of Law.

Where I went to school.

One person who *didn't* attend the Iowa College of Law was Arabella Mansfield. In 1869 law school completion was not a requirement for admission to the bar. Lawyers were admitted through a period of apprenticeship with a lawyer or judge and successful completion of a bar examination. And sitting for the bar examination was limited to "males over 21."

Belle Babb was born in 1846 in Benton Township, 22 miles north and west of Cedar Rapids, Iowa. Changing her first name to Arabella, at 16 she took advantage of the dearth of male students precipitated by the Civil War and attended Iowa Wesleyan College in Mount Pleasant, graduating as valedictorian in three years. Her brother Washington Babb, who graduated with her as salutatorian (the second-ranking student in their class), passed the bar exam and set up a practice in Mount Pleasant. Now Arabella Mansfield following her marriage to an Iowa Wesleyan professor, she apprenticed with her brother in his law practice and in 1869 successfully took the bar exam. She then petitioned the Iowa Supreme Court for admission to the bar.

The Supreme Court ordered that admission to the bar cannot be limited to males. Consequently, Iowa became the first state in the United States to admit women to the bar and, though she was never a practicing attorney, Arabella Mansfield became the first woman in the United States to achieve that status.

By contrast, the United States Supreme Court held in

1872 that nothing in the Constitution required the state of Illinois to admit women to the practice of law. *Bradwell v. State*, 83 U.S. 130 (1872).

When Rosa Parks moved to the front of the bus in 1955, the Iowa Supreme Court had decided *Coger v. Northwestern Union Packet Co.* 37 Iowa 145 (1873) 82 years earlier. Emma Coger, a biracial teacher from Quincy, Illinois, boarded the *S.S. Merrill*, a Mississippi River steamboat, for transportation home. The policy of the carrier was that persons of color were allowed to use the vessel for transportation but could not rent a state room or take meals in the dining room. Ms. Coger's request to pay the full price for a ticket that included these luxuries was denied, and she initially walked away. But she returned and purchased a ticket that identified her as a person of color and limited where she could sleep and eat. She returned that ticket for a refund and persuaded a third party to purchase for her a ticket that did not have these limitations. When she used the ticket to take a place at the ladies' table in the dining room, Ms. Coger was removed forcibly.

Emma Coger sued the carrier for assault and battery, and the jury found in her favor. In the Supreme Court, the carrier challenged instructions given to the jury at trial that the carrier is not required to take passengers or to provide food and that the carrier may place reasonable conditions on the passengers who purchase tickets to travel and dine on the vessel, but that the carrier may not base the conditions on race.

The Supreme Court agreed with the outcome at trial, relying heavily on the unique language in article I, section 1 of the Iowa Constitution that "[a]ll men are, by nature, free and equal." But the Court also found support in the Civil Rights Act of 1866 and the Equal Protection Clause of the Fourteenth Amendment, that had come into effect in 1868.

In 1976, the Supreme Court found that Equal Protection and the right to marital privacy that were the foundation of *Griswold v. Connecticut*, 381 U.S. 479 (1965) and *Roe v. Wade*, 410 U.S. 113 (1973) protected the right of consenting unmarried (and, at the time, heterosexual) adults to engage in oral sex and other acts which were criminalized under then-Iowa Code § 705.1 as sodomy, in *State v. Pilcher*, 242 N.W.2d 348 (Iowa 1976). A quarter century would pass before the United States Supreme Court caught up with *Pilcher* and invalidated sodomy laws in the remaining 14 states where they still existed, in *Lawrence v. Texas*, 539 U.S. 558 (2003).

As a matter of equal protection, the fact that a mother was involved in a bi-racial relationship was found to be an improper factor for the family court to consider in awarding custody of children to the father in *In re Marriage of Kramer*, 297 N.W.2d 359 (Iowa 1980), four years before the United States Supreme Court would experience the same epiphany in *Palmore v. Sidoti*, 466 U.S. 429 (1984).

The potential turning point arose in *Varnum v. Brien*.

Varnum

In any discussion of the landmark decision in *Varnum v. Brien*, 763 N.W.2d 862 (Iowa 2009), two names are immortalized – Varnum and Brien. There were, in fact, twelve plaintiff/appellees in the case. All of them, including Katherine Varnum, had been denied licenses to enter into same-sex marriages. On the other side was Tim Brien, the Polk County, Iowa recorder. I knew Tim Brien, but not well. He and I graduated from the same high school four years apart, so I never met him there. His office was located in the Old Post Office that now functions as the County Administration Building. The stroll on the Des Moines skywalk system that each day brought me to the federal courthouse took me through the County Administration Building. Several times a week I would pass Tim Brien in the skywalk during that passage.

"Good morning, Counselor," Tim would greet me cheerfully. Apparently, he knew who I was and what it was I was doing at the time to put food on the table. But that was the extent of our conversations.

Tim Brien will go down in Iowa judicial history because

he (or perhaps one of his underlings) was the man who refused to provide a marriage license to Katherine Varnum and to the other named plaintiff/appellees. For folks on my side of the political aisle, Tim wore the black hat in *Varnum v. Brien*.

It wasn't that Tim had anything against any of the twelve. It wasn't that Tim necessarily held any predilections for or against gay marriage. As I say, I hardly knew the guy. My guess is that Tim Brien personally was not against gay marriage.

Tim Brien wore the black hat because he wore the badge. He was the county recorder. Among his many other duties Tim Brien, as the county recorder, handed out marriage licenses as he was authorized to do so under Iowa law. Iowa law didn't authorize him to issue a marriage license to Katherine Varnum, or to the other eleven. They knew that. Most likely, they knew that Tim, or his underlings, would say no when they handed in their applications. Like Rosa Parks, or Rosa Parks' Des Moines counterpart Edna Griffin, an African American woman who in 1948 bucked authority and sat down for lunch at the counter at Katz Drug Store, Katherine and the others were blazing a trail. They were setting themselves up as a test case.

Ironically, perhaps, it almost wasn't Tim Brien who would forever wear the black hat in this case. It could have been my friend and high school classmate, Julie Haggerty. In high school she was Julie Schnoebelen. Seven years out of school she married another classmate, Mike Haggerty. Hence the name. Their marriage is, if not the longest, one of the most enduring in our class.

I know for a fact that Julie Haggerty is no opponent of happy marriage, regardless of the marital partners' sexual orientation. Nevertheless...

The *Varnum* case was decided in 2009. The road to the Supreme Court began in 2005, when Katherine was denied a marriage license and, on December 13, filed her petition for declaratory judgment and supplemental injunctive relief in the Polk County District Court. Smack dab between those two milestones, on November 7, 2006, Julie Haggerty was elected

Polk County Recorder. She didn't beat Tim Brien on November 7. She beat a young conservative Republican lawyer named Chris Hagenow. Julie had gone up against Tim earlier in the year in the Democratic primary and had prevailed.

Her victory over Tim had nothing to do with *Varnum v. Brien*. She had worked in the office for several years, and many of the rank and file had grown dissatisfied with Tim's style of management. So Julie and her comrades mounted a *coup d'etat*, in which I have to admit I was an active conspirator. It wasn't that I, as an outsider to the recorder's office, had any personal ax to grind with Tim Brien. And to be honest, in 2006 I knew nothing about Katherine Varnum. Had I known, I would have also recognized that Tim's hands were tied.

But Julie was a homie. One of us. Julie spearheads our extravagant class reunions every five years. While I didn't know her or Mike so well in high school, as members of the cluster of the class of '74 who never left town we have all become close friends over the half century that has passed since graduation. She is smart, pleasant and articulate. She deserved the job, if that's what she wanted.

I have to admit to a few pangs of guilt over the two months or so between the election and her taking office, when I would still pass Tim Brien in the skywalk. I'd still get the cheery *Good morning, Counselor*. Did he know? Did he know I'd ponied up at the fundraisers and marched with Julie in the Beaverdale Parade? From 2007 on, I never saw Tim Brien again.

Because he had the job in 2005 when Katherine asked for the license, Tim garnered the honor of having the landmark decision named after him.

The culprit in *Varnum v. Brien* wasn't Tim Brien. The culprit was Iowa Code § 595.2(1), under which "[o]nly a marriage between a male and a female is valid." That's what Katherine Varnum and the other eleven were fighting.

The Battle Royale that was the *Varnum* case raged in the Polk County District Court for nearly 21 months as various groups clamored to intervene on both sides.

Judge Robert Hanson issued his ruling on August 30, 2007, granting summary judgment for the petitioners. Section 595.2(1) was to be stricken from the Code as unconstitutional and all remaining provisions of § 595 concerning the requirements for marriage would be given a gender-neutral construction and not read in any way that would preclude same-sex marriage. The ruling was an injunction against county recorders such as Tim Brien to stop denying marriage licenses to same sex couples. On the following day, Judge Hanson ordered a stay in the judgment while the case was being litigated in the Supreme Court.

To me at least, the judgment was a surprise. Even if Judge Hanson was correct, he was finding as a matter of first impression that a provision of the Iowa Code was unconstitutional. That decision is normally made in the Supreme Court.

And it would be here. The go-around in the district court was merely a preliminary bout. The main event would be staged in the five-story limestone building that had opened four years earlier sixteen blocks east of the Polk County Courthouse on Court Avenue.

The main event lived up to its billing. By my count, more than 70 lawyers entered appearances on both sides of the issue, and briefs were filed by 26 separate parties and amici. The case went to the Supreme Court *via* notice of appeal on August 31, 2007. Oral arguments were held on Tuesday, December 9, 2008. The decision was announced on Friday, April 3, 2009.

The seven-justice court was unanimous in favor of Katherine Varnum and the other petitioners. Judge Hanson's ruling was correct.

Justice Mark Cady authored a well-crafted decision that was concordant with the inescapable significance of its impact. It is the function of the Court to make such decisions. Under our state constitution, the legislative branch makes the laws and the executive branch enforces them. But it is for the Court to determine whether those laws are consistent with the constitution, which is supreme. The constitution, Justice Cady reminded us, "belongs to the people, not the government or even the judicial branch of government."

He then turned his attention to article I, section 6 of the Iowa Constitution, which is our state's equal protection clause. He discussed the *Ralph* case, Arabella Mansfield, *Clark* and *Coger* as examples of the Iowa Supreme Court taking point in issues relating to equal protection, relying on our own constitution rather than upon its federal counterpart.

For all relevant purposes, the Court found, same-sex couples are situated similarly to opposite-sex couples, the first step in equal protection analysis. Section 595.2(1) differentiated between people based upon sexual orientation. Applying an intermediate level of scrutiny, the Court found that none of the many interests advanced by the government in favor of the § 595.2(1) exclusion were supported substantially by it. Some religions oppose same-sex marriage, Justice Cady recognized, but to allow religious sentiment to trump equal protection would run afoul of the establishment clause in article I, section 3 of the Iowa Constitution.

"We are firmly convinced," Justice Cady concluded, "the exclusion of gay and lesbian people from the institution of civil marriage does not substantially further any important governmental objective. The Legislature has excluded a historically disfavored class of persons from a supremely important civil institution without a constitutionally sufficient justification. There is no material fact, genuinely in dispute, that can affect this determination. We have a constitutional duty to ensure equal protection of the law. Faithfulness to that duty requires us to hold Iowa's marriage statute, Iowa Code section 595.2, violates the Iowa Constitution. To decide otherwise would be an abdication of our constitutional duty. If gay and lesbian people must submit to different treatment without an exceedingly persuasive justification, they are deprived of the benefits of the principle of equal protection upon which the rule of law is founded. Iowa Code section 595.2 denies gay and lesbian people the equal protection of the law promised by the Iowa Constitution."

Iowa was the third state to recognize the legitimacy of same-sex marriage. It took six years for the United States Supreme Court to follow suit, under the due process and equal protection clauses of the United States Constitution, in *Obergefell v. Hodges*, 576 U.S. 644 (2015).

These are the cases that crop up in discussions of the Court's historical willingness to go to the Iowa Constitution to provide more expansive protection in Iowa than what has been given us by the United States Supreme Court interpreting the U.S. Constitution. There are other significant examples, relevant to my line of work, that don't catch the public eye.

The Court I Knew

I practiced in the Iowa appellate courts between 1985 and 1994. There wasn't much of that during my stay. To tell the truth, I don't know that I was even aware of the Court's progressive history before I came on the scene, or that I would ever predict what was to come after I was gone. You just didn't see a lot of it in those years.

My years in the Appellate Defender's office came during the Reynoldson Court and the McGiverin Court, as they would say. W. Ward Reynoldson, who struck me as a very intelligent and deliberate man, was chief justice until 1987 when he was succeeded by Arthur McGiverin, who was very affable but, as I would come to learn, came closer than any other judge to initiating disciplinary action against me.

The setup of the appellate court system was different in those days from what it is today. The Legislature had established the Iowa Court of Appeals just nine years before my arrival, as something akin to the runaway truck ramp on the Interstate in mountainous regions. Appeals went to the Supreme Court, which kept as many as it could handle and siphoned off to the Court of Appeals the cases that were less complex and less consequential. Court of Appeals decisions generally were final, although the Supreme Court had the authority to grant further review and to supersede the lower court's analysis with its own. The nine-member Supreme Court sat in panels of five. Nearly all of the Supreme Court decisions were published, making them precedent for future cases to follow. A small portion of Court of Appeals' decisions were published. As a result, if your case "went up" to the Supreme Court you would likely be making some new law with your case.

Making new law wasn't something you wanted to do a lot of in my day if you were a criminal defense lawyer. There were few victories. You could prepare a full ten minutes of remarks for oral arguments and make it through them virtually unmolested by questions from the justices. If there was a question, it usually came from the justice assigned to write the opinion. Justice James Carter would also toss out a random question, perhaps to keep from dozing off during the arguments. Like many of my observations about the workings of courts to which I had no personal access, some of these may drift far off base. But they represent the conventional wisdom of those of us who practiced in front of the Court during the era I was up there.

In the end, you nearly always lost your case. The opinions generally were brief, and they were affirmances. Most were unanimous. You didn't see many dissents or concurring opinions.

That may not be as unfair as it sounds. Contrary to what you hear in popular culture about "winning a case on appeal," the bar for reversing a district court ruling inherently is a high one. The defendants always lost their appeals because it was the defendants who always appealed. If the defendant is acquitted at trial, the state *can't* appeal. That would be double jeopardy.

Very little history was made during my time in the Iowa appellate courts. When I approached the podium at continuing legal education seminars to present my caselaw update, invariably the introduction was "and here's B. John Burns to bring us the bad news."

Then, almost as soon as I made the lateral jump from

appellate practice to trial practice. the world underwent a dramatic metamorphosis.

It actually began with *Leon*. And *Leon*, and the approach taken to *Leon* by the Iowa Supreme Court, was percolating while I was there. Before *Leon*, there was the *Aguilar-Spinelli* test that was set aside in *Gates*. These were things I had to beat into my head, because they were happening while I was in law school and, more importantly, while I was preparing for the bar exam. They had to do with whether a search warrant was supported by probable cause and could be relied upon validly by police, specifically where it was based upon information provided by a confidential informant.

Under the test devised by the United States Supreme Court in the 60s in *Aguilar v. Texas*, 378 U.S. 108 (1964) and *Spinelli v. United States*, 393 U.S. 410 (1969), a magistrate issuing a warrant must be provided (1) information supporting the reliability and credibility of the informant and (2) information regarding the circumstances relied upon by the informant. From these sources, the magistrate would make an independent determination of probable cause. Then, on June 8, 1983, three weeks after the end of my first year in law school, then-Justice William Rehnquist wrote the majority opinion in *Illinois v. Gates*, 462 U.S. 213 (1983) doing away with the "rigid" *Aguilar-Spinelli* test and replacing it with an examination of the totality of circumstances.

Better for law enforcement. Not so good for criminal defendants.

Just three days shy of 13 months after *Gates*, the Supreme Court essentially proclaimed *to hell with all that*, and in *United States v. Leon*, 468 U.S. 897 (1983) plotted a new course under which a search is valid where law enforcement relied in good faith upon a warrant, even if there arguably are defects in the probable cause. If the warrant *appears* to be valid, the police can do the search. It was devastating news for the criminal defense bar.

Back home in Iowa, however, article I, section 8 of the

state constitution contains its own warrant requirement. And Iowa Code § 808.3 essentially codified the *Aguilar-Spinelli* test. As early as 1987, the Iowa Supreme Court expressed reluctance in *State v. Swaim*, 412 N.W.2d 568 (Iowa 1987) to recognize a *Leon*-esque good faith exception under state law. In the years that followed, the Court made it increasingly clear that the pre-*Gates* test would remain in place for defendants who expressly made their arguments under article I, section 8 and § 808.3, and not exclusively under the Fourth Amendment. In a unanimous ruling on a different issue thirteen years after *Swaim*, Chief Justice Ternus laid out in *State v. Cline*, 617 N.W.2d 277 (Iowa 2000) an exhaustive explanation of the history of the exclusionary rule, the good faith exception in cases like *Leon*, and why the Court rejects such an exception under our Constitution.

It gradually sunk in with even the neanderthals like me that the *Leon* departure wasn't a mere one off and that the Court was eager to blaze its own path, not just diverging from the federal courts' interpretations of parallel rights but also from lines of its own decisions it was now willing to reexamine. I like to say it all started with the Lavorato Court, but some of the changes were already underway when Justice Louis Lavorato was elevated in 2000 from being an associate justice of the Court to chief justice.

What I do remember is Justice Lavorato giving a talk at some small, informal gathering of the local criminal defense bar sometime before the ascension and bringing up, for those who were not aware, the fact that the Court was now receptive to arguments for enhanced protection under state law. You should cite the Iowa Constitution and Code in all of your arguments, he stressed. If you don't, you may be found to have rendered ineffective assistance of counsel.

And it actually went that way once or twice. This was something I bristled about. The traditional notion is that an attorney is not expected to be a crystal ball gazer. He or she is not held ineffective for failing to anticipate some change in the law that would inure to the client's benefit. Having been an appellate defender for nine years, I understand that a claim of ineffective assistance is often the only way to preserve an error to which there was no objection at trial. During that stage of my career, I'm sure I raised ineffective assistance claims on every defense attorney in the state, including (twice) myself. But dammit, if the Court has been getting it wrong over the years and now decides to correct its mistake, it shouldn't be doing it on the backs of some practitioner who honestly gave 100 percent to preserve for his or her client some semblance of a fair trial. I made that point in several of my CLE presentations and in the blog I wrote for several years for the state public defenders association website. It's what got me assaulted by one of the justices at the wake for the three of his colleagues voted off the Court in 2010.

One example of this is *State v. Graves*, 668 N.W.2d 860 (Iowa 2003). Some overzealous prosecutor asked the defendant during cross-examination whether a police officer witness whose testimony conflicted with the defendant's must have been lying. It is improper, the Court found, to ask one witness to comment on the credibility of another. But Graves' attorney hadn't objected. If there is no objection, an issue generally can't be raised on appeal. But if the attorney should have known better, and should have objected, the attorney may be found to have rendered ineffective assistance, and the defendant is awarded a new trial. That's what the Court did.

But the reason Graves' attorney didn't object wasn't because he didn't understand the law. The attorney didn't object because he *was* aware of the status of the law. The same issue had arisen seven years earlier in *State v. Bayles*, 552 N.W.2d 600 (Iowa 1996). In *Bayles* the Court found no basis in Iowa law for a rule that prohibited questioning one witness concerning the credibility of another. Thus Bayles' attorneys were not ineffective in failing to object. Graves' attorney could always ask the Supreme Court to articulate such a rule in his case. But he certainly didn't breach an essential duty to the client when he didn't object because, as the law stood until then, the law wasn't on his side.

And by the way, those two attorneys who weren't ineffective in *Bayles* when they didn't object – one of them was me.

Setting aside the unfortunate use of ineffective assistance as a device to get where they wanted to go, *Graves* was a step forward for the Court. One species of prosecutorial overreaching that went unchecked in my day was now grounds for a reversal of a defendant's conviction.

Here's a big one. The felony murder rule. There are a number of ways that one can commit the offense of murder in the first degree in Iowa, punishable by a mandatory life sentence without parole (unless the defendant has not reached the age of 18 at the time of the offense). In 2003 and the years preceding, there were two. One was to kill another person with malice aforethought and with premeditation, deliberation and intent to kill. The other required no premeditation, deliberation and intent. Its elements consisted of killing another with malice aforethought while participating in a forcible felony. That's felony murder.

As far back as 1982, the felony murder rule was coming under attack. Prosecutors were charging felony murder based upon the predicate offense of willful injury, which is an assault with intent to cause serious injury that does in fact cause injury. What it boiled down to was a ticket for prosecutors to charge defendants with first degree murder without having to prove premeditation, deliberation and intent. The willful injury is a lesser included offense of the murder charge. There is no independent felony. There was no point in even having the premeditated murder alternative.

The Supreme Court rejected a challenge on this ground in *State v. Beeman*, 315 N.W.2d 770 (Iowa 1982). Willful injury is a forcible felony, the Court reasoned, so it can form the basis for a felony murder conviction. A renewed challenge was similarly unsuccessful in *State v. Ragland*, 420 N.W.2d 791 (Iowa 1988).

Undeterred, the defense bar clamored repeatedly for an independent felony rule. I raised the issue myself on multiple occasions and was shot down every time. I had a couple in the works as I prepared to leave the Appellate Defender for John Wellman's office in the Spring of 1994. One of them went up to the Supreme Court for argument while I was still on the job. There were enough of them advancing the independent felony issue that I can't remember today the name of the particular case. Chief Justice McGiverin was on the panel and presided over the argument. I had a couple of issues to present and led off with the one requesting an independent felony rule.

Just a few words into my remarks, the chief cut me off.

"Counsel," he interrupted in a perturbed tone of voice. "We've litigated that issue. It's resolved."

The message I was getting was that I should either move on to another issue or just sit down. I took the road of least resistance. I was starting to detect the odor of a contempt citation.

Whether brought out during the argument or not, the issue was raised. And it didn't stop me from raising it again in one of the very final briefs I wrote before jumping ship. John Fatino, who took over my caseload after my departure, argued that one in the Supreme Court. John subsequently reported back to me that word of my lateral job change apparently had not yet reached the chief justice.

"Where's Burns?" were the first words out of Justice McGiverin's mouth. I think it's possible that the chief came out loaded for bear, ready to just *dare* me to open with the independent felony argument, and went away disappointed from having been denied the opportunity.

That was 1994. Twelve years had passed since *Beeman*, and the battle would slog on for another twelve after that. In the meantime, Bob Rigg and I signed those contracts to author new versions of the Iowa criminal practice manual. In his volume, Bob advocated overruling *Beeman* and adopting an independent felony rule. If you were a young practitioner fresh out of law school, *4 Iowa Practice: Criminal Law* laid out for you the blueprint to join forces with the veterans of the siege on the deeply entrenched bad law concerning felony murder.

But then came Paul Rosenberg. There's something about Paul Rosenberg. It may be that he was the son of Ray Rosenberg, one of the most respected criminal defense attorneys in this neck of the woods. But Paul wins cases. He wins cases that other lawyers don't. When the Iowa Supreme Court tried in 1997 to expand the search incident to arrest exception to the warrant requirement to include searches incident to citations in lieu of arrest, in cases such as *State v. Doran*, 563 N.W.2d 620 (Iowa 1997) and *State v Knowles*, 569 N.W.2d 601 (Iowa 1997) (which was Paul's case), Paul took *Knowles* up to the United States Supreme Court and won a unanimous decision in *Knowles v. Iowa*, 525 U.S. 113 (1998), written by Chief Justice Rehnquist, holding that the interests of officer safety and preservation of evidence that justify searches incident to arrest do not carry similar force with searches incident to non-custodial traffic citations.

So perhaps the Iowa Supreme Court had learned its lesson about butting heads with Paul Rosenberg when he strolled into their courtroom to litigate *State v. Heemstra*, 721 N.W.2d 549 (Iowa 2006), the story of two Milo farmers embroiled in a land dispute that left one of them dead. While the rest of us had taken beating after beating from the Court for even bringing up *Beeman*, the Court handed Paul the keys to the kingdom in a 5-2 decision written by Justice Larson.

"On further reflection," Justice Larson reasoned, "we adhere to the view that willful injury is a forcible felony under Iowa Code section 702.11 and, in some circumstances, may serve as a predicate for felony-murder purposes. For example, if the defendant assaulted the victim twice, first without killing him and second with fatal results, the former could be considered as a predicate felony, but the second could not because it would be merged with the murder. . . Otherwise, all assaults that immediately precede a killing would bootstrap the killing into first-degree murder, and all distinctions between first-degree and second-degree murder would be eliminated."

Heemstra represented a major about-face for the court, resting on a much higher shelf than *Graves* in the trophy case of progressive Supreme Court decisions.

Battle Lines

This was not the Court in which I'd practiced for those nine years. It was different in various respects. It became the Lavorato Court in 2000. And then, when Justice Lavorato retired in 2006, Justice Marsha Ternus became the first woman to be chief justice of the Supreme Court. A 1999 restructuring reduced the size of the Supreme Court from nine to seven justices and increased the Court of Appeals from six to nine judges. The appellate courts went from the model in which all cases went to the Supreme Court, which siphoned off less complex and consequential cases to the Court of Appeals, to a true two-tier system similar to that in the federal courts. Instead of sitting in panels, the Supreme Court decides its cases *en banc*, with all seven justices participating in each case. Most cases are directed to the Court of Appeals, though major cases may go directly to the Supreme Court. Like the United States Supreme Court, the Iowa Court chooses for further review cases that were decided originally by the Court of Appeals. At least from my perspective, it appears that the Supreme Court now has the discretion to select the areas of the law it wishes to develop, and the cases it feels suitable for doing it.

Then along came *Varnum v. Brien*.

While you might not expect a Bob Vander Plaats to take a great deal of interest in whether the State of Iowa allows its police officers to rely in good faith on deficient search warrants or whether prosecutors must prove an independent felony to make their cases of felony murder, it is no surprise that the president and CEO of an outfit dubbing itself "The Family Leader" wanted some say in whether Iowa men should be permitted to marry Iowa men and Iowa women should marry

Iowa women.

One of eight children of a World War II veteran, Vander Plaats was born and raised in Sheldon, Iowa, a town of around 5500 along the Floyd River and bisected by the Sioux/O'Brien County Line. He and his high-school sweetheart, Darla Granstra, headed twenty miles down the road to Northwestern College in Orange City, where Bob majored in education and played basketball on scholarship while Darla majored in accounting. His star rose quickly after college. He and Darla were married and produced four boys. After two years of teaching business at Boone High School, he was recruited to teach business and to coach basketball at Jefferson High School. In 1991 he became principal at Marcus-Meriden-Cleghorn High School before ultimately returning to Sheldon to take the job as principal there. Along the line, he earned a master's degree in education at Drake University.

Bob Vander Plaats was also developing political aspirations. They were molded, at least in part, by the sad circumstance that his third son, Lucas, was born in 1993 with partial pachygyria lissencephaly, a rare brain disease that produces mental and physical disability and requires lifelong 24-hour care. In 2007 Bob would publish a book, *Light from Lucas: Lessons in Faith from a Fragile Life,* about the experience of raising Lucas.

"If it hadn't been for the miracle of Lucas," Bob revealed in his subsequent campaign literature, "we would have never looked beyond where we were."

In 1996, Bob accepted a position as president and CEO of a struggling Sioux City group called Opportunities Unlimited, devoted to providing rehabilitation to youth with spinal injuries and other disabilities. He is credited, at least during his first three years in the position, with turning the organization around and earning national accreditation. In 1997, he was appointed to the Governor's Council on Brain Injuries by his mentor, Governor Terry Branstad. After Branstad stepped down as governor in 1999 (although he returned in 2011 for a six-year encore), Bob Vander Plaats started taking a hard look at party politics. When the bug bites, he told reporters, "it doesn't let go."

He didn't run for the job in 1998. It was Congressman Jim Ross Lightfoot who went up against Mount Vernon attorney Tom Vilsack that year and lost. Parenthetically, I was enjoying a late dinner with my wife at Tumea & Sons Italian Restaurant on Des Moines' south side after playing a show one evening in 1998. I don't know what brought it up, but I made the comment to her in a voice loud enough to be heard through the entire room that "if Jim Ross Lightfoot gets elected, we'll be looking back in nostalgia at the good old days of Terry Branstad." As soon as I blurted it out, I looked over Pam's shoulder to see Jim Ross Lightfoot sitting right there at the next table.

In 1998, I'd never heard of someone named Bob Vander Plaats.

Nor did I pay much attention to him when he ran unsuccessfully in 2002 for the nomination to go up against Vilsack, losing that one to Doug Gross. I did notice him when he lost in the primaries to Jim Nussle in 2006. Nussle brought him on board as his running mate, and they both lost to Democrat Chet Culver.

In 2010, the Republicans must have seen that Culver was vulnerable, because they brought Terry Branstad out of retirement. By now, Bob Vander Plaats was nothing to laugh at, as he garnered nearly 41 percent of the primary vote that year against a relatively conservative candidate who had held the job previously for 16 years, longer than any governor in Iowa history (after his return, Governor Branstad's total tenure exceeded that of any in *United States* history). I have a feeling that the Republican rank-and-file were nervous that year about having Bob Vander Plaats as their standard bearer.

Vander Plaats' impact in the election of 2010 went way beyond the primary votes he attained in his quest to be chief executive of the Hawkeye State.

Every general election ballot in Iowa contains a section for judicial retention votes. Added in 1962, article V, section 17 of the Iowa Constitution provides that a "term" of a Supreme Court justice may be set by the Legislature and may be no less than eight years. The term of a district court judge may be no less than six years. Any judge or justice wishing to remain in office must "stand for retention in office on a separate ballot which shall submit the question of whether such judge shall be retained in office for the tenure prescribed for such office."

The constitution says nothing else about the grounds or reasons that should form the basis for non-retention. An "Iowa Voters Judicial Directory" circulated by the Judicial Branch during the 2020 election said the following:

> Retention elections are intended to focus on the professional competency of Iowa's judges rather than the popularity of individual rulings. In a retention election, voters decide whether a judge should be retained or removed from office. If a judge receives a majority of "yes" votes, the judge serves another full term. If a judge receives a majority of "no" votes, the judge is removed from office at the end of the year.

A list appears on the Judicial Branch website of the benefits of Iowa's merit system of selecting judges and the judicial retention elections:

> Curbs the influence of political parties and special interest groups in the selection of Iowa's judges.
>
> Emphasizes the selection of judges based upon their professional qualifications.
>
> Gives voters the final say about who serves as a judge.
>
> Is the most effective way to ensure fair and impartial courts.

The website goes on to explain that the merit system and retention elections "are designed to foster fair and impartial courts while maintaining judicial accountability through a series of checks on judicial power." As checks on the judiciary, voters who disagree with the Court's interpretation of the law can lobby the Legislature for changes in the law. If they disagree with an interpretation of the Constitution, they can amend the Constitution. Bad behavior by judges and justices can be dealt with through the Judicial Qualifications Commission.

The site doesn't go as far as the judicial directory does in telling the voters not to use the retention elections to vote out judges whose rulings are objectionable to them. I know people on both sides of the political fence who have strong opinions about the way courts have ruled on their pet issues. I have a pretty good idea how they would respond to such advice.

Personally, I don't like term limits for judges. And I've always been leery of judicial retention elections. We vote for the executive. We vote for the Legislature. The majority rules there. It is imperative that there be a check in government that is not beholden to the majority rule. There are times when the oppressed minority needs protection from the majority, whether they are the NAACP or the American Nazi Party.

Someday, I've always argued, these retention elections are going to wreak havoc. Don't worry, they tell me. Only one judge in Iowa had ever been removed, and he was like a judicial magistrate. More recently, a district court judge was voted out in Des Moines, due to general incompetence. I'd been in front of him a few times. He was a good guy, but the voters were probably right on that one. No longer a judge, he joined us in the well of the Polk County criminal defense bar, where he spent the remainder of his career.

But one of these days, I kept arguing, they're going to organize. All hell is going to break loose. Don't worry, my friends kept assuring me.

Well, all hell broke loose on November 2, 2010. Though he'd lost the gubernatorial nomination to Terry Branstad, who unseated Chet Culver that night, Bob Vander Plaats proved me right, and won the most substantial victory of his career.

November 2 was one of those bad nights all around to be a Democrat. A midterm election is nearly always a wake-up call for the party that had been victorious in the preceding general. In 2010 there was major blowback from the Obama victory in 2008. We lost the governor's office. We lost the United States House of Representatives and six seats in the Senate. One bright spot was the re-election of Julie Haggerty as Polk County Recorder, who fortunately took office too late to be the named party in the gay marriage case.

Because the gay marriage case was the story of the evening.

Varnum v. Brien was a unanimous decision of the Court. Three justices on that Court were up for retention on November 2. Justice Mike Streit, my neighbor. Justice David Baker, who graduated Order of the Coif from the Iowa College of Law and who had just come onto the Court two years earlier. And the first female chief justice of the Iowa Supreme Court, Marsha Ternus. All three were voted out.

There is no question why. No other judge at any level lost their retention elections on November 2. None of the three had written an opinion in *Varnum*. Justice Cady, considered by some at the time to be the most conservative justice on the Court and who was not up for retention, wrote the unanimous decision. Justice Streit, Justice Baker, and Chief Justice Ternus simply voted with the majority on this one case out of hundreds that had come before the Court. They lost their jobs. Worst of all, we lost them.

Had they all been up for retention, we would have lost the entire Court.

Unquestionably, Bob Vander Plaats was instrumental in the November 2 coup. On Friday, August 6, 2010, he'd stood on the outside steps of the Iowa Judicial Branch Building and announced that, rather than launch a third-party bid for governor, he would devote his energy to a full-blown campaign to unseat Justice Mike Streit, Justice David Baker and Chief

Justice Marsha Ternus. Five days later he was back on the steps for an 18-minute press conference in which he announced the formation of a group called, ironically, "Iowa for Freedom." The website was already up, he stated, and the resources were available, although he didn't indicate the source of the resources.

"The simplicity," he stated, "is the court stepped out of bounds. Three judges are up for (retention). You don't have to choose which one you vote no on. Vote no on all three of them. And if you're really concerned about your freedom — whether it's your Second Amendment or your First Amendment or your Tenth Amendment or the way you educate your kids or private property or anything else — you want to get involved in this effort."

In the three months that followed, Vander Plaats launched an all-out "Vote No" media assault with well-organized grass roots support. There was little the justices could do in the way of an organized defense without the appearance of campaigning inappropriately for their offices. It can't be said with certainty how large a role he played in the outcome, or whether the three justices would have survived the retention election had he not jumped into the fray. But the conventional wisdom was that November 2 was Vander Plaats' victory, and he certainly ran the victory lap when the votes were counted.

Now CEO of a group called The Family Leader, Bob celebrated with an essay in the December 19, 2010 *Des Moines Sunday Register* calling on the remaining four justices to resign. The November 2 election, he said, was a "clear referendum on failed leadership." In selecting successors to the unseated justices, he advised, Governor Branstad must appoint replacements who "understand" that *Varnum* was unconstitutional and disagree with the outcome.

Thirteen years later, Bob Vander Plaats remains CEO of The Family Leader. While the highly conservative, evangelical group provides advocacy for causes and candidates sympathetic to its views, Bob never returned to the position of visibility and influence that he held in 2010 (although there was some clamoring for the limelight following the Court's June 16, 2023 affirmance by operation of law of an injunction on enforcement of a fetal heartbeat bill in *Planned Parenthood v. Reynolds*).

None of the remaining justices on the *Varnum* panel accepted Vander Plaats' invitation to step down. The last of the four retired in 2022.

Did the 2010 massacre have a chilling effect on what Bob Vander Plaats and other critics characterized as the "activist" Court?

It may be telling that it was Justice Mark Cady who replaced Marsha Ternus as Chief Justice. Though labeled by some observers as the most conservative justice on the pre-2010 Court it was, after all, Justice Cady who wrote the *Varnum* opinion. I don't know that I would rate Chief Justice Cady as the most liberal member of the Court at that point. But he boasted most prolifically, in his case opinions and other writings, of the Iowa Court's proud tradition of diverging from the federal interpretation of parallel rights in interpreting provisions of the Iowa Constitution.

At the very least, Chief Justice Cady was perhaps the swing vote. Three of the survivors of 2010 were Democrat appointees. The three replacements, on the other hand, were selected by Governor Branstad. Justice Cady had been placed first on the Court of Appeals and subsequently on the Supreme Court by Governor Branstad. The general fear was that what would emerge after the purge would be far to the right of even that with which we'd had to contend in the 80s and early 90s.

When the smoke cleared, however, the hits kept coming. Justice Cady occasionally provided the votes necessary to continue to make thoughtful, progressive advances in the law. One thing to keep in mind in reading what I write about court decisions and the judges who render them is that I study all the *criminal* decisions. When I look at a judge as being "liberal" or "progressive," I'm basing it on that judge's rulings in criminal cases. If you handle labor law or family law cases, you may not share my evaluations, and for good reason. And I don't know a damn thing about *abortion*.

But I can say that, though not marching in step with my viewpoint in every case or even in the majority of cases, each of the three replacements has come over to our side on occasion, and each has written a thoughtful opinion or two breaking new ground in protecting the rights of the accused.

The Post-Purge Court

Of the three replacement justices, Justice Edward Mansfield brings with him the most impressive resume. I know he was born somewhere in Massachusetts, which piques my interest. He attended Lexington High School, 36 miles from the house in West Boylston in which I lived from my first year until I was eight, so maybe he was brought up there. Justice Mansfield graduated *magna cum laude* from Harvard in 1978 and from Yale Law School in 1982. He is intelligent and articulate and has a consistent conservative philosophy.

Yet, from time to time, his compass drifts in our direction. Very recently, for example, in *State v. Middlekauff*, 974 N.W.2d 781 (Iowa 2022), in which a slim majority of the Court held that an Arizona Patient Medical Marijuana Registry Identification Card, the issuance of which requires a medical certification, was not a "valid prescription or order" giving rise to the medical use defense under Iowa Code § 124.401(5), Justice Mansfield argued in a three-justice dissent that the Arizona certification and registry card should be considered an "order" under the statute.

And Justice Mansfield wrote *State v. Davison*, 973 N.W.2d 276 (Iowa 2022), finding that imposition of the fixed minimum restitution payment of $150,000 for offenses causing death under Iowa Code §910.3(B)(1) is an increase in the minimum penalty for an offense and thus requires a jury finding that commission of the offense caused the victim's death.

These may seem like small potatoes to the man on the street. But to a lawyer who lived through the Reynoldson and

McGiverin years, they were developments you would witness rarely if at all back then.

I can't avoid noticing that Justice Mansfield, who came into this world eight and a half months after I did, is the next member of the Court to face enforced mandatory retirement. What that means is that all of a sudden I have now reached that point in my life that I am older than the entire Supreme Court (there are still four Justices on the United States Supreme Court who are my elders).

On the other corner of the first row in the current group portrait of the Court sits Justice Thomas Waterman. Justice Waterman himself is no intellectual slouch, graduating Order of the Coif from the Iowa College of Law seven months before I did (although he is three years younger than I am). And while I did my one marathon and gave up running forever, Justice Waterman has seven Ironman triathlons and several ultra-marathons under his belt.

He is a better man than I am. But from my perspective Justice Waterman is the one member of the post-2010 Court, and the present Court, who would fit most comfortably with the Court I faced from 1985 through 1994. He is most vocal in his resistance to splitting away from the federal interpretation of parallel constitutional rights. This may be one of those things that always gets me in trouble, but in my mind, and in my CLE presentations, Justice Waterman evokes the image of a prepubescent Wally Cleaver on the *Leave it to Beaver* series of yesteryear.

Gee, Beav'. Those federal guys are pretty smart. I don't think we should be messin' with their holdings.

In some cases, Justice Waterman seems to brush off extensive analysis from the other side with rather shallow sarcasm. He wrote the majority opinion in *State v. Abu Youm*, 988 N.W.2d 713 (Iowa 2023) finding that law enforcement was justified in entering a residence under the emergency aid exception to the warrant requirement when they responded to reports that shots had been fired and that there was an injured victim. Arriving on the scene, they found a man lying on the balcony outside the residence and several spent rifle shells on the ground nearby. Damage to the window of an automobile parked outside was consistent with gunshot damage. And residents of the apartment objected to their entry. All of this supported a theory that law enforcement may find more injured persons needing assistance inside the residence.

On its face, Justice Waterman's analysis seemed to provide reasonable support for entry without a warrant. Justice Matt McDermott, however, disagreed. To make the facts of Abu Youm's case fit the community caretaking exception, he said, required "a contortive magnification of some facts and minimization of others to get the emergency aid exception to fit. But the glass slipper simply won't oblige." Justice McDermott pointed specifically to the fact that officers took their time in seeking access to the building and other behavior inconsistent with a pressing need to render emergency assistance.

"Would the dissent prefer," Justice Waterman snapped back, "that the officers upon arrival immediately sprint upstairs and force their way into the apartment?"

My reaction to that was that, if police *really* think there's someone bleeding to death in the apartment upstairs, sprinting upstairs and forcing their way into the apartment sounds to me like a damn good plan. So yes.

For people like me who care about such things, the Court took a major step forward in 2022 in *State v. Crawford*, 972 N.W.2d 189 (Iowa 2022). In all the time I've been an attorney, to raise an argument on appeal that a defendant's conviction was not supported by enough evidence on every element of the charge to even place the case before the jury it was necessary to make an oral motion for judgment of acquittal at the close of the state's evidence, and then again at the close of trial. As time went on, the principle was refined to require that in the motion for judgment of acquittal the lawyer must specify the manner in which evidence was insufficient. If you didn't do these things, you couldn't argue to the Supreme Court that there was insufficient evidence to support your client's conviction.

That all went out the window with Justice Christopher McDonald's opinion in *Crawford*. Because it is the duty of the appellate courts to assure that the defendant receives a fair and impartial trial and because, in taking a case to trial, the defendant inherently asserts that the evidence is insufficient to support conviction, the four-justice majority ruled that the failure of the defendant to move for judgment of acquittal during trial does not preclude an appellate challenge on the ground of insufficient evidence.

This was the status of the law until the 1970s, Justice McDonald noted, when the Court began requiring motions for judgment of acquittal to preserve sufficiency claims. The theory before that point was that the Supreme Court cannot approve a verdict that is not supported by substantial evidence. When that was taken away by decisions requiring motions for judgment of acquittal, defendants had to resort to arguing that trial counsel was ineffective in not making them. But starting in 2019 defendants were precluded by law from raising ineffective assistance claims on appeal. It was always the case that motions for judgment of acquittal were not required to preserve sufficiency claims in bench trials. What *Crawford* did was to extend that notion to jury trials.

To me, *Crawford* was good law.

In his partial dissent, Justice Waterman seemed to take it personally.

"After reading the majority opinion," he posits, "one might think the members of our court during the 1970s and early 1980s were a bunch of dummies . . . That claim should surprise us because the justices who served during that time period are widely regarded as among the court's finest in its history."

Widely regarded by whom?

I have never thought of anyone who has served on the Iowa Supreme Court at any time during my career as a "dummy." But the *finest in the Court's history*? Anyone who views those years as a Golden Era of Iowa jurisprudence, from where I stand, simply wasn't there. The fact that Justice Waterman articulates those views in a separate opinion, a common phenomenon today, puts him in a class above what I saw "during that time period."

And we've gotten good results from Justice Waterman, right from the start.

I have to say my blood ran cold on July 29, 2011 when I read the first line of what may have been his first opinion in a criminal case, in *Anderson v. State*, 801 N.W.2d 1 (Iowa 2011), coming down in favor of a defendant.

"Ours not to reason why," he complained at the outset, dredging some dicta from *Holland v. State*, 115 N.W. 161 (1962), paraphrasing Tennyson's "The Charge of the Light Brigade." "[O]urs but to read, and apply. It is our duty to accept the law as the Legislature enacts it."

Oh. Is *that* how it's going to be? By reversing the Court of Appeals and the district court, of course, Justice Waterman had already proved himself more progressive than most of the jurists I faced in my nine years with the Appellate Defender. But is doing the right thing *so* distasteful that he equates himself with a British light cavalry officer galloping off to certain death as a consequence of a misinterpreted order? This guy has to hold his nose to reverse a conviction? Is this what we've got in store for us now?

But then I read *Anderson*. And I saw exactly what he was talking about. Pursuant to *North Carolina v. Alford* (Iowa's version of a no contest plea), Michael Anderson had pleaded guilty in 2004 to two counts of enticing away a minor and received a total sentence of imprisonment of not to exceed ten years. The sentence was suspended, and Anderson was placed on probation. Initially he would live in a residential facility and would then return home under supervision and electronic monitoring. In 2006 it was discovered that Anderson, who was 37, was dating a 16-year-old girl, in violation of his conditions of release. Additionally, he was frequenting pornographic and dating websites. Probation was revoked, and he was ordered to serve his ten-year prison sentence.

The question before the Court had to do with the amount of credit he would receive on his prison sentence for time he had spent on release. The district court and the Court of Appeals found that he was entitled to credit for the time spent in the "jail-like" residential facility, but not for time he was at home on monitoring and supervision. But Anderson pointed out that Iowa Code § 907.3(3) was written in such a way that a defendant is entitled to credit for time spent under most levels of supervision, even if he is not in custody. While it didn't make much sense, Justice Waterman was compelled to rule in his favor. In 2012, the Legislature fixed the problem and amended § 907.3 to allow credit for time in a residential facility, but not for time on supervised release.

Over the dozen years that followed, the remainder of the justices who comprised the *Varnum* Court have been replaced by Terry Branstad and Kim Reynolds appointees. In 2018, Justice Bruce Zager became the first of the three 2011 replacement justices to retire from the Court, creating the first vacancy since the purge. By 2022, the entirety of the Iowa Supreme Court was now populated by justices appointed by Republican governors. The expectation was a Court more consistently conservative than at any point in recent history. At least in the areas that draw my attention, this hasn't entirely been the case.

Perhaps the most intriguing addition to the Court, from my perspective, has been Justice Christopher McDonald. Justice McDonald wasn't the first Justice appointed by Governor Reynolds. Justice Zager's seat on the bench was filled by Susan Larson Christensen. We'll talk about her later. Justice McDonald came on board five months later after Justice Daryl Hecht announced his retirement, necessitated by a battle with cancer to which he would succumb in 2019.

Born in Bangkok in 1974 to a father who was a United States serviceman and a mother from Vietnam, Justice McDonald was the first person of color to serve on the Supreme

Court. His credentials were unassailable, graduating Order of the Coif and as valedictorian from the University of Iowa College of Law, followed by a clerkship with Judge David Hanson of the Eighth Circuit Court of Appeals. He sat on the Iowa Court of Appeals for five and a half years before he ascended to the Supreme Court.

At the start there were some ominous bright red flags swirling around Justice McDonald. The one that rattled me right to the core was his concurring opinion in *State v. Brown*, 930 N.W.2d 840 (Iowa 2019). *Brown* was the Iowa Court's golden opportunity to part company, under article I, section 8 of the Iowa Constitution, with the United State Supreme Court's Fourth Amendment ruling in *Whren v. United States*, 517 U.S. 806 (1996) that a law enforcement officer is justified in executing a pretextual stop, pulling over a vehicle where there is probable cause to believe the driver has violated a traffic law, even though the *true* subjective reason in the officer's mind is not a valid ground for a stop. There had been some hints in earlier opinions that, when the right case came along, the Iowa Court would be willing to break with *Whren*.

By the time the right set of facts presented itself, however, in *Brown*, the makeup of the Court had changed to a point at which the promises of the past no longer held currency. A 4-3 majority of the Court found, just as it would have found under *Whren*, that a stop is valid under article 1, section 8 of the Iowa Constitution when a reasonable officer would have probable cause to believe the subject committed a traffic offense. The dissenters were the three pre-purge justices remaining on the Court.

There was nothing remarkably bad or good about then-Justice Christensen's majority opinion which, following the realignment of the Court, was not unexpected. But Justice McDonald's special concurrence read as a harbinger of things to come.

One of the consistent melodic themes played over and over in the preceding decade by litigants appealing to the Court to carve out greater protection under the state constitution is that the federal court's interpretation of the Bill of Rights sets the *floor* beneath which the states may not go in interpreting parallel rights in their own jurisdictions. The states are free to adopt the federal standards as their own, and they are free to offer *more* protection. Increasingly, the Iowa Court had been accepting the latter invitation.

It was George Bernard Shaw (and later Senator Robert F. Kennedy) who uttered "'Some men see things as they are and say why. I dream things that never were and say, why not." In a sense, Justice McDonald's reasoning in *Brown* followed that logic. Our duty, he wrote (in so many words), is to interpret the state constitution independently. Fine, I thought. But he goes on. So why do we look at the federal protection under the federal Constitution as the *floor*? Why *can't* we provide less protection?

What?

We can't provide less protection than what the federal Constitution gives us because the federal Constitution is *there*. Isn't that right? Nearly all of the substance of the Bill of Rights has been incorporated to apply to the states. Iowa law enforcement, prosecutors and courts must follow the U.S. Constitution. So even if we say *we're not giving you everything you get in federal court under our constitution* we still have to dole it out under theirs.

So why are you even having these thoughts? What's going on in the mind of Justice Christopher McDonald that he feels compelled to spread them over the pages of a Supreme Court decision? What does he have on the drawing board for us?

The *Brown* concurrence scared the living bejeezus out of me.

"More clearly than ever," I wrote in the caselaw outline I prepared for my 2019 CLE presentations, "the final decision of what essentially was the 2018 Iowa Supreme Court term illustrates how important it is to take gubernatorial elections seriously. With the swearing in of Justice Christopher McDonald this year, the golden era of Iowa criminal jurisprudence that had lasted approximately a quarter century ground to a complete stop. The effects are unmistakable."

It wasn't just *Brown*. Justice McDonald directed some effort in his partial dissent in *State v. Veal*, 930 N.W.2d 319 (Iowa 2019) to taking issue with the United States Supreme Court holding in *Taylor v. Louisiana*, 419 U.S. 522 (1975) that a "jury from a representative cross section of the community is an essential component of the Sixth Amendment right to a jury trial." *Yeah, but after 44 years that genie's not going back in the bottle. Why is he saying these things? What does he have up his sleeve?*

I was not complimentary of Justice McDonald in 2019.

A year later, when Chief Justice Mark Cady died unexpectedly and Justice David Wiggins retired, Governor Reynolds appointed Dana Oxley and Matthew McDermott to the Court. My first impressions of Justice Oxley were that she seemed to be joining Justice McDonald in many of his written opinions, which did not bode well for her. Or us. Justice McDermott, a quiet, dignified fellow member of the Blackstone Inn of Court, seemed to be coming down quite a bit on the other side of them.

In what may have been his first majority opinion in a criminal case, for example, Justice McDermott held in *State v. Schiebout*, 944 N.W.2d 666 (Iowa 2020) that a person who writes a check on an account upon which she is not authorized to engage in transactions is not guilty of theft by check under Iowa Code § 714.1(6) absent substantial evidence that she knew the check would not be paid when presented, since such knowledge is an essential element of the offense. Justice Oxley's dissenting opinion was joined only by Justice McDonald.

In the natural quest to identify for my audiences who is with us and who is not – who are the "Allies" and who form the "Axis" – I was alerting to the squabbles that seemed to be cropping up in the writings of Justice McDermott and Justice McDonald as evidence of what I called the "Battle of the Mickey D's." The two traded attacks in *State v. Shackford*,

952 N.W.2d 141 (Iowa 2020), in which Justice McDermott made a very case-specific ruling that the Court had jurisdiction to modify or vacate a civil judgment requiring the defendant to repay costs of incarceration after the defendant's conviction was reversed. Justice McDermott tossed a few darts in Justice McDonald's direction for a dissenting opinion that was "neatly divided up by asterisks," where it was "really just one argument." More substantially, when Justice McDonald castigated him for not citing a recent unpublished Supreme Court decision Justice McDermott responded, rightfully in my opinion, that non-published decisions are not precedent.

But then things took an unexpected turn.

There was *State v. Wright*, 961 N.W.2d 396 (Iowa 2021).

Back in 1988, the United States Supreme Court ruled in *California v. Greenwood*, 486 U.S. 35 (1988) that a person has no expectation of privacy in trash left out for pickup. The warrantless seizure of trash, therefore, did not violate the Fourth Amendment. But then, all of a sudden and out of the blue (for me, at least, though not for Colin C. Murphy of the Gourley Rehkemper Lindholm firm, who made the argument), the Iowa Court comes down in *Wright* with a holding that the practice does violate the search and seizure provision of article I, section 8 of the Iowa Constitution.

And it's Justice McDonald who authors the majority opinion. He hasn't forgotten what he wrote in *Brown* – questioning the notion that the federal interpretation of a parallel federal provision is the floor beneath which the state cannot go in evaluating the protection provided by its constitution. He repeats this in the *Wright* majority, but in a footnote adds the caveat that local officials are nevertheless bound not to go below the level of protection afforded by the federal constitution, because it's there. And, just like that, I'm okay with his *Brown* concurrence.

I've already mentioned *State v. Crawford*, 972 N.W.2d 189 (Iowa 2022), in which the Court unexpectedly rolled back a rule created in the late 70s and early 80s by justices who, in the words of Justice Waterman, are "widely regarded as among the court's finest in its history" requiring criminal defendants to file motions for judgment of acquittal to be able to appeal their convictions on ground that the evidence was insufficient to support them.

That, too, came from Justice McDonald.

I don't know if Justice McDonald is aware of my caustic criticism of him in 2019 and 2020. I don't know if he even knows who I am. But by 2021 I was beginning my CLE lectures with public apologies for having rushed to judgment on him and for all the nasty things I said about him.

Maybe I apologized too soon.

On March 31, 2023 the Supreme Court decided *State v. Burns*, 988 N.W.2d 352 (Iowa 2023) (no relation). After enjoying a meal at a Manchester, Iowa Pizza Ranch in 2018, Jerry Burns left behind a used plastic straw. Jerry was a person of interest in a 1979 homicide. Without a warrant, law enforcement seized the straw and tested it, and found DNA that was possibly consistent with DNA found on the victim's dress. Burns argued on appeal, among other things, that he had a privacy interest in the DNA on the straw, and that its warrantless seizure and subsequent admission into evidence violated both the Fourth Amendment and article I, section 8 of the state constitution.

A five-justice majority did not buy Burns' argument, which is not terribly surprising.

But Justice McDonald wrote a concurrence in *Burns* that put me back in the 2019 frame of mind.

In it, he launched into a full-frontal assault on the exclusionary rule. It's not the first time such arguments have surfaced. But it was a detailed, scholarly opinion. There is nothing in the text of the Constitutions, state or federal, that mandates exclusion of evidence based upon police misconduct. Police misconduct in the collection of evidence has little to do with the defendant's guilt or innocence. That sort of thing. If you have a beef with the way police acted during their investigation, sue them. It shouldn't be a get out of jail free card.

I don't like hearing rhetoric like that from Supreme Court justices. Especially the young ones we expect to have around for a while.

But here's the rub.

Five weeks later, the Court decided *Burnett v. Smith*, 990 N.W.2d 289 (Iowa 2023). Truck driver Cory Burnett is suing an agent of the Iowa Department of Transportation for arresting him without probable cause. He can do that under *Godfrey v. State*, 898 N.W.2d 844 (Iowa 2017) in which the Court authorized aggrieved parties to sue the government directly for constitutional violations.

It was unanimous. Unless the Legislature creates some vehicle for a lawsuit against the government, the constitution is not self-executing, and one may no longer sue the government directly for damages. The gist of *Burnett* is that the remedy for governmental misconduct lies in exclusion of evidence, among other things.

Justice McDonald didn't write *Burnett*. But he signed on, with all the others. But none of the others joined his concurrence in *Burns*. If Justice McDonald had his way, there would be no remedy for a constitutional violation. No money. No exclusion. Butkus.

The one other thing I have to say about Justice McDonald is something that Justice McDermott brought out in their little skirmish in *Shackford*. It's one of my pet peeves. The rules of the game, I admit, have changed a little. Considering that nearly three decades have passed since I practiced in the Iowa appellate courts, this may come down to being more about me being a dinosaur about some things and about Justice McDonald being on the cutting edge.

Before 2001, unpublished decisions of any court could not be cited in a Supreme Court brief. Currently they may not be cited as controlling authority. There are some revisions to the Iowa Rules of Appellate Procedure that are working their way up. If they survive, it will still be the case that unpublished decisions are not controlling authority, "but they may be cited as providing persuasive reasoning."

Justice McDonald regularly cites a good number of unpublished Court of Appeals decisions in his opinions. I always wonder if there is some point he is trying to make by doing that. I realize he was one of those guys for five and a half years. No one knows better than he does how hard the Court of Appeals judges work and the standards they strive to meet. Maybe he is trying to push the envelope to give them more recognition. Maybe Justice McDonald had some input in including the "persuasive reasoning" language in the proposed new rule. I can only speculate.

As I mentioned earlier, I've always felt that there was some utility in allowing the appellate courts to issue rulings and opinions that do not see the light of day. No judge, justice or anyone in proximity to the courts has ever said a word that would confirm my suspicion. That's just what it is. Pure speculation. I've always felt that keeping the unpublished decisions under wraps gives the courts an option to "do the right thing." There are cases in which you might want to reach a just and equitable result for a sympathetic client, but you don't want to make bad law. There are cases that scream out for making good law, but their ugly facts militate against it.

What comes to mind in my personal experience is actually not the best example, because all the cases are in fact published. But they illustrate what I'm getting at.

It all has to do with Iowa's speedy indictment guidelines under Iowa Rule of Criminal Procedure 2.33(2)(a). With some very limited exceptions, if the accused is not indicted (or, more commonly in Iowa, charged by trial information) within 45 days of arrest, the charge for which he or she is arrested must be dismissed. From the very beginning of my career, it's always amazed me how rigidly this one is enforced. The Court, over time, has played with the definition of "arrest" to give the state a little leeway. But for the most part, if the speedy indictment deadline, the speedy trial deadline, or the umbrella rule that requires trial to commence within a year of arraignment are not met, the case is dismissed. Forever.

It's not constitutional. There are many cases, some involving defendants represented by me, in which the state and federal courts have looked at delays in bringing persons to trial that went on for decades, and have found that they do not run counter to the constitutional rights to speedy trial and due process. It's not something passed by the Legislature. It's a mere court rule, but our Court takes it seriously. When I moved into federal court, I saw cases that were dismissed on speedy trial grounds. But they were dismissed without prejudice, meaning the government had the authority in most cases to initiate a new prosecution as long as the statute of limitations had not run.

But not in Iowa. In Iowa, there are some offenses so onerous that there is no statute of limitations. Jerry Burns was prosecuted in 2018 for a murder committed in 1979, because there is no limitation for murder. Had he been indicted 46 days after his arrest, however, or brought to trial 91 days after indictment, he would go home a free man absent some showing of good cause or delay attributable to the defense.

The story I'm talking about begins with a 1989 case called *State v. Van Beek*, 443 N.W.2d 704 (Iowa 1989). It involved three men arrested in a Rock Valley tavern for possession of cocaine. When law enforcement spoke to the county attorney about the arrest, they were instructed to release the defendants until the substance with which they were arrested could be tested. The defendants were "unconditionally unarrested" until the lab reports came back establishing that the substance was, in fact, cocaine. *Then*, nearly two months after the encounter in the tavern, a complaint was issued and the men were arrested. The trial information was filed within a week.

Sioux County Trial Judge Terry Huitink found that what was then the Rule of Criminal Procedure 27(2) speedy indictment period was triggered by the arrest in the bar, and ordered the charges dismissed. The Court of Appeals affirmed the dismissal. The case then went up to a five Justice panel of the Supreme Court.

New law was made.

The four-justice majority in *Van Beek* found, as a matter of first impression, that there is "an inherent prosecutorial right" to unconditionally arrest a suspect, at least before his or her initial appearance or preliminary hearing, when the defendant has not been held in custody for an extended period of time. If the prosecutor decides subsequently to file the charge, it is that arrest that triggers the then-Rule 27(2) deadlines. Justice Louis Schultz explained the Court's reasoning in the majority opinion:

> Following their unconditional release, defendants were under no more hardship than any other citizen. They were not subject to incarceration, anxiety while awaiting trial, or the social stigma that may accompany one criminally accused. The only on-going aspect of this incident was the analysis of the evidence seized. This placed defendants in the same situation as any citizen similarly under investigation but not charged with a crime. Unless or until formal criminal charges were filed against them, neither the defendants, nor the public in general, could have a legitimate interest in the prompt processing of a nonexistent case.

The sole dissenter was Chief Justice Arthur McGiverin, who did so without a written opinion.

Two years after *Van Beek*, 11-year-old Rosalyn Barnes disappeared after a church picnic in Des Moines. Her body was discovered early the following morning. The investigation focused quickly on Charles Edward Lasage, and Lasage was arrested the following day for a traffic violation and for murder. The arrest was, according to the written opinion, "the result of miscommunication between the police and the department of criminal investigation," which needed time to get its ducks in a row before subjecting the prosecution to the speedy indictment and speedy trial deadlines. After a few short hours Lasage was released unconditionally without having appeared before the magistrate.

In one of the grisliest cases of our careers, Jim Whalen represented Lasage at trial and I handled his appeal. We argued, among other things, that the state failed to file the trial information within the Rule 27 speedy indictment period. His unarrest truly wasn't "unconditional."

The case went before the Court of Appeals, being one of the last I submitted before transferring from the Appellate Defender to the Des Moines trial office to replace Jim Whalen, who was moving to the Federal Defender's Office. *State v. Lasage*, 523 N.W.2d 617 (Iowa App. 1994) came down several months after my departure.

Ironically, the unanimous opinion of the three judges in *Lasage* was written by Judge Terry Huitink, who'd been reversed for freeing the three defendants in *Van Beek* and who had just been appointed by Governor Terry Branstad to the Court of Appeals.

Judge Huitink followed *Van Beek* in affirming Lasage's conviction and life sentence.

> When a person is taken into custody, he or she is arrested for purposes of rule 27(2)(a). *State v. Van Beek*, 443 N.W.2d 704, 706 (Iowa 1989). However, if it is decided that no charges will be filed, there is no obligation to take a defendant in front of a magistrate in accordance with Iowa Rule of Criminal Procedure 2. *Id.* A release without charges is equivalent to a dismissal, provided the release is unconditional. *See id.* A dismissal tolls the speedy trial clock; likewise, an unconditional release without charges tolls the speedy information clock. Only when the charges are refiled does the clock start anew. *Id.* Lasage was released within hours of his arrest, an arrest which was the result of miscommunication between the police and the department of criminal investigation. After

this he was not subject to any of the evils rule 27(2)(a) was designed to protect against. Rather, Lasage was placed in the same position as any individual under investigation but not charged with a crime. *See id.* Rule 27(2)(a) did not apply to Lasage's initial arrest as he was unconditionally released without charges being filed.

I was out of the picture at that point. In my absence, Lasage applied for further review of the Court of Appeals' ruling. The application was submitted without argument on September 14, 1994.

One day before that, a seemingly inconsequential appeal of a defendant's conviction of operating while intoxicated was submitted directly to the Supreme Court. Like *Lasage*, the defendant in *State v. Davis*, 525 N.W.2d 837 (Iowa 1994) challenged his "unconditional unarrest" being used as a prosecutorial shield against dismissal under Rule 27. Considering the Court's decisive holding in *Van Beek*, followed just weeks before by the Court of Appeals, one would expect a rapid affirmance.

But the decision in *Davis* did not come rapidly. Three months passed.

Charles Lasage's application for further review was denied in the second week of November. The deadline for rehearing passed in early December. On December 21, the very first Supreme Court decision date after Lasage's murder conviction became final, the Court announced its decision in *Davis*.

It was a marvelous decision. Chief Justice McGiverin, the lone dissenter in *Van Beek* but who did not author an opinion in support of his dissent, wrote for a now unanimous, *en banc* Court. *Van Beek* was wrongly decided. *Van Beek* was overruled. The reasoning was lofty and inspirational.

> Once the defendant is handcuffed, booked, and detained for a time, the defendant then could

be released by the state until it could collect sufficient evidence or make up its mind at its convenience to file a trial information or obtain an indictment.

* * *

An arrest of a citizen is a serious matter. It should not be done unless the peace officer or the state has probable cause to do so. Once an arrest is made, the state should be required to follow through on the time requirements for a speedy indictment and processing of the case pursuant to rule 27(1) and (2). To do otherwise generates disrespect for the law by the authorities.

It also threatens abuse of citizens' rights. A defendant remains anxious as to when "the other shoe will drop" by an indictment or trial information being filed against the defendant. The case did not become nonexistent as far as defendant was concerned...

Neither is a defendant placed "in the same situation as any citizen similarly under investigation but not charged with a crime."... The local newspaper reported that defendant had been arrested on a complaint for OWI, first offense. Defendant had a right by virtue of rule 27(2)(a) to know that forty-five days after his arrest his waiting period would be over. A person who is the subject of an investigation but not of an arrest does not have a similar right.

Justice McGiverin did not mention Charles Lasage in his opinion in *Davis*. Perhaps it is self-evident to the man on the street that our system would jealously protect a citizen from having to wonder when "the other shoe will drop" when that citizen is charged with drunk driving, but not when he is charged with the brutal murder of an eleven-year-old girl. After

35 years in this line of work, I guess my mind is just wired differently.

I see now as I dive back into those choppy waters that the first person who appeared to grasp the inconsistency was then-acting Chief Justice Mark Cady in his dissent fifteen years later in *State v. Wing*, 791 N.W.2d 243 (Iowa 2010), a case in which the defendant's conviction of possession with intent to distribute a controlled substance was dismissed on *Davis* grounds. The analysis that had evolved to that point, Chief Justice Cady argued, "totally ignores the absence of any charges and disregards the purposes of speedy indictment. Not only is such a loose standard unnecessary and detached from the purpose and aim of the right to a speedy trial, it is largely unprincipled and capable of inconsistent results." As evidence of the "inconsistent results," Chief Justice Cady pointed specifically to the disparate outcomes in *Davis* and *Lasage*. What led him to these cases was *my* tirade about them in *4A Iowa Practice: Criminal Procedure*. That warms the cockles of my heart.

And Chief Justice Cady wasn't saying these things because he felt Mr. Lasage should have been released with an apology. His point was that the current definition of "arrest," for speedy trial purposes, had gone off track. Rather than seeing arrest as a set of circumstances under which a reasonable person would believe that his or her freedom was curtailed, a Rule 2.33(2) arrest should be deemed to occur when the suspect is brought in to answer on the filed charges.

Because the law drifted, in the dozen or so years following *Wing*, in the direction advocated by Chief Justice Cady in his dissent, my hurt feelings about how Charles Lasage (and specifically my argument in his case) were handled by the Court are now academic. Neither Davis nor Lasage would have an argument to make under the status of the law today.

So why bring it up?

This is the class of circumstances under which a non-published Court of Appeals opinion would have been optimal. When my *Lasage* brief was making its way through the appellate courts, I have no idea whether somebody there took a look at it, then took a look at Davis' brief and thought *damn. We need to fix what we did in Van Beek. But we sure the hell aren't letting that character back out on the streets* (Charles Lasage wasn't going back out on the streets anyway. While his appeal was still pending, he was shipped to New York to be prosecuted for a nearly identical homicide of a young girl near Niagara Falls). They could have followed *Van Beek*, waited for Lasage's case to conclude, then go to town on Davis. They could do just what they did, without publishing the Court of Appeals opinion in *Lasage*. No one would be the wiser, except me. I'd still be seething about it. But sooner or later, I'd get over it. Charles Lasage died in 2018.

That's the utility of having non-published opinions and keeping them under wraps, from my perspective. Maybe the Court doesn't see it that way. Justice McDonald apparently doesn't. It's harder to bury things like that now, in the electronic age. It's prudent to pay close attention to Justice McDonald. As the second youngest member of the Court, it's likely that he will be around longer than most of the others, and he's not afraid to take giant steps. Some of them are helpful to people in my line of work. Some are not. We just find out every Friday.

To a lesser degree, I also initially miscast Justice Dana Oxley as someone who blindly would follow Justice McDonald. She has since distinguished herself as an intelligent, independent thinker. What first grabbed my attention was her dissent in *State v. McGee*, 959 N.W.2d 432 (Iowa 2021). The case involved the constitutionality of the warrantless drawing of blood from a subject who was partially incapacitated. Justice Mansfield wrote the majority opinion approving the taking of blood from McGee. There was a separate concurring opinion from Justice McDermott.

In her dissent, Justice Oxley made a point I'd been wanting to make as far back as I can remember. It has to do with Iowa Code § 321J.2(1)(c). Under Iowa law, it is illegal to operate a motor vehicle while under the influence of alcohol, a controlled substance, or any combination of the two, or to operate a motor vehicle while having a blood alcohol content of .08. But it is an equivalent offense under § 321J.2(1)(c) to operate a motor vehicle when "any amount of a controlled substance is present in the person, as measured in the person's blood or urine." It doesn't matter if the defendant is under the influence or impaired, as long as there's a trace of it in that person's system. Personally, I don't partake. But if I did, and if I used marijuana today, it possibly could show up in my blood a month from today.

My personal lexicon categorizes that as a "bullshit" law.

Justice Oxley used different terminology in her *McGee* dissent. The rapid decay of alcohol in the blood system over time creates an exigency that justifies a warrantless blood test for alcohol. Such is not the case with THC, the active ingredient in marijuana. Justice Oxley gets it.

In 2022, Justice Oxley found in *State v. Stevens*, 970 N.W.2d 598 (Iowa 2022) that, while the indications of a drug dog may supply probable cause for a search under the automobile exception to the warrant requirement, they do not alone justify the search of the person of passengers in the automobile.

And while Justice McDonald was using his concurring opinion in *State v. Burns*, 988 N.W.2d 352 (Iowa 2023) to call for the elimination of the exclusionary rule, Justice Oxley wrote in a thoughtful dissent that there are some unique expectations of privacy beyond those inherent in one's "persons, houses, papers and effects" recognized in *Katz v. United States*, 389 U.S. 347 (1967). The notion was applied by the Supreme Court in *Carpenter v. United States*, 138 S. Ct. 2206 (2018) to location information stored digitally in cellular telephones. The same reasoning should fit the plethora of personal information stored in the DNA molecule. A person who abandons a used plastic drinking straw at a Pizza Ranch does not, in Justice Oxley's mind, abandon his privacy interest in matter locked securely in the mitochondria of each cell of his body. She also joined most of Justice McDermott's multi-faceted dissent.

Not all of Justice Oxley's votes and written opinions in

criminal cases have favored the accused. Like those from Justice McDonald, some have represented what in my opinion are huge steps backward. But from a roster of justices selected entirely by two Republican governors, there have been some formidable and unexpected victories. And the hits keep coming.

Commentators on the goings on in the courts love to put jurists in boxes. This one is liberal. This one is conservative. This one was appointed by a Democrat. He must be liberal. This one appointed by a Republican must be conservative. Considered at the outset of his tenure to be the most conservative justice on the Court, the Branstad appointee who was the author of *Varnum v. Brien* and the champion of the Iowa Court's proud history of carving out new protections under the state constitution was regarded, at the time of his unexpected death, to be one of the most liberal. It's a perception that was perhaps instrumental in his statutory demotion, which I'll discuss later.

But I'm done with the boxes, for at least the time being. Justice Waterman appears to be conservative, though he continues to go our way from time to time. Justice Mansfield is clearly conservative, but at the same time deliberate and pragmatic.

For the rest of them, I throw my hands in the air. We feared Justice McDonald. Then he turned around and gave us some of the most formidable gifts we've received from anyone on the bench. At the outset, it looked like Justice McDermott was going to step up as the counterbalance to Justice McDonald. But there are times we get the latter and the former goes against us. Sometimes they line up together in a dissent or as teammates in a fractured majority.

It's fun to watch. You don't know what they're going to do, and who's going to do it. Generally, however, after everything that's happened things still seem to be moving forward in a positive direction.

It's hard to know what Governor Reynolds thinks about that. We'll talk about that later. My conclusions about the positive direction of the court, however, are limited to what I care about, which is criminal justice. Perhaps Governor Reynolds doesn't care too much about warrantless trash pulls, or whether a defendant must move for judgment of acquittal to preserve a sufficiency argument for appeal. Bob Vander Plaats? Maybe it was all about same sex marriage with him, and about abortion with the governor. I don't know. I live in my tiny universe. We'll also talk about abortion later.

What I will say is that the last consistent, unabashed, committed light of liberalism on the Iowa Supreme Court flickered out on June 2, 2022.

The Little Guy from the Fryer Argument

Remember me talking about the *Fryer* argument? The case I worked on in the prisoner assistance clinic during my final semester at the Iowa law school? The case that helped me get my first job with the Appellate Defender because Charlie, the boss, had represented one of Allen Fryer's brothers in the appeal from his conviction in the same murder case. Charlie extended the job offer on Friday. I started the bar exam on Monday, and finished it on Wednesday. Then I hightailed it to Iowa City to await the results and to begin preparing (provided I passed the test) for my first court appearance the following Monday – an oral argument in the Eighth Circuit Court of Appeals to be held in front of the *whole Iowa Law School*.

Remember the guy the attorney general sent down to argue against us? The little guy with the movie star good looks who spoke eloquently and methodically as he thumbed with relaxed confidence through a looseleaf notebook. Remember that guy?

Brent R. Appel remained Deputy Iowa Attorney General for another year before going into private practice with Dickinson, Mackaman, Tyler & Hagan P.C. After 18 years there, he went into partnership for about a year with my law school classmate Steve Wandro. In 2006, Governor Tom Vilsack appointed him to fill the seat vacated with the retirement of Iowa Supreme Court Justice James Carter. Fortunately for all of us, that seat was up for judicial retention in 2008 and not 2010.

It seemed ironic to me that a man I first came to know as a tenacious prosecutor would distinguish himself, even during the relatively liberal Lavorato and Ternus Courts, as their most progressive member. But as the *Varnum* Court withered away after 2010, Justice Appel stood out more and more as the liberal voice crying in the wilderness. As the voice grew louder, the dissents he authored also grew in length.

In a sense, it made my life somewhat difficult. Every Friday there would be multiple 90-page slip opinions for me to read and digest for my caselaw updates and for *4A Iowa Practice: Criminal Procedure*. In some of them Justice Appel wrote for the Court, but others would consist of a 15-page majority opinion by a different justice followed by his 75-page dissent or concurrence. Everything he wrote was a law review article, replete with an exhaustive analysis of the common roots of the issue being decided, the statutory or constitutional text, a comparison of the holdings of various jurisdictions that had come down on the issue and law review articles and other commentary exploring the policy considerations in play in the case. Every Appel opinion was a treatise. To this day, a young lawyer preparing a trial brief or appellate brief raising a novel issue is well-advised to consider a Justice Appel opinion as the starting point for research. It's all there. If I went into as much detail exploring the nooks and crannies of criminal procedure as Justice Appel did in his opinions, *4A Iowa Practice: Criminal Procedure* would be a 16-volume set, and not a 1200-page "pamphlet."

On July 13, 2022 Justice Brent Appel turned 72. At 72, Iowa judges are subject to mandatory retirement. If they choose, they may remain on the payroll until the age of 78 as part time senior judges. Justice Appel instead elected to join the faculty of the Drake Law School as a lecturer and jurist in residence. I can't think of anyone more suited to imparting knowledge to prospective attorneys than the author of so many well-researched and organized opinions.

It was the end of an era in the Iowa Supreme Court that began with the ascension of Justice Louis Lavorato to the position of chief justice. Thirteen years after *Varnum*, Vander Plaats got his wish. They're all gone now.

It's an all-Republican Court now (at least a Court composed of justices appointed by Republican governors).

Is it the Court that Governor Reynolds and the Republican Legislature pray for each night before they go to bed?

THE ACTIVIST COURT MEETS B. JOHN BURNS

1985 into 1986 was a rough patch for me.

There's a song on my 2015 album *Forty Years Ago Today* called "Years That End With Five." They haven't been my best. My dogs died in 2005 and 2015 (the impetus for the song). 1975 was the year I dropped out of school without a definite plan and stumbled around in a morose fog for four or five months wondering if I was damned to spend the rest of my life working as a Pinkerton security guard.

The remainder of 1985 after I passed the bar, swore the oath in Justice Louis Schultz' cramped Iowa City office, argued the *Fryer* case in the Iowa College of Law and started my job with the appellate defender sits perched like the avenging angel atop my Christmas tree of miserable years that end with five.

There is, I've heard, a lot of pressure in law school. That's very true, but it's self-imposed pressure. Nobody else's life hangs in the balance, dependent on how you perform on a Corporations II examination. It's just you. That all changes when they swear you in. There are people now for whom the prospects of any meaningful future rest fully on your being prepared and knowledgeable and willing to invest the hours necessary to attain for them a favorable result. They trust you.

For me, the epiphany soon arrived that I had chosen a field of practice in which, at least in 1985, there would be few victories. If any. The Supreme Court rarely reversed criminal convictions in 1985, and they didn't do it that year in any of my cases. I had to come to grips with that.

The icing on the 1985 cake, however, was Eleanor. The third romance of law school, which carried me from March 11, 1983 right through graduation and the bar exam. This was the one that stuck. Two thirds of my law school experience.

There is nothing like college romance. A campus is a petri dish for sprouting romance. You have access to each other all day, every day. You don't shovel snow or mow grass or do a lot of driving, so you savor the changing seasons rather than battle them. The cultural opportunities were infinite. The Alfred Hitchcock Summer Film Series. The Fred Astaire Summer Film Series. The Symphony. Ray Charles. Sara Vaughan. Independent foreign films at the Bijou Theater in the Union. Dance lessons.

And you are so young.

Suddenly it's over. And for the first time in our lives as a couple, we are out in the real world. I'm living with my parents in West Des Moines. Eleanor's entire family is back in Memphis, Indiana, eighteen miles north of Louisville. With one exception. She has a 30-year-old cousin, Marcie, living in an apartment in Pleasant Hill, a small suburb just east of the Iowa Fairgrounds. Marcie and Eleanor have nothing in common and, to be honest, don't like each other terribly well. But Eleanor's Aunt Penny, Marcie's mother, impressed upon her the importance of looking out for one's kin when they're thrown into an unfamiliar environment. It could happen to you. Marcie didn't see anything like that ever happening to her, but she had a guest bedroom. How long would it last, anyway? Soon enough, Eleanor would find a position and get her own place. And the sole reason she was even in the Des Moines area rather than back home in Indiana was the presumption held by everyone, including me, that it wouldn't be long before Eleanor and I tied the knot and I'd be taking her off Marcie's back.

Marcie's apartment was about a half hour drive from my

parents' house. Eleanor and I saw each other now maybe twice a week. Most other nights there would be a twenty-minute phone call. And there was less to discuss in each call.

I had a job, and Eleanor was still looking. That didn't help.

It didn't take long for the little glitches in our personalities (particularly mine) that we were willing to overlook during law school to inch toward center stage. The insecurity that grew from being in the first truly long-term relationship of my life made me even more controlling, moody and manipulative than I naturally am. Eleanor didn't need that, and the arguments in favor of staying together quickly shrank on the balance sheet in relation to those for calling it quits.

As 1985 wore on, I watched the romance that I'd pegged to be a life-long commitment wither gradually and excruciatingly on the vine. Eleanor's job search had broadened to a geographic circle that included cities far from Des Moines. By the end of the year it was apparent even to me, who three years earlier essentially had earned an Olympic gold medal in clinging to a relationship that had long since gone belly up, that this one wasn't coming back. Thoroughly heartbroken, I resolved not to reenact the months of desperate and pathetic stalking in which I'd engaged the last time out.

By mid-1986, she was gone. I think she settled in Cleveland, where she'd completed her first year of law school before coming to Iowa.

Eleanor was really the final link between me and my college days. I was now fully entrenched in the real world. I had a job as a lawyer. I was all at once an eligible bachelor, untethered to any spouse or girlfriend. I had my own apartment on Fleur Drive near the Airport. I had a brand-new car, a tiny late-model Renault Alliance. It was time for me to don the brave face and to move the hell forward.

It was a sensation that harkened back to the days just after Baby Lester and the Buggybumpers disbanded, bringing to an end my idyllic life on the road, or back to that weekend during my first semester in law school when I'd just broken up with Imelda. Whether it was in Iowa City or Des Moines, or in Sevastopol for all that mattered, my entire social life revolved around Eleanor. Even when it was just the late evening phone calls. What do I do? Who do I know?

My life was once again an empty slate. I drifted for quite a while.

In the days before computer-assisted research, my job with the appellate defender's office regularly brought me to the ornate State Law Library in the Iowa Capitol Building, just through the tunnel from the Lucas Building, where I worked. It's all there in bound volumes, the decisions of the appellate courts in Iowa and every other state, and those of the federal courts, going all the way back to the Civil War. There were countless afternoons of rifling through them in search of the ones that might support an articulable position favoring one of my clients. When I started doing the caselaw updates at seminars and writing *4A Iowa Practice: Criminal Procedure*, I would bring in lists of recent cases that had come to me as slip opinions to find their official Northwest Reporter and United States Reporter case citations. I logged hundreds of hours of research in the State Library.

Especially when the Legislature is in session, the Capitol Building is like Grand Central Station. All three branches of government are vibrant with activity at the same time. Tourists and classrooms are led through the Statehouse wings to view the relics of Iowa history on display in every corner and to witness democracy in action.

There was one Friday afternoon in the fall of 1986. Still unattached and grieving the demise of what had once thrived between Eleanor and me, I had to run over to the library to check one or two case opinions before calling it a week. As I emerged from the tunnel in the Capitol basement on my way to the grand staircase, I passed a woman who seemed to know me.

Actually, she did know me. She called me by my name.

And she stopped for a little conversation. I had no idea who she was. It wasn't a matter of placing the face. It wasn't like *where do I know her from?* I didn't recall ever seeing this woman before. She was an attractive woman with close cut blonde hair, actually quite a bit like Eleanor's. Very friendly. She may have been slightly older than I was. But she knew me and, from all the signs, she seemed to *like* me.

Since the breakup, I'd done little with myself besides just go to work and come home. I wasn't out meeting a lot of people. I'd been training in taekwondo for about a year, and there were a few incidents of struggling to identify people in their street clothes who, it would turn out, I knew from the dojang. But she wasn't one of them.

It could have been the *lawyer* thing. Some women, I'd been told, are impressed by that. Even, I suppose, if you're a public defender. It's like being a minor celebrity. It might be something I'd have to start getting used to. But you wouldn't expect that in the Statehouse, where *everybody's* a lawyer.

I was overthinking it, as I was accustomed to do. It was Friday, near the end of the workday. Rapidly approaching was another weekend with no plans. And here was this opportunity, just dropped on my lap. And I was about to let her walk away, without even making an effort.

It could be perfectly casual. *I'm about to knock off for the day. Do you have dinner plans? Do you want to grab a drink? Would you like to go for a cup of coffee?* Something down that line. One of those things. But vestiges remained of the socially awkward John Burns who, before Eleanor, was more at ease approaching a coiled viper than he was asking a woman for a date.

Do it, John. Ask her now, before she walks away. Do you want to be single forever?

I almost did.

Then suddenly it washed over me. Fortunately. Mercifully.

At the very moment I stepped right to the precipice of what would have been certain professional suicide, I recognized her. I know *exactly* who this woman is.

About three months earlier, Governor Terry Branstad had

appointed 38-year-old Linda Kinney Neuman as the first woman to sit as a justice on the Iowa Supreme Court. Ten years before that her aunt, Helen Kinney, had been the first woman to sit as a circuit court judge in DuPage County, Illinois after being the first woman in DuPage County history to serve there as an assistant district attorney. There are people you don't approach on a Friday afternoon and invite out for a drink. Thankfully I hit the brakes just before I drove up to the edge of the cliff. I have a good idea how that one would have played out.

Had I been accorded some due process, a reasonable opportunity to be heard, I may have been forgiven for not realizing who it was I had accosted. I don't think I attended Justice Neuman's swearing in. There would have been, at most, two oral argument weeks between then and our encounter in the Capitol basement. The majority of my cases were going to the lower-tier Court of Appeals. What is baffling is that she knew who I was.

As far as I recall, that was the only direct conversation I had with Justice Neuman out of court. Ever. She once sent me a complimentary letter following the publication of an essay I had written for the *Des Moines Register*. She was an excellent justice. Completely moderate in her views, it wasn't instantly predictable where Justice Neuman would come down in a case. She was pleasant and respectful to the attorneys in oral arguments.

The story I've heard is that, during the last private meeting of the Court when Justice Neuman retired 17 years later, Justice James Carter serenaded her at the table with a song called "Linda." There is a standard entitled "Linda" written in 1942 by Jack Lawrence during the Second World War. First published after he left the service, its subject was his lawyer's one-year-old daughter. "Linda" was a hit for the Ray Noble Orchestra and over the years has been covered by such icons as Jan & Dean, Bing Crosby, Perry Como, Willie Nelson and Frank Sinatra. The young Linda in the song grew up to be married to Paul McCartney, the Beatle, for 29 years.

It's a sweet, upbeat tune.

I hope to God *that's* the "Linda" that Justice Carter sang to Justice Neuman during their last meeting together on the Court.

Because, you know, *I* have a song called "Linda." And it's been played in public a few times. It the one and only John Burns original that was performed by Baby Lester and the Buggybumpers when we were on the road. As a matter of fact, the night that Dolly Parton's rhythm section filed into the Holiday Inn lounge after their Albuquerque concert and sat in with us for our final set, while the Harlem Globetrotters danced on the floor beneath us, one of the songs we played was "Linda."

My Linda has a very, very salacious set of lyrics. It's a song that, had it been written about a one-year-old girl (which it wasn't), would put me in prison. At the very least, it would make me a target of investigation. Singing that song to an associate justice of a state supreme court would certainly place my license to practice law in more jeopardy than awkwardly asking her out for a drink.

My first meeting with Justice Neuman's successor on the Court was far less amiable. I was attending the Thursday evening "wake" at the Iowa Bar Association Building for the three justices voted off the Court in the 2010 judicial retention elections following the unanimous 2009 same-sex marriage decision in *Varnum v. Brien*. In the midst of a conversation with a friend, I was slugged on the back by somebody standing behind me.

It wasn't injurious. There was no pain, nor did it appear to be calculated to inflict pain. It was calculated to get my attention. I turned around to see him standing there. Though he'd served as a Supreme Court justice for over seven years, I hadn't met him before. He wasn't the only one, as it had been 16 years since I'd left the appellate defender's office and ten since I'd made the jump to federal court. I extended my hand.

"I'm John Burns," I introduced myself. But he rebuffed the handshake.

"I know who you are," he barked. "You keep writing that

shit."

"You've got to understand about me –," I began, intending to explain that there is always going to some loudmouth like me out there with the criticisms. But it could be a lot worse. I didn't get the chance. He cut me off.

"No. You've got to understand about *us*. I don't write those opinions. The *Court* does."

Being who I am, the snarky response mechanism was already kicking into gear.

"Well, I'd like to *see* that," I came really close to saying, but he stalked off before I had the opportunity.

"What's *his* beef?" I wondered.

By then, I'd long come to realize that I had allies and foes on the bench, some of whom I'd never met. The West practice manual wasn't really a source of the enmity. When I first signed on to write it, the West representative told Bob and me to feel free to take a position where I had one. The book is going out mostly to defense lawyers, and part of its *raison d'etre* is to stimulate advocacy in unexplored terrain. So buried within the hundreds of pages of case cites and court rules were a few of my opinions about the way things *should* be.

There were the one or two instances of me crossing the line in my rhetoric back when I practiced in the Iowa Supreme Court. The remark about the chief justice coming down off the bench and donning the mantel of advocacy may be the closest I ever wandered to earning an ethics complaint.

The real minefields for me were my caselaw updates and the outlines that I prepared for them, and the blog. After I left the state public defender system to chart a new course in federal waters, stepped down as president of the Public Defender Association and ceased publication of the monthly *PDA Update*, I was contacted by Peter Persaud in the Iowa City Public Defender asking if I wanted to do a daily blog on the Public Defender Association website, to keep the less experienced practitioners up to date with developments in the law. Why not, I told him.

Soon the blog went the way of my caselaw updates

at CLE seminars. About thirty percent of their content was an exchange of useful information, with the remainder being a showcase for my over-the-top theories about the law and anything else about which I needed to vent. And my misguided and often self-destructive attempts at humor.

It was a little unsettling being confronted at the "wake" by this particular justice. Ideologically, he and I were on the same side of the aisle. Even for the ones who weren't, I'd become in many respects a *cheerleader* for the Court. Most of what I'd been writing and saying was complimentary and, in my view, should have been unobjectionable to members of the Court.

When these little manifestations of displeasure filtered back to me from the Court, what always moved me most about them was that the justices were paying any attention to what I had to say about them. Who was I, anyway?

What had stuck in this justice's craw, I learned down the road a bit, were a few things I'd written about ineffective assistance. I knew all about ineffective assistance. There's the rule that a party can only argue on appeal the issues that his or her attorney has "preserved" by making motions or objections raising them in the trial court. The way around that (at least until the Iowa Legislature stepped in with a rule that you can't do it anymore) is to argue that the reason the motion or objection wasn't made was because the attorney who didn't make it was incompetent. That attorney, you argue, rendered ineffective assistance. Your client, consequently, was denied his or her Sixth Amendment right to counsel.

I could write the book on ineffective assistance alone. Routinely I brought, or attempted to bring, issues before the appeals courts that were not preserved in the trial courts by using the mechanism of ineffective assistance. I've mentioned already that in my time as an appellate defender, I probably pinned the ineffective assistance tail on every attorney in the state, including myself (twice). You come to recognize ineffective assistance as an error preservation tool, and not a personal affront to the trial attorney.

To be effective, however, an attorney needs only to make motions and objections that invoke the law, *as it is*. Even as a legal fiction, no attorney should be deemed incompetent for not following the law *as it should be* but isn't.

After my practice before it came to an end, I saw the Supreme Court becoming more progressive in its interpretation of constitutional principles in criminal cases and, in doing so, making drastic changes in the law. From my perspective that's a good thing. But they were doing it on the backs of defense attorneys who'd done nothing wrong. Under the law, as we proclaim it today, the client was denied the protection of a constitutional or statutory right. But the lawyer didn't file a motion or make an objection asking that the law be applied in this manner. We're going to consider the issue anyway, the Court writes, by finding that the trial lawyer was ineffective. But the *real* reason the lawyer didn't make the argument was that the law said something different at the time of trial. Nevertheless, there is now a written published opinion out there making the express finding that this lawyer did not perform an essential duty and thus did not meet the standards of competency required under the Sixth Amendment.

My feeling is that the Court should take responsibility for its own mistakes. If you want to change a bad law to make it better, go for it.

This was the type of rhetoric that incited one Supreme Court justice to "assault" me at the wake for the three deposed justices in 2010.

It's not the only time my blog got me in trouble with a judge.

Twelve years ago, my cousin died. A nationally ranked heavyweight bodybuilder and one of my personal heroes, my cousin had recently completed a sentence in the federal criminal justice system for activities relating to a controlled substance upon which competitive body builders sometimes rely in their training as a substitute for steroids. There was a time, not so far back historically, when it was not an illegal controlled substance. My cousin took responsibility for his offense and paid his debt without giving testimony against his friends.

One morning not long after his release, my 42-year-old cousin lay down for a few minutes and didn't wake up.

I had a few things to write about him in my blog. I was proud of him, what he'd made of himself, and how he handled himself facing the charges. One of the frightening prospects of incarceration is that of losing relatives while you're locked up. It happened to my cousin, when his father passed away about halfway through the ordeal.

There was some wrath in that blog entry, directed mostly towards the folks who put my cousin in prison. The United States Attorney in that district was someone who apparently fancied himself as a stalwart crusader against organized crime. My cousin was a big, muscular, ruggedly handsome man with a long Italian surname. But he was a small player in a small case and, according to media accounts, the prosecutor was trotting him out like he had ensnared John Gotti. I didn't pull a lot of punches in that one. I had things to say about this United States Attorney and a few about United States Attorneys in general.

A year after my cousin died, a new judge was appointed to sit in the federal district court in which I now practiced. Before that, she had served as the United States Attorney in a different district. I had met her once in that capacity.

A reception was held in the new judge's honor in the same hall in which I'd sustained the kidney punch from the Iowa Supreme Court justice two years before. After attending a monthly Inn of Court meeting across town, I pulled into the parking lot of the Bar Association Building where I was approached by a local prosecutor.

"I just want you to know," the prosecutor informed me. "The new judge just pulled John Courter aside and told him she'd heard about a blog he'd written about the United States Attorneys. She wasn't going to tolerate any of that unprofessionalism in this district."

"That wasn't Courter," I laughed. "That was *me*."

"I *know*. That's why I'm telling you."

"Well, I'd better go in there and straighten this out right now."

I took my place at the tail end of a long line of well-wishers. It was funny she thought it was John Courter writing the blistering attacks on the United States Attorney. At the time, John Courter himself was an Assistant United States Attorney. Why would he do that?

I made it to the front of the line and shook the judge's hand.

"I'm John Burns," I introduced myself. "And I have a blog."

For the seven years after that, I had a very good working relationship with that judge.

My wife turned 30 four months after I met her in 1987. To celebrate, I took her to Shogun, the teppanyaki restaurant in West Des Moines where the chefs prepare your food at the table, Japanese-style. Our chef, who goes by the nickname Duke, was born in China, moved to Vietnam at a young age, then emigrated to the United States after the war. It was a lot of food and, on what I was earning at the time, wasn't cheap. But we returned, again and again. When Shogun went out it was replaced by a similar operation called Tokyo. Tokyo was short-lived. In 1996 Cy Gushiken, one of the original chefs from Shogun, opened the restaurant as Ohana Steakhouse.

Our visits to Ohana progressed to the point that, for the past two decades, we have visited Ohana once or twice each week. We have come to know intimately many of the chefs and staff at Ohana, as well as some of the other customers. Dinner at Ohana has become one of the cogs in the machinery of our day-to-day routine.

Often seated at tables with strangers, you become acquainted with people with whom you would not otherwise come into contact. It's a microcosm. Some are hardened criminals. Some are local celebrities. Some are celebrities on a grander scale.

I met Max Collins once at Ohana. Max is the graphic

novelist who wrote the Warren Beatty *Dick Tracy* film and Tom Hanks' *Road to Perdition*. The Slipknot guys originally are from this neck of the woods and, like all the cool people in town, apparently do come into Ohana. Maybe I've eaten at a table with them, but I wouldn't know them without their masks.

We went in one Saturday over a weekend during which a major pro-am golfing event was being held six miles away at Glen Oaks County Club. It may have been the Principal Charity Classic. At the same time we arrived, Japanese golfer Isao Aoki came in with his entourage.

Over the course of his career, Isao Aoki won a total of 80 golf tournaments. His crowning achievement, however, was shooting 244 at the 1980 U.S. Open Golf Tournament, one shot better than Jack Nicklaus' record of 245 in 1967. What kept him from returning to Japan with the trophy was Nicklaus' score of 242 in that same 1980 tournament. Aoki took second place.

As a reward for our patronage at Ohana, we were seated at the table with Aoki and his men. Head chef Ken Hale prepared a special seared tuna dish off the menu for the guests, in which we were invited to share. I loved it. My granddaughter loved it. But my wife, who would rather be drawn and quartered than put sushi in her mouth, made a valiant effort to take a bite and pretend to enjoy it. She wasn't going to win an Academy Award for *that* performance. Her efforts were well-appreciated entertainment for the Asian guests.

In December 2022 we celebrated Pam's 65th birthday, and the 35th anniversary of our first dinner there, at Ohana. With Duke as our chef.

We went there one evening in 2015 or 2016 during State Fair Week. I'd played shows on two of the stages that afternoon and rather than pig out on Fair food I came home, got the wife and went to Ohana. They seated us with three generations of one family. There was the matriarch, her son and the grandchildren.

It came out early in the dialogue that the son was a

drummer and had also played a show that day with a band. I let them know that I'd been out there as well. He wasn't just a drummer, it turned out. He was also an agent for the Iowa Division of Criminal Investigation. I knew him by name in that capacity.

"I think I know you," the woman claimed. That always makes me feel good, to be recognized as a musician, after all I've invested in it over the years. "Aren't you a lawyer?"

Shit.

"Among other things."

"Don't you do the caselaw update at CLE seminars?"

"That's me."

"They're so *entertaining*."

Now I was sorry I didn't recognize this woman.

"Are you an attorney?" I asked.

"I'm actually a judge. You wouldn't know me. I'm from western Iowa. Perhaps you know my dad."

"Maybe. Who's your dad?"

"Jerry Larson."

BOOM!

"Jerry Larson? Are you talking about *Justice* Jerry Larson, on the Supreme Court?"

"That's my father."

"You're telling me that Justice Jerry Larson is your father."

"That's right."

"Justice Larson – he *hates* me."

"No, he doesn't. My dad doesn't hate anyone."

"He hates *me*. I guarantee it. You ask him. He'll tell you."

There was no question about that one. I've had my friends and my foes on the bench. But there's been no one more adamant, more vocal about their dislike for me than Justice Jerry Larson. That news has trickled back to me through several tributaries.

Before the Dahl's grocery store across N.W. 86th Street from my development went out of business I ran into one of the three justices who would later be taken out in the 2010 judicial retention elections. He was, at the time, the one member of the Court with whom I had the closest personal relationship. As I did from time to time, I subjected him to some good-natured ribbing about the members of the Court not citing *4A Iowa Practice: Criminal Procedure* more frequently in their written opinions.

"We use it quite a bit," he stressed. "As a reference."

"But when you cite it in your opinions, that sells books."

"Well, I'll get the word out."

"Anyway, I know why the Court doesn't cite my book in your opinions."

"Why is that?"

"Because Justice Larson got you all together and told you not to."

"Yeah, he's still hurting about that 'larceny' remark," he explained.

Oh, wow.

That flushed the scales from my eyes about a few things. I was kidding about Justice Larson not wanting the Court to cite my book as authority, but apparently I touched on something. And the reference to "that 'larceny' remark" told me that once again I'd said something that had filtered back up to the Court.

It had just slipped out during one of my caselaw updates a few years earlier. But it went over really well and was a source of pride for the wannabe standup comedian who lives inside of me.

"There is no offense called larceny in the Iowa Code," I had told the assemblage at a CLE seminar in one of the Amana Colonies roadside hotels. "Are there any of you here who remember when there was larceny in Iowa?"

There was a small handful of old-timers who did.

"Okay. What were the elements? What does a prosecutor have to establish beyond reasonable doubt to get a larceny conviction?"

It's a lot like theft. There must be a taking of property. The property must belong to another person. The property must be taken without the owner's consent. And the defendant must take the property with the intent to deprive the owner of it permanently. Something like that.

"Oh, that's not how *I* define larceny," I come back. "Under *my* definition larceny occurs when you (1) have a case on appeal in Iowa, (2) the case is routed initially to the Court of Appeals, (3) the Court of Appeals rules in your favor in a righteous, well-reasoned decision, (4) then the Supreme Court takes it up on further review and takes the victory away from you, and (5) Justice Larson writes the majority opinion. *Larson-y*."

Prolonged, enthusiastic laughter. I *scored* with that one.

Of course, it wasn't entirely fair to Justice Larson. In my day, *all* the justices predictably ruled against whatever my colleagues and I were advocating for. But after Justice Louis Lavorato was named chief justice and the Court became more responsive to what I saw as meritorious arguments for change, Justice Larson grew consistently open-minded to at least listen. He was coming down frequently on our side.

I'm not the only attorney who does criminal caselaw updates at CLE seminars. One attorney who had worked with me in two offices and who ultimately settled in as a bureau chief in the attorney general's office bumped into two justices in the lobby of the Plaza building a day or two before he was scheduled to deliver the update at a seminar for judges.

"Are you going to be saying bad things about the Court?" one of them asked my friend.

"No," the other, Justice Jerry Larson, chimed in. "That's *Burns*."

It was just several months after that dinner at Ohana during State Fair week that I once again ran into Judge Susan Christensen, as she waited for a table at Ohana.

"I asked my dad," she informed me. "He really *does* hate you."

That's the last conversation we had. Interesting things have happened since then. Her father, who had served on the court longer than any justice in Iowa history, passed away two days before her birthday in 2018. Had he died five months later, he would have lived to see his daughter take a seat on the Supreme Court bench, attired as she took the oath in his judicial robe. Seventeen months after that, she became chief justice of the Iowa Supreme Court.

Susan Christensen was the third woman to sit on the Supreme Court. The second was Chief Justice Marsha Ternus, one of the three victims of the 2010 judicial retention elections.

You know the first.

A REPUBLICAN STATE

My family moved to Iowa from Massachusetts in 1964 when I was eight years old. Numerous times in the early years I'd hear my father tell people that Iowa is a Republican State. I didn't understand why he would say this, because we arrived late in the first term of office of a widely popular Democratic governor. What I didn't realize until recently was that Harold Hughes had been a lifelong Republican right up until 1962, the year he was elected to office. He made the transition not long after he freed himself notoriously from the shackles of alcoholism, a disease he helped others battle during most of his adult life.

In coming here, we left behind us an unequivocally Democratic state, the home of the 35th President who was martyred almost exactly a year to the day prior to our departure. We were, to that point in time, lifelong Democrats. As seven- and eight-year-old boys in early '64, during our first conscious election cycle, my friend Mike and I played Johnson and Goldwater the way other youngsters played cowboys and indians or cops and robbers. I was relegated in that exercise to champion Barry Goldwater. We crafted hand-drawn campaign signs -- Mike's out of the cardboard that had been inserted in his father's shirts by the drycleaner and mine out of two pieces of scrap lumber nailed together, which we swung at each other like Medieval huntsman's axes. The nail that held my sign to its handle was a rusty one. I drew blood in the skirmish, and Mike was off to the doctor for a tetanus shot.

My father strayed in 1980, when he caught a ride on the Reagan prosperity train which rapidly and substantially beefed up his net worth. His drift back began during the Obama years and, with the advent of the Trump Administration, he made a complete return to the Democratic fold.

But saying that Iowa was a Republican state in 1964 held an entirely different meaning from saying that Iowa is a Republican state today. The few times I've let myself be drawn into a political argument with one of those people in recent years, the one that slithers out quite often is "Don't forget. Lincoln was a Republican. The Republicans freed the slaves. The Democrats wanted to *keep* slavery."

My response?

It's true. We call that irony.

Roles change in a century and a half.

The New Party

Back in the days before Highway 218 between Mount Pleasant and Keokuk were four-lane divided as part of the cross-country Avenue of the Saints, my monthly road trips to and from the Iowa State Penitentiary in Fort Madison brought me through the tiny Washington County town of Crawfordsville, Iowa. At least in those days, a sign on the outskirts identified the town as "The Birthplace of the Republican Party." There is, it turns out, some veracity in that boast.

Apparently, some disgruntled members of the conservative Whig Party held a secret meeting in February 1854 to discuss creating a new political party. Though not ardent abolitionists, they opposed the spread of slavery into new territories and were concerned by what at the time was being called "Slave Power," the inordinate concentration of political power in the hands of southern slave owners. The secret conclave took place in Crawfordsville, hence the town's claim of being the birthplace of the party (parenthetically, Crawfordsville is a mere 21 miles due south of Riverside, Iowa, which advertises itself as the *future* birthplace in 2233 A.D. of Captain James Tiberius Kirk, commander of the U.S.S. Enterprise in the early *Star Trek* series).

The group went public on March 20, 1854 with a meeting in a schoolhouse in Ripon, Wisconsin. Consequently, Ripon also bills itself as the Birthplace of the Republican Party. The first time they called themselves "Republicans" was at a July 6 gathering in Jackson, Michigan. So, unsurprisingly, Jackson holds *itself* out as the Birthplace of the Republican Party.

If not the actual birthplace of the GOP, therefore, Iowa can proudly lay claim to being the locus of its conception. Maybe that's what Dad was talking about.

A lot more Republicans than Democrats have occupied the Governor's Mansion over the history of the state. There have been thirty Republican governors and ten Democrats. Two of those Democrats served before there even was a Republican Party and the number of Republicans may more accurately be 31, if you consider the fact that Terry Branstad left the job and came back twelve years later. And the Republicans hold a clear edge in what wrestlers would call "riding time," the total number of minutes in control of the governor's office. Leaving in 1983 after fourteen years, Bob Ray had been the longest-serving governor in the history of Iowa. When Branstad, his successor, stepped down in 1999, he'd surpassed Ray by two years. But when he finished his second run in the job after six more years, the combined total made him the longest-serving Governor *in the history of the United States*. Democrat Robert Fulton, on the other hand, held the office for only 15 days. As lieutenant governor, Fulton served out the remainder of Harold Hughes' term when Hughes was elected to the United States Senate. By my count, Iowa has been governed by Republicans for 123 years, and for 38 by Democrats. Iowa has sent 27 Republicans to the United States Senate, and 11 Democrats. In the United States House of Representatives, Iowa has been represented by 129 Republicans and 54 Democrats. In 2023, our entire delegation to the House and the Senate, and our governor, are all Republicans. The Republican Party holds overwhelming majorities of 34-16 in the Iowa Senate and 64-36 in the Iowa House.

What is baffling about these numbers is that 31.16 percent of the 2.16 million voters in Iowa are registered Republicans while 30.47 percent are registered Democrats. That's a difference of slightly more than one half of one percent. Yet the Republican Party currently has an ironclad grip on all the elected branches of government. I don't have an explanation for that. Perhaps the Republican message resonates more effectively with the 37.55 percent of the voters who are unaffiliated. In many respects, they do a better job of getting out the vote. Or maybe they are more skilled in seeing that the redistricting maps are drawn up in such a way that they favor Republican candidates. You tend to see it that way if, like me, you've been voting since 1974 and have grown conditioned over the course of a half century to a routine of seeing your candidates spiral down in flames (except the rare occasions you vote for *their* candidates).

There have been a few fleeting moments over the course of my lifetime as a voter in which the Red Tide has seemed to be abated. 1988, for example. Remember Michael Dukakis? He carried ten states plus the District of Columbia. One was Massachusetts. Dukakis was from Massachusetts. He was their governor. Another one was Iowa. Iowa? Why? I don't know. It was hefty margin in Iowa, too. 54.7 percent for Dukakis to 44.5 percent for Vice President George H.W. Bush.

I know that Jerry Crawford backed Dukakis. Jerry is a Des Moines lawyer who over the years acquired the reputation of being a Democratic kingmaker. It is said that each of the candidates he supported in the Iowa Caucuses went on to be the Party's nominee (he also held part ownership in a horse that won the 2022 Belmont Stakes). Jerry is reputed to be a close personal friend of Bill and Hillary Clinton. With his pale complexion and white hair, I suspect he is a useful golfing partner for the former President. Any potential snipers would have a fifty percent chance of targeting the wrong quarry from 200 yards out.

In 1988, Jerry picked Dukakis. Jerry's wife, Linda, had

been my boss for four years. She's from Massachusetts. Maybe that had something to do with the governor's emergence as "Jerry's kid" in the race. I have no doubt that Jerry was instrumental in boosting Governor Dukakis to a third-place finish in the Iowa Caucuses, but I'm not so sure he had the clout to sway the voters of Iowa in the general election. Whatever the reason, the Iowa numbers were a gratifying enclave in an otherwise abysmal evening for Democrat voters.

Prior to that year, Iowa had come down on the Democratic side only five times after Lincoln and the Civil War.

Then there was Obama, and all was good in the world. I latched on to Senator Barack Obama after hearing him speak at Beaverdale Park on July 4, 2007, and worked my butt off on his Iowa Caucus campaign. Everyone expected Hillary Clinton to walk away with that one and the question was how close we could come to her numbers. Of course, Jerry Crawford supported Hillary. He was a friend of Bill's. But Hillary didn't win the Iowa Caucuses. She didn't come in second. John Edwards came in second. We won big that night, and felt that we'd truly made history. And when the election came around, we carried Iowa by almost ten points over a formidable, respectable Republican opponent who carried himself with class and integrity. Four years after that, we again carried Iowa against another formidable, respectable Republican opponent who carried himself with class and integrity.

In my mind, we turned a corner in 2008. All of us.

I guess I rushed to judgment a little on that one. The 2010 midterm elections, especially the judicial retention elections, were a bitter wake up call. In both the 2016 and 2020 General Elections, the Democratic Presidential candidates were bested in the Iowa voting booths by nearly ten percentage points. Had our opponent been a formidable, respectable type like those nominated by the GOP in 2008 and 2012, who carried themselves with class and integrity, the results would have been palatable.

But he wasn't.

And an unignorable majority of Iowa voters bought into it. My father was right. Iowa remains a Republican state.

Like I've said, casting Iowa as a Republican state during my wonder years means something entirely different from what it is today.

As I was growing up, the model of "extreme" Republican conservatism in Iowa was Congressman H.R. Gross. Serving in Congress from 1949 to 1975 (when he was succeeded by a young up-and-comer named Charles Grassley), this World War I veteran turned journalist was no pillar in the Civil Rights Movement. Though he voted against the Civil Rights Acts of 1957 and 1964 and the Voters Rights Act, he did vote in favor of the Civil Rights Acts of 1960 and 1968 and for the 24th Amendment prohibition of poll taxes. The cornerstone of his political philosophy, however, was frugality. He voted against most measures that had a price tag. The nuns who taught me at Sacred Heart School spoke of H.R. Gross as if he was possessed by Satan.

Few Iowans would disagree with me when I say that the most beloved political figure in our history was a Republican. He was the most affable and reasonable politician I've observed at any level during my adulthood, at least prior to the arrival of Barack Obama.

A Beloved Republican

In 1968, our Democratic Governor Harold Hughes decided to run for the open seat in the United States Senate vacated by Republican Bourke Hickenlooper, who was retiring at the age of 73. Like Hughes, Hickenlooper had served as governor of Iowa before running for the Senate. In his day, Bourke Hickenlooper was regarded as a conservative, yet he voted for the Civil Rights Acts of 1957, 1960 and 1965 (he voted against the Civil Rights Act of 1964), and for the 24th Amendment to the Constitution that barred the requirement of paying a potentially discriminatory poll tax before voting.

Attorney Robert Dolph Ray, a former chair of the Iowa

Republican Party, ran against State Treasurer Paul Franzenbug to succeed Hughes as governor. Ray won the election decisively.

Fifty-five years later, in the current political climate, we hear Democratic office holders being assailed by Republican opponents as being "too liberal for Iowa." The fact of the matter is that a review of the accomplishments of several of the Republican leaders of the late 60s and early 70s would cast them as being more progressive than most 21st Century Democrats. As the war in Vietnam and Indochina drew to its conclusion, Governor Ray invited 1,400 Tai Dam refugees to resettle in Iowa. It was a move that was not universally popular, and one that today would probably make him a pariah in some pockets of the Republican Party. For years he continued to advocate on behalf of the Southeast Asian refugees and was selected as a delegate to the 1979 United Nations Conference on Refugees in Geneva. The SHARES program that he played a part in founding raised a half million dollars for Southeast Asian refugees, a number that would be four times as much in today's dollars.

He was also instrumental in the passage of the Iowa Burials Protection Act of 1976, the precursor to the federal Native American Graves Protection and Repatriation Act.

Regardless of the R behind his name, Bob Ray was on the best side of every issue. The only persons I ever heard speak about him disparagingly were the poor fools saddled with the dubious task of running against him. If you ask me any question today about James Schaben, I'll tell you honestly that I don't know who that person is. On November 5, 1974 I was six months past my 18th birthday and, under the authority vested in me three years earlier by the 26th Amendment, I walked into a voting booth for the first time. And I didn't vote for James Schaben.

I voted for the Republican.

I voted proudly for Robert D. Ray. And four years later, seven days into a month that would culminate in all my dreams of a career in music taking a fiery nosedive, I didn't vote for

Jerome Fitzgerald either. In the 48 years I've been eligible to vote I've exercised the privilege three or four dozen times, if you include primaries and the odd-year county elections. You can count all the Republicans for whom I've voted on the fingers of, if not one hand, most certainly two. There are maybe two for whom I've voted *twice*.

I would vote for Bob Ray if he was on the ballot today (five years after his passing). In his golden years, I would pass Bob Ray regularly in the Des Moines skywalks.

"Good morning, Governor," I would greet the aged gentleman.

"How are you doing?"

"I'm doing well. How are you?"

It was like running into an old friend. I'm sure it happened to him hundreds of times every day, just like that. The warm smile. The pleasant, familiar voice. This man was, in his day, the longest-serving governor of the state in which I've lived 90 percent of my life. This is the man who, after the Jimmy Carter miracle in 1976, was courted by Republican presidential aspirants during Caucus season for his support or at least a photograph together in front of the butter cow at the Iowa State Fair. There were occasional suggestions of a Cabinet position. Senator Howard Baker teased us with the idea of a Vice President Bob Ray at a time when there were still people alive who could remember a day that, had Franklin Roosevelt died five months earlier than he did, a Vice President from Iowa would have become our Commander in Chief. Bob Ray was a national figure. But in the 35 years that followed his service, he remained the favorite uncle you'd pass on the skywalk and exchange a few words. And you'd go back to the office and home that evening and brag about it for the rest of the day. Even a crusty old Democrat like me.

And when he stopped being governor, Bob Ray didn't just retire. To fill the hours of his days, he took a job as Chief Executive Officer of Life Investors Incorporated, a Cedar Rapids insurance company.

After that he was Batman. Whenever Gotham City needed rescuing, Commissioner Gordon would flash the Bobray logo on the low-hanging clouds and our perennial hero would come to the rescue. When former Iowa Democratic Party Chairman Arthur Davis resigned in 1997 for health reasons after 15 months as mayor of Des Moines, Bob Ray stepped in as interim mayor. The following year he returned to his *alma mater*, where he had earned his business degree and his law degree, to replace Michael Ferrari as interim president of Drake University.

I have never been a Republican, and I never will be. But I was content to make my home in a Republican state governed by the likes of Robert D. Ray.

Life After Bob

Bob Ray was succeeded in the post by his lieutenant governor. The conventional wisdom, I believe, is that being lieutenant governor is a "shit job" and the only reason you do it is the aspiration to transition one day to being governor. I don't know how often that happens, but it did here.

While the administration of Bob Ray made it a positive experience to live in a "Republican State," the theme for Terry Edward Branstad's many years at the helm, at least in my mind, was *we can do a hell of a lot worse*. That's certainly been proven out.

I have mixed feelings about Terry Branstad. Rather than saying that Terry Branstad is everything Bob Ray wasn't, I think the converse is more accurate. Bob Ray was everything Governor Branstad isn't. Bob Ray was outgoing, approachable and instantly likable. When I saw him and when I observed him in the media, Governor Branstad seemed shy, socially awkward and uncomfortable in his own skin (sometimes I think those characterizations apply just as well to me). Where Bob Ray was a visionary, Governor Branstad is a pragmatist. I know he is politically conservative, and that we disagree on many issues. I generally don't fault somebody for that. The Iowa voters knew the direction in which Governor Branstad leaned, and they kept bringing him back. Longer, as I say, than any other governor in the history of the United States.

From my limited perspective, it didn't appear to me that Terry Branstad enjoyed the game of politics. I think he understood it, and made himself visible to the voters with frequent public appearances. Parenthetically, that's a lesson Chet Culver, the second Democrat to follow after Branstad stepped down, never learned. I may be wrong, but it appears to me that once you've got the job it's yours to lose. Chet Culver seemed to eschew the gladhanding, and almost willfully handed the scepter back to Branstad twelve years after he first left office. I also suspect that, when it was apparent they could win it back, the reasonable thinkers in the Iowa Republican Party saw what was approaching on the horizon and lured the seasoned centrist to leave a job as President of Des Moines University, a college of osteopathic medicine, and come back for an encore.

But he didn't approach the politicking with any degree of joy or humor. Once, during my running days, I entered the inaugural Governor's Cup, a ten-kilometer race beginning and ending at the State Capitol Building. Like most of them, I finished in the middle of the pack. Before the race, held on a gubernatorial election year, Jerry Crawford gave me a t-shirt to wear. On the front was a caricature of Terry Branstad inside a red circle with a slash across his face similar to the logo for the film *Ghostbusters*. The inscription read *Branstad Busters*: *I ain't afraid of no governors* (an allusion to the film's title theme). At the conclusion of the race, I changed out of the sweaty shirt into one of the event's t-shirts, rolled it up and carried it up the stairs to where the governor was dutifully signing t-shirts and other memorabilia. He signed it for me.

"What does your t-shirt say?" the Governor of Iowa inquired.

"You don't want to know."

He grabbed it out of my hands, unrolled it, and threw it back at me in a huff when he saw what he had just signed.

Bob Ray wouldn't do that. He couldn't. There wouldn't be a t-shirt like that when Bob Ray was governor.

One interesting bit of trivia about Terry Branstad is that his second cousin is Democratic United States Attorney General Merrick Garland, the judge nominated by President Obama to fill the seat on the United States Supreme Court vacated by Antonin Scalia when he died in 2016. At that time, the Senate was controlled by a narrow Republican majority. With the Presidential Election just nine months away, the Senate Judiciary Committee, chaired by Iowa's own Charles Grassley, put the brakes on the confirmation process on the off chance that a Republican candidate would beat Hillary Clinton in November and take the first step towards nudging the ideological balance of the Court to the right.

According to a statement from his office at the time this drama was playing out, Governor Branstad had written a letter in support of Garland's appointment to the powerful D.C. Circuit Court of Appeals, but the two had never met face-to-face until earlier in 2016.

Though he had not read any of Judge Garland's rulings while on the Court of Appeals bench, the governor announced that he supported the committee's tactics, because he trusted Grassley.

For the most part, Branstad kept the ship of government sailing on an even keel. Changes were incremental, undoubtedly a product of the split control of the two branches of government between the parties. This may be a reason why the accomplishments of even the Nixon Administration seem liberal in comparison with the output of recent Democratic administrations in Washington. Nixon had to compromise with a Democratic Congress. Perhaps Branstad was in the same boat. Personally, I'm never comfortable seeing one party, even my own, in control of all the branches (in a nutshell, that's what this book is about).

Being who I am and what I do, I was most worried about the death penalty. In an era when the national consensus seemed to be going the other direction, Governor Branstad was mouthing some rhetoric suggesting that he might have an interest in bringing capital punishment back to Iowa. We came perilously close in the early 90s, when the Legislature held open hearings to consider the reinstatement of the death penalty in the state. I can't say what Terry Branstad would have done had a bill landed on his desk. He is, as I say, a pragmatist. Like Bob Ray, Governor Branstad had a law degree from Drake University, and he had practiced law for a period of time before immersing himself in politics. He even dabbled in criminal defense. I think he understood the economic costs of bringing capital punishment back to the state, along with the political price he might pay for such a move. I think Terry Branstad always kept an eye on the opposition.

I'm not going to say it was all roses and daffodils with Governor Branstad. No, he didn't bring back the death penalty (which had been abolished in Iowa in 1965), but he did what he could to flaunt his conservative credentials. One of the dynamic areas of constitutional litigation over the decade beginning in 2010 had to do with harsh sentences meted out to defendants who committed their offenses as minors. In *Graham v. Florida*, 130 S.Ct. 2011 (2010) the United States Supreme Court held that a life sentence without parole for a non-homicide offense was grossly disproportionate to the seriousness of the offense where the offense was committed prior to the defendant's 18th birthday, and thus violated the Eighth Amendment proscription of cruel and unusual punishment. At that age, many youths have not yet developed the capacity to make decisions with consequences that will follow them for the remainders of their lives. *Graham* was followed two years later by *Miller v. Alabama*, 132 S.Ct. 2450 (2012) which invalidated statutes providing for mandatory life sentences with no possibility of parole for juveniles who commit homicide offenses. *Miller* was made retroactive to apply to defendants previously sentenced to mandatory life terms for crimes committed as juveniles, in

Montgomery v. Louisiana, 136 S.Ct. 718 (2016).

Terry Branstad saw the writing on the wall and was not about to go quietly into *that* good night. Every last soul languishing away in Fort Madison or Anamosa for murders committed decades earlier as juveniles would now be brought back and potentially set free. On July 26, 2012, the day after *Miller* was decided, Branstad issued an order commuting all life sentences for inmates affected by the *Miller* holding to a uniform term of incarceration of 60 years without the possibility of parole or commutation. In accompanying statements, the governor made it clear that the purpose of the order was to assure that none of the affected inmates would ever be eligible for release from prison. He issued the following commutation order in *State v. Ragland*, 836 N.W.2d 107 (Iowa 2013), a case involving a 17-year-old boy who encouraged two of his friends to engage in a fight with another group of boys in Council Bluffs in 1986. One of the friends struck Timothy Sieff in the head with a tire iron, and Sieff fell and died. The boy who struck Sieff pleaded guilty to second-degree murder at a time when there was no limitation on parole eligibility for that offense, and was out in three years. The other boy who *was* involved in the fight received an equally brief sentence. Jeffrey Ragland challenged the murder charge at trial, was convicted, and received the sentence of life without parole. The true assailant wrote letters to the Pottawattamie County Attorney taking full responsibility for the killing and pleading for leniency for Jeffrey Ragland. Yet Ragland remained in prison for a quarter century with no viable hope for relief:

> WHEREAS, in the recent case of Miller v. Alabama the United States Supreme Court ruled that states cannot mandate life sentences without the possibility of parole for murderers who committed their crimes before the age of eighteen; and
> WHEREAS, now after the Court's ruling, up to 38 dangerous juvenile murderers will seek

resentencing and more lenient sentences; and
WHEREAS, it is a serious violation of federalism for the federal supreme court to throw out long-standing Iowa sentences; and

WHEREAS, the Eighth Amendment to the United States Constitution prohibits "cruel and unusual punishments," which allows the Court to ensure the method of punishment does not violate constitutional rights, but does not allow them to substitute their own judgment for that of the duly-elected legislature on issues of proportionality and public safety; and

WHEREAS, in the Miller v. Alabama opinion the court used "evolving standards of decency that mark the progress of a maturing society" to justify their decision, but ignored the fact that first degree murder itself violates the most fundamental right of a free society—the right to live; and

WHEREAS, unlike elected and accountable Iowa legislators, the Supreme Court has not had the opportunity to hear from the friends and family members of the victims of first degree murderers, nor do they live in the Iowa communities affected by their ruling; and

WHEREAS, first degree murder is an intentional and premeditated crime and those who are found guilty are dangerous and should be kept off the streets and out of our communities; and

WHEREAS, the penalty for second degree murder, a lesser offense, is fifty years in prison; and

WHEREAS, an appropriate sentence for first degree murder is life in prison, evidenced by the fact that when the General Assembly changed criminal penalties for other crimes committed before the age of eighteen the sentence for first degree murder was not changed; and

WHEREAS, after the decision in Miller v. Alabama, the decision about whether a juvenile first degree murderer will be released, or remain in prison, is taken away from the legislature, and given to judges, it is imperative that action is taken to ensure our public safety.

KNOW YE, that by virtue of the authority vested in me by the laws of the Constitution of the State of Iowa, I, Terry E. Branstad, Governor of the State of Iowa, do hereby COMMUTE the sentence of Jeffrey K. Ragland # 0803013, who after being found guilty of the crime of Murder in the First Degree in violation of Iowa Code section 707.2 from events occurring on or about August 16, 1986 was transferred by order of the Pottawattamie County Court to the custody of the Iowa Department of Corrections for a term of imprisonment of life without opportunity for parole, to a term of life with no possibility for parole or work release for sixty (60) actual years, with no credit for earned time.

When Ragland was brought in to be resentenced under *Miller*, the prosecution argued that *Miller* no longer applied because Ragland was no longer ineligible for parole. Branstad's order made him parole-eligible at 78, within months of the average life expectancy of American males. The district court ignored the commutation order and resentenced Ragland to a term of life with the possibility of parole after 25 years. The Supreme Court affirmed the more reasonable sentence. For all practical purposes, Chief Justice Cady recognized in the majority opinion, Ragland's sentence following Branstad's commutation order was equivalent to one of life without parole. Governor Terry Branstad's effort to thwart the will of the United States Supreme Court was itself thwarted by the Iowa Supreme Court.

Jeffrey Ragland was granted parole on February 9, 2017 at the age of 48. That was twenty days before the inauguration of Donald J. Trump as the 45th President of the United States. Trump's presidency is significant because it was the event that lured Terry Branstad out of Terrace Hill on May 24, with an appointment as the Ambassador to China, after a total of 22 years, four months and 13 days on the job, the longest any person has ever served as the governor of an American state.

It had actually been 34 years since he first took office, but there was that twelve on sabbatical. As I say, I suspect that Branstad was enticed back into the arena by moderate Republicans worried about the direction in which the party might be turning. In Branstad's absence, Bob Vander Plaats had twice attempted to win the Republican nomination, and the third time might be the charm. A year after the announcement of the decision in *Varnum v. Brien*, Vander Plaats' sphere of influence was reaching its zenith in 2010, fueled by his seizure of the issue in his active (and ultimately successful) campaign to unseat three sitting Iowa Supreme Court justices.

Bob Vander Plaats wasn't the most troubling personality emerging as the face of the Iowa Republican Party in northwestern Iowa.

In 2005, I was asked by a friend if I had a band that could play at her daughter's wedding reception at the Summerset Winery just north of Indianola, Iowa. What I was able to put together was what we touted as the first and last reunion of Baby Lester and the Buggybumpers. I brought Lester in from Omaha to play lead guitar and vocals, along with our original drummer, Steve Wilkinson. On bass, I hired Iowa Rock and Roll Hall of Famer Joe Hernandez. My co-worker Tim Ross-Boon, who had fronted several bands in his day, played rhythm guitar and did vocals. I thought we put together a pretty good show, and it was an enjoyable day all around. Steve's bus was parked on the rural property of Joe's brother R.J., who graduated a year behind me in high school. We all hung out there after setting up at Summerset to await the gig. What I didn't know that afternoon was that it would be the last time I would ever see Steve or Joe, and the last time I would play in public with Baby Lester.

The groom in that wedding had a famous uncle. Fifth District Congressman Steve King. Just starting his second term, Steve King had made himself well known throughout Iowa, and was already a name recognized across the United States. And not for good reasons. I wrote a rock song I thought I could work up with the band called "The Downside to Democracy," but we didn't get around to playing it. From the bandstand, I observed Congressman King jockeying to make his way to the stage during the toasts. He's not a large man, and it looked to me like the family was throwing elbows and doing everything they could do to keep him from speaking.

Steve King was, at the time, an embarrassment to all Iowans outside the Fifth District (later the Fourth District due to redistricting that followed the 2010 Census). He was a polarizing figure who made even conservative Republicans squirm in the days before personalities like Marjorie Taylor Green, Matt Gaetz and Lauren Boebert popularized caustic, extremist right-wing views to the extent that less than a decade later King might now be perceived as being more mainstream in his views and perhaps be regarded as a leader. But his toxic notoriety led the National Republican Congressional Committee to withdraw its funding for his campaign in 2018 and led the Republican Steering Committee to remove him from all of his committee assignments in 2019. Finally, in 2020, King was defeated in a primary by a more respected conservative.

The removal from his committee assignments came after a *New York Times* interview in which he mused, "White nationalist, white supremacist, Western civilization—how did that language become offensive?" Of the countless racist, nationalist comments made by King during his career, the one reference to immigrants from the south that garnered the most prominence was that "[f]or every one who's a valedictorian, there's another 100 out there who weigh 130 pounds—and they've got calves the size of cantaloupes because they're hauling 75 pounds of marijuana across the desert." A confederate flag was displayed on his desk in Washington until August 2016 when two Des Moines-area police officers were ambushed in Urbandale, Iowa by an individual who two weeks earlier had created a disturbance by waving the Stars and Bars at an Urbandale High School basketball game.

In 2010, King purchased $80,000 in radio advertising to advocate the removal in the judicial retention election of the three justices who participated in the same-sex marriage decision in *Varnum v. Brien*. When the United States Supreme Court fell into line with *Varnum* six years later in *Obergefell v. Hodges*, he suggested that the House should pass a non-binding resolution advising the states that they need not follow *Obergefell*.

I wanted to view 2010 as an aberration, as the peak of evangelical conservatism in Iowa. A survey of the damage done by Bob Vander Plaats and his followers would be an inducement to Democrats to work harder to get out the vote, and to Republicans to rescue their party before it was driven off the cliff by the extremists. I thought that was why we were getting Branstad back.

Who knows what deals were made to facilitate the second coming of Terry Branstad and who the players were who made them?

Kimberly Kay Strawn

For six years, I was making snide comments on the social media about "the Puppet." That's the nature of being the lieutenant governor. Nobody really wants to be the *lieutenant governor*. If you've got something going for you, if you've got a career, if you've got prospects, you're not going to abandon them all to be a sidekick. There are two reasons why a person would agree to be lieutenant governor. One is that you've got no better way to bring home $103,212 a year. The other is that you expect it to lead to your someday being the governor. It worked for Terry Branstad, after all. Not too many others, in my lifetime.

When you saw this woman walking six steps behind Terry Branstad at every public function, it didn't strike you that this was someone destined to ascend to the throne. Unless he died or something. If I was Branstad, I don't think I would select for my running mate a font of charisma who may one day turn around and challenge me for my job.

Kimberly Kay Reynolds, *nee* Strawn, born two years to the day before President Barack Obama, was a natural for the role. In all the various paths that have led others to the top of the political heap in our state, I don't know of any whose history in government consisted of eighteen years as the treasurer of a county with just under 10,000 residents and three years in the state senate. But with Chet Culver out of office and Terry Branstad back in the saddle, we once again had a governor who could be seen out in public. And, like I say, if the governor was there the lieutenant governor was never far behind.

We all have a list, I suppose, of old friends we've lost over the past decade because of the vast political chasm that's formed on the surface crust of our society. One of mine called me out on the social media on the day of the 2016 Iowa Caucuses for posting a photo I had taken in my office building of the governor with "the Puppet" in tow. I don't know if my friend had some personal acquaintanceship with Kim Reynolds, but he lofted a "we all know your politics, John" at me and we cut each other off as social media contacts. I don't know that my label for Kim Reynolds was necessarily political. It just seemed to fit the lieutenant governor who was tacitly present with the governor at all public functions. As long as she held that job, I don't think I ever heard her speak. I couldn't say what her views were, if she in fact had them. She was a puppet. That's how she came across to me, and I had fun with it.

So when Donald Trump put Terry Branstad on that slow boat to China to be our ambassador there, when he was replaced by the first female governor of Iowa, and when I first discovered what her voice sounded like, what the voice revealed was my first taste of Kim Reynolds' views on the issues. In time, I would learn rapidly just where she stood.

Now let me say this about that. I try not to vilify people just because their politics differ from mine. Close acquaintances of my philosophical ilk do that. They have derogatory nicknames for public officials on the other side. The other side certainly does that to us. I live in a state where the majority of people disagree with me on many topics. Many are smart, likeable people who have shown me much kindness and generosity.

At my last high school reunion, cornered on all sides by a herd of classmates who had crossed over politically to the dark side, they challenged me to say one positive thing about President Donald Trump. I can't do that. You're so far over to the left, they accused, that you can't admit to a single iota of the good he's done for our country. You're blinded by the anger and hate. If that's what you think, you don't know me. I'm the guy who wrote a supportive letter to the editor about Richard Nixon back in 1974, at the age of 18, expressing the opinion that one day President Nixon would be remembered for the strides he made both in areas of domestic and foreign policy. I'm the guy who accepted a VIP seat at a Ronald Reagan rally at the Cedar Rapids Airport on September 21, 1984, who carried on so frenetically that I (and my compatriots) earned one of those nervous side waves that Reagan liked to dole out. I saw the good in those guys despite the fact that, at least in Reagan's case, I disagreed with so much of what came out of their mouths.

I can't do that with Trump. And I never will. That's all I'll say about that.

Ask me instead about Kim Reynolds. There are things to respect about Kim Reynolds, I'll be the first to acknowledge.

The first has to do with the drinking. It's no secret that, over a very short period of time in 1999 and 2000, Reynolds was twice convicted of operating while intoxicated. After the second conviction she sought inpatient treatment, and she has been clean since then. She took that bull by the horns and conquered it. I respect that.

Another involves her persistence in pursuing higher education. Some people make light of her stop-and-start college career. I don't. After graduating from high school in 1977, Reynolds took classes at Northwest Missouri State University. Over the years, she attended three separate community colleges, and enrolled in 2012 in the Bachelor of Public Administration program at Upper Iowa University. Finally, in 2016, she was awarded a bachelor's degree in liberal studies at Iowa State University while she was lieutenant governor. There's always a part of me that's going to derive some humor out of making an arch conservative explain a college degree in "liberal studies." But the story here is that Kim Reynolds didn't quit. She plugged away at it for nearly 40 years and earned her college degree. It's not easy, I would imagine, doing that while managing a marriage, three daughters and a day job. It's a sign of character and I respect her for that.

There was one incident on a Monday in early 2023 in which I observed a flicker of humanity in the governor that induced me to view her in a more favorable light. Shortly after noon on January 23, an 18-year-old man appeared at the Starts Right Here facility for troubled youth on the near south side of Des Moines brandishing a 9-millimeter handgun with an extended clip and gunned down two of the participants, in what has been described as an ongoing gang dispute.

The assailant also shot William Holmes, the founder of Starts Right Here. Subjected as a youth to intra-family sexual abuse and violence, the 50-year-old rapper known as Will Keeps affiliated with a Chicago gang for protection at the age of 13. Coming to Des Moines in his 20s, Holmes became involved in mentoring youth with backgrounds similar to his. Those efforts developed into the Starts Right Here program, which in late 2019 and early 2020 took possession of offices used previously by the Social Security Administration. He filled them with classrooms, a recording studio, a weight room and other activities that would draw youngsters off the street.

On its website, Starts Right Here keeps a tally of its successes. The focus is on high school age youth with troubled backgrounds. Seventy percent are minorities. As of June 24, 2023, for example, the program boasted that its participants have passed 341 and a half classes and have earned 170 and a half credits. Twenty-eight have graduated.

The opening of the south-side facility was attended

by Des Moines Police Chief Dana Wingert and by Governor Reynolds, who pledged to continue to assist Holmes in growing the project.

Then January 23 happened. At a time in which mass shootings appear to be cropping up everywhere, the violence at Starts Right Here instantly grabbed the attention of the community and the media. The entirety of the five o'clock news that evening seemed to be devoted to the story. The local media outlet that I was watching happened to have a camera in the governor's face the moment she was informed that there had been shootings, that there had been fatalities, and that the rapper Will Keeps was seriously injured (not much was disclosed at the outset about the nature of Holmes' injuries or whether they were life-threatening. It came out later that he was shot in the hand and the hip and continues to recover).

What I observed on Governor Kim Reynolds' face was shock. She was stunned and at a loss for words. She appeared to tear up. It was genuine. We've seen politicians like Ronald Reagan and even Bill Clinton who are gifted with the talent to summon a tear at the opportune time. This wasn't that. This was the visage of someone who'd suffered a personal loss. She *cared* about this guy. This evangelical conservative Republican was visibly shaken by the shooting of a former gangster rap artist from Chicago who'd been out there trying to set a handful of wayward youth on the right track.

Unless Kim Reynolds experiences some political epiphany and does a one-eighty on her priorities and agenda, I can't imagine that I will ever vote for her. But after January 23, I can't help liking her personally, if even just a little.

That may wear off in time.

The one attribute I admire most begrudgingly is her effectiveness. Once she inherited the seat from Branstad, I finally did hear what her voice sounded like and discovered where she leaned politically. From the start, she's been crystal clear about her priorities as governor and, with a very, very friendly General Assembly, has had little difficulty working through her agenda. I don't like it, but I respect it.

Like I say, she's crystal clear. If there were any questions about that, they were answered in 2018 when she first had to run for the seat Branstad had bequeathed her a year earlier. Governor Reynolds made an unequivocal statement with the selection of the co-chairperson of her campaign.

Steve King.

The racist white supremacist who had consistently embarrassed the people of Iowa was, she claimed, "a strong defender of freedom and our conservative values." Only after she won the election did Governor Reynolds suggest that King should think about modifying his rhetoric.

Until he turned against her in 2023, as he has a history of doing, Governor Reynolds remained closely aligned with Donald Trump.

For the most part, Governor Reynolds has used her mandate to take the giant steps to further her intensely right-wing policies. It is truly a mandate. On the national scale, our two most recent Presidents have used their elections to further the agenda of their base. Although he took office by acquiring the requisite number of votes in the Electoral College, Donald Trump lost the popular vote in 2016 by a substantial number (the same was true to a lesser degree with George W. Bush in 2000). In 2020 President Joe Biden brought home both the popular vote and a win in the Electoral College. At the same time, Donald Trump garnered more votes than any *successful* candidate in history before President Biden (making him in my view the Isao Aoki of American politics). Neither victor walked away with the level of support that would justify running the table in his policy decisions.

But, especially in 2022. Kim Reynolds was racing under the unmistakable green flag. Her reelection margins have been decisive, and she has successfully packed the Legislature with, not just Republicans, but socially conservative and widely evangelical Republicans. And she has wielded that hammer without hesitation.

Although she has not yet been successful in attaining an increase in the inherently regressive Iowa sales tax, she and the Legislature have embarked on a mission to abandon the more progressive state income tax. The tax cuts have been accompanied by a massive reorganization of Iowa state government that reduced the number of cabinet-level state agencies from 37 to 16 and eliminated a slew of positions that at the time were vacant. To me, it is clearly within the governor's prerogative to do this. The governor is the state's chief executive, and streamlining the Executive Branch as a cost-saving measure and to promote efficiency is not necessarily a negative, provided there is no correspondent reduction in services. Back in my appellate defender days, I was asked to serve on a committee focused on "Zero Balance Budgeting" in Iowa state government. While I didn't understand it much at the time, my guess is that the objective was to find ways to streamline state government to make it more cost effective. I don't know that much came out of the Zero Balance Budgeting push in the early 90s. And I don't know how much study preceded the 2023 state government reorganization. But Kim Reynolds had no difficulty pushing it through the Legislature.

What the governor and the Legislature have done in the area of education to bolster their evangelical credentials, however, threatens in my opinion to both drive up costs and to lay public education in Iowa to waste. At a time when Iowa's former position as one of the top five states in United States for public education has dwindled, she and the Legislature have implemented a program enabling students to withdraw their shares of the education budget in the form of vouchers that can be used to attend private schools. School voucher measures appeal to conservative parents concerned that their children are being indoctrinated in elementary school with liberal teachings and age-inappropriate matter relating to sex. I don't disagree with the notion that parents have a right to know what their children are reading and being taught and that they should not be exposed to subject matter geared more toward more mature minds. It's one of those gray areas where there is no easy fix, but siphoning resources out of our public school system to assuage the concerns of our most socially conservative constituents is likely to have devastating consequences for public education.

A measure passed in 2019 concerning higher education is another one that, on its face, I fully agree with. The bill requires our state universities to foster free speech in and out of the classroom regardless of the content of positions taken by their professors, students and other speakers. One of the true benefits I received as a student at the University of Iowa was being exposed to an array of ideas, some of which ran dramatically counter to mine. That's an integral part of the educational process. I don't know, however, that the University of Iowa should be forced to hire and grant tenure to a biology professor who tells 18-year-old freshmen that human beings and dinosaurs lived together 10,000 years ago after God rested on the Sabbath, if this is what they're getting at.

But that apparently wasn't the motivation underlying the free speech on campus bill. It was similar to one passed on the federal level and signed enthusiastically by Donald Trump. When I hear that, my natural reaction is *what's going on in this picture*? What are they *really* after?

The answer comes in section 3.3 of Senate File 274, under which "a public institution of higher education shall not deny any benefit or privilege to a student organization based on the student organization's requirement that the leaders of the student organization agree to and support the student organization's beliefs, as those beliefs are interpreted and applied by the organization, and to further the student organization's mission." Apparently, the University of Iowa had acted to defund a group calling itself "Business Leaders in Christ," after it refused to permit one of its members, who was gay, to sit on its board. That was the *raison d'etre* for SF 274.

Two years later, the governor signed House File 744, that required First Amendment training for university officials and discipline, up to termination, for college officials who violate the First Amendment rights of students and others. I think perhaps that one man's freedom of expression may be another's oppression.

The Reynolds Administration and Legislature have taken aim at LGBTQ+ youth with bills that prohibit any discussion of their status in schools and that ban schoolbooks containing discussion found offensive to the moral leanings of the right. Potentially life-saving gender-affirming care for transgender youth is prohibited. God help the 17-year-old transgender high school senior who wants to run the 4x100 relay at the State Track Tournament.

A major theme of Reynolds' 2022 re-election theme was that she kept businesses and schools open during the COVID-19 pandemic, a disease that claimed the lives of 10,000 Iowans, 1.1 million Americans and just under 7 million human beings worldwide, by battling aggressively against efforts to contain the disease. In May 2021 she defiantly signed bills denying state aid and contracts with government agencies and private businesses who attempted to protect themselves and their clientele by requiring proof of vaccination, and barring mask requirements in schools and businesses operating on public property. In July 2023, she unveiled the new state logo to appear on roadside signage, bearing the slogan *Iowa, Freedom to Flourish*, a nostalgic allusion to her commitment to thwarting any mandates designed to combat the disease that would infringe on the "freedoms" of pandemic deniers.

Much of her rhetoric and actions have centered on the issue of abortion. On Friday, May 4, 2018, she signed a bill that would prohibit medical personnel from performing an abortion on a fetus that had a detectable heartbeat, which in the opinion of some experts comes about six weeks after conception. It was, at the time, the most restrictive regulation of abortion in the United States. An attempt to pass similar legislation in South Carolina failed on that same day.

"I believe that all innocent life is precious and sacred," Governor Reynolds proclaimed as she signed the fetal heartbeat bill which would in effect ban virtually all abortions in Iowa. "And as governor, I have pledged to do everything in my power to protect it. And that's what I'm doing today."

At the time she signed it, the fetal heartbeat bill was a rebel cry. As *Roe v. Wade* was still the law of the land, the bill was destined to be struck down. And it was struck down on January 22, 2019, when Polk County District Court Judge Michael Huppert entered a permanent injunction barring its enforcement. But then on June 24, 2022, *Roe* was overruled by the Supreme Court in *Dobbs v. Women's Health Organization*, 142 U.S. 2228 (2022) and the issue was sent back to the states. On August 11, 2022, Attorney Alan Ostergren filed a motion to dissolve the 2019 injunction, reportedly at the behest of Governor Reynolds. The motion was denied on December 12 by Polk County District Court Judge Celene Gogerty in a 16-page ruling. Judge Huppert's injunction was based on the 2018 decision in *Planned Parenthood v. Reynolds ex rel. State*, 915 N.W.2d 206 (2018) which found that access to an abortion was a fundamental right under the Iowa Constitution. That decision was overruled a month before *Dobbs* was announced, in *Planned Parenthood v. Reynolds ex rel. State*, 975 N.W.2d 710 (2022). Abortion was no longer a fundamental right under the state constitution, requiring strict scrutiny analysis, but the Court applied the intermediate scrutiny test of *Planned Parenthood v. Casey*, 505 U.S. 833 (1992) that invalidated a restriction on abortion that placed an "undue burden" on a recipient. In *Dobbs*. Judge Gogerty found, the United States Supreme Court set aside the finding in *Roe* that abortion was a fundamental right, but not the undue burden test of *Casey*. Consequently, *Dobbs* was not a substantial change in the law that would justify removing the injunction. There were also procedural reasons for keeping the injunction in place. Judge Gogerty's ruling went rapidly to the Iowa Supreme Court.

On June 16, 2023, the Iowa Supreme Court left Judge Gogerty's ruling in place by "operation of law." Of the seven justices on the Court, three voted to affirm Judge Gogerty's ruling and her analysis. Three voted that *Dobbs* changed the law to an extent that the fetal heartbeat bill was now constitutionally valid and could be enforced. Justice Dana Oxley recused herself in the case without explanation. The *Des Moines Register* speculated that she did so because at some point she had participated in the case as an attorney for one of the named parties. It is a common though not mandatory practice of the appellate courts that a case is affirmed by operation of law when the judges or justices are split evenly. The decision of the lower court stands as the law of the case and the action of the appellate court has no precedential effect. For these reasons, it is rare for appellate judges and justices to issue written opinions (particularly extensive ones) in evenly split cases.

In the June 16, 2023 *Planned Parenthood v. Reynolds* order, there were extensive opinions. But there is no binding holding of the Court. The injunction simply remains in place. There is no fetal heartbeat law in Iowa. There is no opinion from the Iowa Supreme Court telling us whether a restriction on abortion does or doesn't place an undue restriction on a person's rights under the Iowa Constitution, or whether that remains the test. The Legislature can pass a new bill with the same provisions, and we can let the Court reveal the answer. Provided that none of the named parties were former clients of a sitting Supreme Court justice, it is likely to be Justice Oxley who breaks the tie.

Governor Reynolds was heartbroken.

"To say that today's lack of action by the Iowa Supreme Court is a disappointment is an understatement," she mourned. "Not only does it disregard Iowa voters who elected representatives willing to stand up for the rights of unborn children, but it has sided with a single judge in a single county who struck down Iowa's legislation based on principles that now have been flat-out rejected by the U.S. Supreme Court. There is no fundamental right to abortion and any law restricting it should be reviewed on a rational basis standard — a fact acknowledged today by three of the justices. Still, without an affirmative decision, there is no justice for the unborn."

The governor did not take the loss lying down. She summoned the Legislature back for a July 10 special session, which produced a new fetal heartbeat law. That Friday, she took the opportunity to sign the bill publicly during a "Family Leader Summit" organized in Des Moines by Bob Vander Plaats as a forum for candidates for the 2024 Republican nomination for President. Noticeable in his absence was Donald Trump.

The signing of House File 732 was accompanied by a long self-congratulatory address which concluded with the following:

> We read in Scripture that the Author of life wants to give "a future and a hope" to all his children. Who are we to stand in his way?
>
> With the self-evident answer to that question in mind, I've never been prouder to sign a bill into law.
>
> Thank you for standing for life, the most fundamental of our rights.
>
> God bless you, and God bless the great state of Iowa.

After that, there was another injunction. And another appeal.

In my nearly sixty years as a resident of this "Republican State," Iowa has run the gamut from being the cradle of the party that managed to put an end to the institution of slavery, to being the home of Robert D. Ray, to being a state that presently ranks with Florida and Arizona as being among the most extreme right wing in the country. At its masthead is the first woman governor of Iowa, who gained such prominence among others in her party for her response to the COVID pandemic that she was selected to deliver the Republican response to President Joe Biden's March 1, 2022 State of the Union Address.

In a few respects, I will admit, Governor Reynolds has

displayed some political independence. She was instrumental in helping restore voting rights to convicted felons whose sentences had been completed. She has some empathy for Iowans in that position, she has indicated, stemming from her two OWI convictions about twenty years earlier. And after the United States Supreme Court decision in *Obergefell*, she indicated publicly that the matter of same-sex marriage was now settled and, contrary to the Republican Party platform, wasn't something she intended to pursue any further. Does this resolve the Republicans' beef with the Iowa Supreme Court? We'll get back to that.

THE NEW RULES

I'd heard they were coming.

I heard they might be massive. The last time there was a massive overhaul of the Iowa Rules of Criminal Procedure was 1976, when the Legislature adopted the new Iowa Criminal Code to come into effect in 1978. There were no rules of criminal procedure in our state courts prior to 1976. One critical difference between myself and Professor Ron Carlson, who authored the procedural chapters of the *4 Iowa Practice*: *Criminal Law & Procedure* manual that was replaced by my book, was that while I was touring the Holiday Inns of the United States in 1976 with Baby Lester and the Buggybumpers Professor Carlson was consulting with the Iowa Legislature as they drafted rules that have remained in effect for nearly a half century.

I had mixed feelings about the adoption of new rules. There's always this sense of *if it ain't broke* combined with my experience that any time a collection of judges, prosecutors and one or two token defense lawyers meet to devise "improved" rules, only mischief can ensue.

And I'll be honest. When I hear talk about a complete recasting of the rules, what I see in the future is a shitload of work for me. The substantive portion of my 2022 volume is 1159 pages long. My best estimate is that scattered throughout those pages are 500-600 cites to the rules of criminal procedure. Even if all they do is renumber the rules, like they did in 2002, I have to go through and modify those 500-600 cites. Where substantive changes are made, it is necessary to add new paragraphs and sections, remove the superseded ones and explain how the practice of law has changed because of the modifications. And I have to sound like I know what I'm talking about.

When that happens, it can be a full-time job. For the first fifteen years *4A Iowa Practice: Criminal Procedure* was out I *had* a full-time job, to put it mildly. And since I have left that world, I am actually more pressed for time meeting the self-imposed demands of music and writing than I ever was before. There are those points in the chronology of every year by which content must be submitted, and the closer it is to those deadlines that I get my hands on the changes, the more pressure there is on me to incorporate them into my book. And they have to go in. A book like *4A Iowa Practice: Criminal Procedure* only has value if it provides reliable access to current law.

The Task Force

The first step in the process was the creation by the Supreme Court, on April 3, 2018, of the Iowa Rules of Criminal Procedure Review Task Force. The task force's objectives were (1) to streamline and amplify the rules, eliminating ones that were outdated, (2) to reorganize the rules (ughh), (3) to bring the rules in line with recent court decisions and statutory changes, (4) to fill in any gaps in the current rules and (5) to make other substantive changes.

The initial makeup of the task force included Justice Edward Mansfield, four district court judges, a staff attorney from the Supreme Court, four state and federal prosecutors, six defense attorneys employed either as public defenders or in private practice, and one professor from each of Iowa's two law schools.

The task force submitted to the Court its proposed revisions to rules governing trials of indictable cases in November 2019. Proposed rules for simple misdemeanor cases came in February 2020 along with some modifications to the 2019 proposed rules. On March 30, 2020, just as the great COVID-19 pandemic was starting to take wing, Chief Justice Christensen entered an order circulating the proposed revisions for public comment. The deadline for comment was June 30.

My introduction to the new rules, however, had come a month earlier. On February 5, Bob Rigg forwarded to me an invitation from the Polk County Bar Association to a brown bag lunch at the Polk County Courthouse on Tuesday, February 25 to introduce the local legal community to what was in the works. It was my first time in a courtroom since I'd left the federal defender seven months earlier, and one of the handful of times I'd been inside the Polk County Courthouse since I'd left the state system in 1999.

Several task force members were there, including Justice Mansfield. I also ran into Judge Steve Colloton, who has sat on the Eighth Circuit Court of Appeals since 2003. It was interesting to me that he was there. If he'd ever practiced in state criminal court it would have been for a very brief period of time. The time he was in a position to do so was the two years he'd been a partner in the Belin firm in Des Moines from 1999-2001. Justice Mansfield had also been at Belin during that time, which may be the reason Judge Colloton showed up for the brown bag lunch.

There were two years we had been adversaries, in a sense. For a time after the Obama Administration drew to a close and Judge Jane Kelly's star was no longer positioned as high in the sky as it had been, Judge Colloton was my one acquaintance with the best chance of climbing the ladder the furthest. Apparently, Judge Colloton was on Donald Trump's short list for the United Supreme Court. If that were to happen, I would have my footnote in history. After law school at Yale, Steve Colloton went on to clerk for Judge Laurence Silberman of the D.C. Circuit and then for Chief Justice William Rehnquist of the United States Supreme Court. After a year in the Justice Department in Washington, he worked as an Assistant United States Attorney in Cedar Rapids for eight years, during one of which he was an associate to special prosecutor Ken Starr. Then he joined the Belin firm, and remained until he was appointed by George W. Bush in 2001 to serve as United States Attorney for the Southern District of Iowa. That's where I knew him. He approached the position more as an administrator than a practitioner, and we had very little courtroom interaction.

But two years later, when President Bush nominated Steve Colloton to serve on the Court of Appeals, there was a seven-month lag between the date of his appointment and his 94-1 confirmation by the Senate. Knowing that his tenure as United States Attorney would soon be drawing to a close, he filled in where he was needed.

On Tuesday, May 13 of that year, I was in St. Paul arguing a couple cases before the Eighth Circuit Court of Appeals. In one of them, there were six issues to be resolved. Whoever had written the brief for the government in *United States v. Walterman* was unable to attend the oral argument, so United States Attorney Steve Colloton argued the case in her place. He also handled at least one other case scheduled during that session.

Then we all went home and, as always, waited for the Court to decide.

Senate approval came on September 4, and on September 10 Steven Michael Colloton was sworn in to replace David Hansen on the United States Court of Appeals for the Eighth Circuit. From what I've heard, Judge Colloton took a week or two vacation before starting in his new position, and was away on September 16, when the Court announced its decision in *Walterman*. It was a good decision – for me. I won on a rather consequential issue, and it was an unexpected result. A few months passed before I ran into Judge Colloton in the parking lot of the United States Courthouse Annex, where he had set up his judicial office.

I congratulated him on his ascent, and we exchanged a few words about how he'd enjoyed the position thus far and about when I might expect to be arguing cases in front of him. I wished him good luck as I approached the annex and he walked toward the Courthouse. Just before I reached the door, Judge Colloton wheeled around and got my attention.

"Do you think they're ever going to come with a decision

in *Walterman*?" he asked.

It goes without saying that he and I are ensconced on opposite ends of the philosophical spectrum. But I've always said that we could do a lot worse than Steve Colloton on the United State Supreme Court. He's ten times smarter than I am, and he is intellectually honest. If an argument has merit, I trust someone like Judge Colloton to be receptive to it. But that little exchange in the Courthouse parking lot in the autumn of 2003 would be my footnote in history if Judge Colloton was ever appointed to SCOTUS.

As far as I can tell, I was the last attorney who faced him as an adversary in a courtroom. And I *beat him*. And the icing on the cake is that *I got to be the one to tell him about it.*

And today, for some reason, he attended a brown bag lunch at the county courthouse called to discuss changes in the state rules of criminal procedure.

The meeting was informal. The centerpiece was a power point presentation put together to be disseminated on March 30 that emphasized the most significant changes arising out of the proposed rules.

The Original Proposal

There wasn't much I considered earthshaking in that power point. Of course, earthshaking wasn't what I was concerned about. I was concerned about *quantity*. How much work is this going to be for me?

The first objective of the task force had been to streamline the rules. What they did in that respect, according to the presentation, was to hold the state rules side by side with the federal rules to see what guidance could be drawn from the latter in redrafting the former. In the course of its deliberations, the task force had managed to pare down the word count of the rules by 20 or 25 percent even taking into account the new rules that were adopted. Removing provisions for bills of particulars, bills of exceptions, motions for a change of judge, and a rarely used process for selecting a jury in a case's original venue then moving the trial to another were all touted as serving that end. Streamlining was further accomplished by striking the words "closed circuit" from each reference in the rules to "audio visual closed circuit system." Three pages of the power point presentation listed individual rules that were either rewritten or removed to shorten the total length of the rules.

The one slide discussing the task force objective of reorganizing the rules was the most welcome to me. Yes, certain rules were transferred to different sections where they most logically belonged. However, "a tension exists here because we didn't want to change the basic numbering scheme too much. Lawyers and judges need to know where to look for things. So the indictable offense rules are generally not renumbered. Old rule numbers are usually retained." The task force didn't come right out and say *we're retaining the old rule numbers as an act of courtesy to B. John Burns*. But thank you, anyway. The task force was not as hesitant to renumber the simple misdemeanor rules "[b]ecause of their brevity." I could live with that.

The power point noted ten changes made to reflect developments in the caselaw and two bringing the rules in line with new statutes. Before pleading guilty to a drug possession charge, for example, the defendant must be advised by the court that one punitive consequence of a conviction of this offense is a revocation of his or her driving privileges. *State v. Fisher*, 877 N.W.2d 676 (Iowa 2016). A particular colloquy between the court and the defendant was now required before the defendant could waive his or her right to a jury trial and admit to a prior criminal conviction that would have the effect of enhancing the defendant's sentence for the current charge. *State v. Harrington*, 893 N.W.2d 36 (Iowa 2017). The speedy indictment deadline would now run from the time the defendant is brought to answer before a magistrate and not from the time the defendant is detained by police. *State v. Williams*, 895 N.W.2d 856 (Iowa 2017). The 2019 legislation that limited the right to appeal convictions based on pleas of guilty was addressed in the proposals.

One slide addressed the task force's objective of filling in perceived gaps in the rules in areas like guilty plea colloquies, sentencing procedures and the circumstances under which the presence of the defendant could be waived.

The bulk of the presentation concerned what the task force characterized as a "few" substantive changes to the rules, with slides covering what it believed to be the most significant revisions.

Under the proposed new rules, initial appearances could be held in person or by interactive video and could be waived in writing. Challenges to the makeup of a grand jury (in the relatively rare cases where the defendant is indicted by the grand jury rather than charged by trial information) would be similar to those made to the makeup of the jury at trial. All grand jury proceedings would be recorded either by a court reporter or electronically. For speedy indictment and speedy trial purposes, when the Electronic Document Management System rejects the filing of a trial information that has been approved by the court, the date the indictment was approved is treated as the filing date.

Multiple defendants charged together in one indictment could move for separate trials where they believe prejudice would result to their cases. Any fact that could increase the defendant's minimum or maximum sentence must be set out in the indictment or information.

Consistent with the practice in federal court, the proposed rules would require that defendants be placed under oath before entering a plea of guilty. The plea colloquy must contain a disclosure of the elements of the offense and all punitive consequences that would result from a conviction including immigration consequences. Counsel would be entitled to question the defendant. The terms of a plea agreement, whether or not it was in writing, would have to be placed in the record and the defendant would have to be clearly apprised of the mechanics of a plea agreement that is subject to the approval of the court.

If both parties agreed, the defendant would be permitted to waive the use of the presentence interview and to proceed directly to sentencing.

Motions to continue trials would no longer be discouraged under the proposed rules, and the courts would have more flexibility in setting deadlines where the defendant waives speedy trial. These proposals obviously were a response, even prior to the pandemic, to the burgeoning dockets and the dwindling pool of available counsel willing to accept appointments. Certain classes of cases would no longer be given priority.

The defendant would be required to notify the state of all affirmative defenses, and to identify all expert witnesses who have examined the defendant for any purpose, not just for insanity and diminished capacity. The state would then be given the opportunity to have the defendant examined by its expert.

Timely written motions to suppress would be required to cover all allegations of illegally obtained evidence, and not just those claiming Fourth Amendment violations, absent a showing of good cause.

The time for taking depositions would be expanded to allow them up to a date at least 30 days before trial. Following *State v. Folkers*, 703 N.W.2d 761 (Iowa 2005), the defendant would be permitted to be absent during deposition questioning about the identity of the perpetrator.

The disclosure of grand jury testimony would be a compulsory part of discretionary discovery. The duty of reciprocal discovery would be automatic for defendants who request discovery, with no requirement for the state to obtain a court order.

Subpoenas could be served electronically, but not by a party to the case. Subpoenas would be issued only by the clerk of court, and not by a magistrate.

The court would have the discretion to approve a written pretrial stipulation of the parties without a formal hearing.

In the past, there have been no rules controlling what has

come to be called a "trial on the minutes," in which the parties stipulate to the minutes of testimony as the evidence in the case. The court reviews the minutes and enters a verdict of guilty or not guilty based upon them. This comes up where the parties are more concerned about litigating some legal issue regarding, for example, the admissibility of certain evidence. As a general matter, a plea of guilty waives an issue that might be raised on appeal. And, to this point in history, there had been no such thing as a conditional guilty plea, under which a defendant could enter a plea of guilty yet still preserve a legal issue for appeal. Trying the case on the minutes saves time and judicial resources, especially where it is apparent to everyone that the defendant will be convicted on the evidence.

The court would engage the defendant in a colloquy similar to that used in a guilty plea proceeding to satisfy itself that the defendant understands that he or she is waiving all rights to a jury trial, to confrontation, to put on evidence supporting any defense, and to testify at trial. In a trial to the bench on the minutes, the proposed rules would require that, absent a waiver by the defendant, the court's verdict be rendered in open court and on the record.

A potential juror could not be disqualified from the panel on the ground of a prior felony conviction if the juror's voter rights have been restored or ten years have passed since the later of the defendant's conviction or release from confinement. During *voir dire*, jurors would be questioned on sensitive subjects outside the presence of other panelists. When a juror expresses a personal bias on issues such as race, religion, etc., the court could question the juror to clarify the response but would not be permitted to attempt to rehabilitate the juror. Counsel on either side, however, could attempt to rehabilitate the juror. The identity of alternate jurors would not be disclosed until deliberations, at which time they would be excused.

The parties would not be permitted to waive the reporting of any portion of the trial, except for *voir dire* in misdemeanor cases. This provision makes sense to any attorney who has handled criminal appeals or postconviction relief proceedings on either side. Participants at the district court level occasionally don't spot the issues or fully appreciate the dimensions of the issues they do raise that are fleshed out on appeal. Absent a verbatim transcript, it can be difficult to reconstruct what went on below.

The admonition given to the jury prior to being excused would be expanded to include warnings about exposure to the social media. In its deliberations, the jury would not be provided with the discovery depositions or any items of evidence that would create a risk of harm. If the jury had a question during deliberations it would have to be made in writing and answered on the record.

Immunity granted to a witness would, under the proposed rules and following *Allen v. Iowa District Court*, 582 N.W.2d 506 (Iowa 1998), be both transactional and use immunity. This means not only that the witness would be guaranteed that his or her cooperation could not be used against him or her in court, but also that the witness would not be charged with the offense that is the subject of the cooperation.

Absent an objection by the state, the proposed rules would allow defendants to waive the submission of offenses that are lesser to and included in the charged offense.

All exhibits would be retained until 60 days after completion of the defendant's sentence and could not be disposed of during the pendency of a postconviction relief proceeding.

The jury would be required to answer special interrogatories on findings that increase a defendant's minimum or maximum sentence and, unless waived by the parties, on issues regarding accomplices. Consistent with *State v. Mumford*, 338 N.W.2d 366 (Iowa 1983), the court would have the discretion to return inconsistent verdicts to the jury for reconsideration. Parties could agree in misdemeanor cases to the submission of written verdicts.

Procedures to be followed in sentencing hearings are set

out in the proposed rules, including a requirement that the victim be permitted to address the court last, and that the advice to the defendant about his or her appeal rights include the admonition that a conviction following a plea of guilty may be appealed only if there is good cause to do so.

The district court would no longer be required to rule on a defendant's motion for new trial within 30 days, and could grant a motion for judgment in arrest of judgment only upon a showing that it is more likely than not that the defendant would not have pleaded guilty in the absence of its grounds. An illegal sentence may be corrected at any time, but only after notice to all parties and an opportunity to be heard.

The court would have the authority to have any person in the courtroom searched for weapons or other prohibited items, with no required showing of probable cause.

Consistent with *State v. Young*, 863 N.W.2d 249 (Iowa 2015), the right to appointed counsel would extend to any defendant facing incarceration. It would also apply to proceedings relating to the correction of illegal sentences. Limited appearances by privately retained counsel would be prohibited in cases in which counsel has been appointed to represent indigent defendants. In any proceeding in which the defendant has a right to counsel, the right would extend to certiorari proceedings challenging the outcome.

The task force proposed removing language that the defendant has no right to choose appointed counsel but that the defendant's request for a specific attorney would be given consideration.

The proposed rules would eliminate the discretion of the district court to dismiss a prosecution *sua sponte* for good cause. Such a dismissal could come only on motion of the state. The one-year speedy trial deadline could be waived only by the defendant, either on the record or in writing.

So this is what they came up with.

As the proposed rules are unveiled in the power point presentation, I'm not thinking so much about their substance.

It's not likely that I'll ever again appear in court as a practicing attorney. My mind is on the play clock. The 2020 edition of *4A Iowa Practice: Criminal Procedure* comes out in April. It's February 25 (the brown bag lunch at the Polk County Courthouse). I submitted my final revisions two days ago. What I saw today isn't necessarily the proposed rules. The chief justice's order circulating them for comment had not yet been issued. That wouldn't come for another month. The comment period, once it begins, would last 90 days. It's likely that there would be revisions once the comments are received and reviewed. At the very earliest, the new rules would come into effect in mid-summer.

How do I prepare for that? Even if the print edition of the manual released in April is instantly out-of-date, I could jump as soon as possible to make the digital Westlaw version accurate. But it would be imprudent to do that now. What I've got in my hands are not the new rules. They're a draft of a proposal. After the comment period had run, the rules might look completely different. This is a major undertaking by the Court. I have no idea how many months will pass before they come up with something I can incorporate into my book.

All I can do is keep an eye on the play clock. December and February -- the annual deadlines. If the new rules come in 2020, hopefully they'll come out in September or October. That would give me plenty of time to sit down and work them in before December 10, when my revisions are due. If not by then, perhaps December or January, and I can get them into my final revisions in February. But there's really no idea. There's absolutely nothing I can do in the meantime.

Public Comments

In the meantime, the COVID-19 pandemic made its landfall in the United States, including Iowa, and the attention of the legal community, particularly the Supreme Court, was diverted to other matters. On June 25, 2020, the chief justice entered an order extending the comment period on the new rules of criminal procedure by two weeks, to July 14.

The legal community did take it seriously.

The "Public Comments Regarding Chapter 2 Amendments" is 251 pages long, and the comments came from 24 sources. Three were received during the original 90-day comment period, while 20 came in during the two-week extension. And one was received from Wapello County Attorney Reuben Neff on July 21, a week after the comment period had expired, but appeared to have been considered fully with the others. 2020 was a difficult year for all of us.

The first set of comments received by the Court came from several attorneys from the Iowa attorney general's office. The proposed requirement that grand jury proceedings be reported contains an exception for the grand jury's voting, they pointed out, but not for its deliberations. The latter should be incorporated into the new rule. It would benefit both parties, in some cases, to allow the defendant to be absent for more than just questioning regarding identification during depositions. The parties should be able to agree to waive the defendant's personal presence. There should be a rule punishing as a contempt of court the redissemination of minutes of testimony. The assistant attorneys general were concerned about permitting convicted felons to serve on juries and advocated for extending the right only to convicted felons whose voting rights have been restored. In the alternative, they suggested, convicted felons should be allowed to serve once they are no longer under supervision, not on the sex offender registry and not serving the special lifetime sentence of parole for sexual offenders.

A letter from the executive director of the Iowa County Attorneys Association mirrored many of the assistant attorney generals' concerns.

The Iowa Association of Justice and several of its board members submitted extensive comments. One of the board members, Nicholas Sarcone, told a compelling story from an interesting perspective. In late 2017, he recalled, Sarcone and several others from the IAJ Criminal Core Group requested a meeting with Chief Justice Mark Cady to discuss the possibility of redrafting the Iowa Rules of Criminal Procedure. Based upon his experience as a practicing attorney in Florida and a survey of the discovery practices in other states, Sarcone believed that Iowa had fallen behind much of the United States in several respects.

Chief Justice Cady agreed to a meeting, during which Sarcone made his pitch covering "various topics we felt were inhibiting our abilities as criminal defense attorneys to do our jobs." The chief justice "listened intently" and "asked excellent questions."

"The entire presentation," Sarcone explained, "was an effort to modernize and level the playing field between the State and the Defendant. In short, we point out the deficiencies and suggested remedies. It seemed at the time Justice Cady was in agreement something should be done. He closed by telling us he would discuss the matter with the Court."

When the Court subsequently announced the creation of the task force, Sarcone was pleased, "although I was concerned that a committee would get bogged down in conflict between prosecutors, defense attorneys and judges and ultimately not be able to do much of anything."

Not long afterwards, Sarcone ran into Chief Justice Cady in the Capitol Building. The chief justice approached him, shook his hand and "told me that I should be very proud of myself and that I was the reason the Criminal Rules Committee had been formed. It goes without saying I was proud, proud to be complimented by Justice Cady whom I admired greatly."

"That was then," he complained, "and of course this is now."

The proposed rules, in Sarcone's view, furthered none of the objectives for which the committee was formed. Without going into any detail besides statements at the outset of his letter that he was interested in changes regarding defense subpoenas, discovery and the availability of conditional guilty pleas, he incorporated by reference the comments of the IAJ.

"What I feared about the committee process," he said, "ultimately came true."

The IAJ submitted 17 pages of objections. The first concerned discovery depositions. The existing Rule of Criminal Procedure 2.13(1) allows defendants to depose all witnesses listed on the indictment or information or notices of additional witnesses. Rule of Criminal Procedure 2.13(2) allows for the deposition of prospective witnesses not covered by Rule 2.13(1) if necessitated by the very general "interests of justice and the special circumstances of a case." The rule also authorizes the production of documents relating to the witness's deposition testimony. Under proposed Rule 2.13(6) the only special circumstance that would apply to the defense would be to perpetuate testimony of a witness anticipated to be unavailable at trial.

The proposed rule, the IAJ argued, is unclear in many respects, including who is a "prospective witness" and whether the new rule would still authorize the production of documents. Potentially, it could hinder the defendant's ability to prepare a defense and the truth-finding function of the criminal justice system.

A major area of concern is the ongoing disparity between the parties in their ability to conduct a meaningful fact investigation. This was one of the topics Nick Sarcone and his cohorts addressed in their meeting with Chief Justice Cady. It's a touchy subject that was becoming an issue during the five years I practiced in the Iowa state trial courts between 1994 and 1999. When my investigators and I needed to gather records that were not in the possession of the state (phone records, school records, etc.), the entities that held them often told us that they could only release them if there was a subpoena for them. Our office would then prepare a *subpoena duces tecum* that had been signed by the clerk of court and serve it on the custodian of the records.

When I first came on board there after my nine years in the pristine universe of appellate practice, it surprised me how well this worked out for us. A subpoena duces tecum requires a witness to appear at trial or other another hearing and to bring along certain specified documents that will be discussed during the witness's testimony. There's nothing in the rules that allowed the defendant in a criminal case to subpoena documents for investigative purposes, to see what one might see. Strictly followed, the existing rule enabled the party using the subpoena to see what the witness had in his or her possession only when the witness appeared at the trial or the deposition. The prosecutor, on the other hand, has *unlimited* subpoena power, especially before charges have been filed. There's nothing in the way of the government getting what they want as part of their investigation.

The United States Supreme Court held in *Brady v. Maryland*, 373 U.S. 83 (1963) that the government has an obligation to turn over to the defense any evidence in their possession that is exculpatory, that might prove the defendant's innocence. There are other rules and practices that allow for discovery of additional evidence in the government's possession. But if it's not in their possession, the defendant has no recourse under *Brady* or the rules.

So I always wondered how we were able to use these subpoenas in our investigations to gather evidence that might or might not be used at trial. I imagined that, in the Courthouses in which I was practicing, the inequity inherent in the plain language of the discovery rules was evident to all the parties. There was, I assumed, a tacit understanding that, provided we didn't abuse the privilege, the rules might be bent a little.

But the tacit understanding apparently wasn't universal in other districts across the state. I was hearing stories about prosecutors in the rural counties south of Des Moines who were moving to quash subpoenas duces tecum issued on behalf of criminal defendants for purely discovery purposes. The defense bar was fighting back vigorously, arguing that the state was impinging on their right under the rules and the constitution to conduct meaningful discovery.

For a hearing in a rural courthouse on a state's motion to quash, one defense attorney felt it might be a good idea to call me as an expert witness to testify that defendants are entitled under law to use subpoenas duces tecum as an investigative tool. As the author of *4A Iowa Practice*: *Criminal Procedure* and a frequent lecturer at CLE seminars, she thought, I would be an effective expert in support of her cause.

I balked at this.

In the first place, the *judge* in any court proceeding is the expert on the law. It did not strike me as a good way to make friends and influence people for me to walk in and hold myself out as having knowledge superior to that of the judge. Secondly, she was on the wrong side of the law. There is nothing in *Brady* or in either the Iowa or United States Constitutions that vests a criminal defendant with a right to use a subpoena to gather evidence from a source that is not the government. There was certainly no right of this nature in the rules.

I had a real sick feeling that by stirring the pot in Podunk, Iowa I could be screwing up the good thing we had in Des Moines. If I take the stand there and testify that this is how we're doing it here, someone with the power to make it stop would step up and stop it.

That's exactly what happened. But without my help.

I'd like to say I was able to appeal to the better angels of that lawyer's nature. I went down there and sat in the lobby all morning. At lunchtime, they sent me home. I don't think the lawyer backed off. I think the judge disallowed me as an expert witness. That's what I'd do if I was that judge.

I made it through my five-year stint in Polk County without losing the luxury of using subpoenas duces tecum for investigative purposes. Lawyers in the rural counties were not so fortunate, but they continued to fight the good fight. It obviously made sense to them, as it did to me, that there should be at least the semblance of a level playing field and that, from time to time, a defendant might like to muster an adequate defense. In 2017 two prominent defense attorneys, Angela

Campbell and John Sandy (now a district court judge) brought the issue before the Iowa Supreme Court. The result in *State v. Russell*, 897 N.W.2d 717 (Iowa 2017) was what I expected.

The door slammed shut to the use of subpoenas duces tecum as a discovery tool.

It was perhaps the *Russell* decision that precipitated Nick Sarcone's invitation to the chief justice soon afterwards to meet with the IAJ criminal justice core and discuss redrafting the rules of criminal procedure. "[C]hanges to the Subpoena Rule (2.15)" was one of three topic areas he offered for discussion.

The disparate access to investigatory subpoenas was near the top of the IAJ comments on the proposed rules. Before or after initiation of a case, prosecutors are allowed to depose and subpoena evidence from any witness, while defendants have no mechanism to obtain even exculpatory evidence from a non-listed witness. The types of evidence for which investigatory subpoenas would be useful include surveillance footage, cell phone records, email and social media communications, and business records.

Limiting access to subpoenas duces tecum to trial witnesses makes the trial process more cumbersome for everyone, as the defendant's first opportunity to view the subpoenaed evidence comes at the time of the witness's trial testimony. Parties have more power to subpoena evidence in civil cases than they do as defendants in criminal prosecutions.

The IAJ expressed concern about requiring that a defendant be placed under oath prior to entering a plea of guilty and allowing all the parties, including the prosecution, to question the defendant. Any questioning by the prosecutor beyond that establishing a factual basis for the guilty plea "creates a situation that is ripe for abuse without any legitimate purpose."

The judge should retain the ability to dismiss *sua sponte* a prosecution in the interest of justice, the IAJ argued, in cases involving prosecutorial misconduct, repeated discovery violations by the state, and other abuses of this nature.

The other general topic mentioned by Nick Sarcone in his letter to the Court was "a new rule for conditional pleas." Iowa has not formally permitted conditional pleas of guilty, in which the defendant saves the state the time and expense of a jury trial while preserving the right to appeal an adverse pretrial ruling to the Supreme Court. The defendant pleads guilty with the understanding that he will be able to argue the merits on a motion to suppress, etc., to the appellate court. If the appeals court rules in his or her favor, the plea is vacated, and the case returns to the district court to either be dismissed or brought to trial *sans* the objectionable evidence. Conditional guilty pleas are utilized in federal court. A defendant in Iowa must resort to a trial on the minutes, the procedures for which were set out in the rules proposed by the task force. The IAJ comments contained a suggested procedure for taking conditional pleas, including a provision that "[s]uch reservation of a defendant's right to have an appellate court review the adverse determination of a specified pre-trial motion shall, in all cases, constitute good cause for appeal of that issue after judgment is entered on the guilty plea. A defendant who prevails on appeal may then withdraw the plea." This language was necessary in view of 2019 legislation resulting in the Iowa Code § 814.6(1)(a)(3) denial of the right to appeal a non-class A felony conviction based on a plea of guilty unless good cause is shown.

On the topic of discovery, the IAJ noted that 46 states have more liberal discovery rules than Iowa and submitted a proposed Rule of Criminal Procedure 2.14 that would tend to level the playing field with respect to discovery. It would include a prohibition of the practice of some prosecutors of conditioning a favorable plea agreement on the defendant foregoing requests for disclosure of evidence.

The IAJ concluded its presentation with a review of American Bar Association standards that place a duty on defense counsel to investigate a case entrusted to him or her. Changes to the rules should be geared toward enabling the Iowa defense bar to meet those standards.

In its comments, the NAACP noted that the exclusion from jury service of convicted felons has been shown to have an adverse impact on persons of color. While it lauded the task force for removing the lifetime ban on jury service, the ten-year ban in the proposed rules remains excessive. Any concerns the government may have that convicted felons harbor anti-prosecution bias can be addressed effectively through *voir dire*. Circumstances that a potential juror harbors actual bias based upon age, creed, sex, race or similar factors should be included as bases for challenges for cause. If individualized *voir dire* is necessary to flesh out these concerns, it should be facilitated regardless of the additional time it may take to conduct it. A requirement that all proceedings be reported should include *voir dire*.

Story County Public Defender Paul Rounds objected to the proposed requirement that the defendant be placed under oath before entering a guilty plea as having a potential chilling effect on a defendant who otherwise desires to resolve his or her case with a plea, but fears subjecting him- or herself to possible perjury charges when valid grounds arise for withdrawing the plea. Abolishing the bill of particulars would eliminate a tool that is "essential to defendants receiving fair notice of the charges against them." While the rules governing bills of exception are, from his perspective, rarely used, Rounds argued that the device should not be fully eliminated. He feared that the additional access to the defendant by government-retained experts would be subject to abuse and "further erode the defendant's right to remain silent and right to counsel." The requirement that notice be given of additional defenses would be damaging to the defense, whose role at trial "is often one of a counterpuncher" and can't effectively plan strategy until the government has made its case. Rounds joined the chorus protesting the inequitable access between the parties to subpoenas duces tecum.

State Public Defender Jeff Wright worried that the

proposed rule prohibiting the service of subpoenas by a party precluded the public defender from using its investigators for that purpose.

Appellate Defender Martha Lucey requested a rule requiring that the names of all co-defendants appear on the initial appearance order to enable new counsel to discern any potential conflicts with existing clients. A preliminary hearing should be cancelled if the trial information or indictment are filed prior to the hearing dates. Along with others, Lucey objected to the elimination in the proposed rules of the judge's discretion to allow a defendant to withdraw a plea of guilty upon showing of good cause. She joined the IAJ in advocating for a rule permitting conditional guilty pleas to preserve issues for appellate review. The portion of the guilty plea colloquy in which the defendant is notified of the consequences of the plea should also include notice of non-punitive consequences such as victim restitution and registration as a sex offender. Where the defendant is notified that once a plea of guilty is entered there is no right to withdraw it, the defendant should also be advised that under certain circumstances withdrawal may be permitted. Lucey, too, objected to placing defendants under oath prior to taking their guilty pleas. Extending the rule to misdemeanants would require notarized signatures on written guilty pleas. During the plea hearing, the court should question the defendant only on subjects relevant to the charged offense, and the prosecutor should not be allowed to question the defendant directly. Motions for bills of particulars should be retained. Safeguards should be placed upon the testimony of any experts retained by the state to examine the defendant to protect the privilege against self-incrimination. Defenses for which the defense is required to provide notice should be limited to those defined in the Iowa Code or in the caselaw. Defendants should have prerogative to waive their presence at a deposition.

In the proposed rules, Lucey argued, the task force "misses an important opportunity to establish a procedure which would permit the defendant to utilize a subpoena duces tecum for investigatory purposes." She submitted a proposed rule which would allow parties to issue subpoenas duces tecum, giving notice to other parties. If notice to other parties would have the effect of disclosing otherwise privileged defense strategy, *ex parte* subpoenas would be filed under seal. Like the State Public Defender, Lucey asked for a more clear definition of who constitutes a "party" precluded from serving subpoenas. Does it include the prosecutor or defense counsel?

Persons with prior felony convictions would not be disqualified from service, under Lucey's alternative proposed rule, if it can be established through some source including the juror's testimony that his or her voting rights have been restored and that he or she is no longer on any form of supervision as a consequence of the conviction. Jury selection should take place in open court and, absent valid reasons for closing the proceeding, in public view. If jurors are subject to prosecution for perjury for giving false answers during *voir dire* they should be advised of the possibility at the outset.

Lucey emphasized that all proceedings, including *voir dire*, should be reported in all indictable cases, and that waivers should not be permitted. Exhibits should be retained until the limitation period for postconviction relief has passed. Notice should be given to all parties within 90 days of the destruction of any evidence.

Though rarely utilized, Lucey argued against the proposed elimination of the rule permitting a district court to grant a new trial on grounds not raised in a posttrial motion. She also asked that the rules not include the language permitting vacation of a defective guilty plea only if it is established that the plea would not have been entered absent the defect. Bills of exceptions are rare, she admitted, but occasionally are necessary to preserve error for appeal, and should not be eliminated.

The decision as to whether to appear personally or on video, in Lucey's view, should be left to the defendant and should not require approval by the prosecutor. The proposed rule permitting searches of all persons present in the courtroom without probable cause or reasonable suspicion, in her opinion, would violate the Fourth Amendment to the United States Constitution and article I, section 8 of the Iowa Constitution.

The proposed rules would eliminate the court's discretion under Iowa R.Cr.P. 2.33(1) to dismiss a case on its own motion in the interest of justice. Lucey asked the Court to retain the old rule. A waiver of speedy trial should be made only by the defendant personally and not, as the proposed rule would allow, by the defendant or defense counsel.

One proposed rule would require a defendant to appeal a simple misdemeanor to the district court before requesting Supreme Court review. Lucey pointed out that Iowa Code § 814.6(2)(d) provides that under certain conditions some simple misdemeanants may obtain direct discretionary review in the Supreme Court. The new rule should be consistent with § 814.6(2)(d).

The Midwest Innocence Project weighed in on a number of changes that were proposed and a few that were not and, in its view, should have been included. The Project objected to proposed limits on the court's ability to grant motions for new trial and argued that actual innocence should be included as a ground for new trial. There is no reason to require a defendant to be placed under oath before pleading guilty, exposing him- or herself to perjury charges if it is withdrawn. The abolition of bills of particulars "will prevent pre-trial negotiations, increase discovery demands and lead to wrongful convictions." Restrictions on defendants' subpoenas duces tecum for discovery "constricts a defendant's due process and prevents investigation, a key process in the truth-seeking process." A proposed rule eliminating the requirement that the defendant be present at post-indictment investigation interviews, the Project argued, violates the Sixth Amendment of the United States Constitution and article I, section 10 of the state constitution. The most acceptable discovery practice would be an open-file policy. The elimination of the requirement that the government produce audio and voice recordings of the defendant and recordings of grand jury testimony "moves Iowa in the wrong direction." In support, the Project called the Court's attention to 323 wrongful convictions obtained as a result of false confessions. All confessions should be recorded, and all recordings of the defendant should be disclosed to his or her attorneys in discovery.

What I've set out above is a sampling of the comments received by the Supreme Court in the 104 days (111 counting the letter from the Wapello County attorney) following the dissemination of the proposed Rules of Criminal Procedure. Nearly all were fair-minded and well-thought-out observations of professionals aligned with the defense, the prosecution and the adjudication of criminal cases.

There were some common themes. One objection coming from both sides of the aisle was to the requirement that the defendant be present personally during discovery depositions and that one's presence could be waived only during questioning involving identity. Though not limited exclusively to these issues, the concerns of the criminal defense bar seemed to group around the three invoked by Nick Sarcone when he initiated the late 2017 meeting with Chief Justice Mark Cady that, according to the chief justice, served as the launch pad for the task force. At the outset, Nick envisioned "changes to the Discovery Rule (2.15), Subpoena Rule (2.14) and a new rule for conditional pleas."

The task force, in Nick's estimation, had fallen woefully short in these areas. But the proposed rules were, *possibly*, just the first step in the process. The ball was in the Court's court now. The Court could receive all 251 pages of public comment, thank the commentators for their time, and adopt the rules in the form proposed by the task force. Verbatim.

Or they could carefully review the input and modify the proposed rules accordingly. It could take months, especially since the Judicial Branch was now preoccupied with the task of riding out a pandemic of which no visible end was in sight.

Or the Court could simply decide to punt and leave the old

rules in place.

I will admit that I studied the public comments with a lot more intensity in 2023 as I prepared this book than I did in July 2020. Whatever the Court decided would go into the manual. Until then, there was nothing I could do but sit and watch the play clock. There was no news.

December 2020 came and went. Nothing on the new rules. I prepared and submitted my revisions for the 2021 edition of *4A Iowa Practice: Criminal Procedure*. February 2021 came and went. Still nothing. When the manual was released in April 2021, I lamented in the author's introduction that the "author expected to report in the 2021 volume on a substantial rewrite of the Iowa Rules of Criminal Procedure currently ongoing. The process, however, has been slowed by the pandemic and will not be concluded by the time of publication."

When the deadline arrived eight months later for revisions to the 2022 volume, I began to wonder if the new rules were ever going to come to life. I'd stopped worrying about the immediacy of getting them into my book. A year and a half had passed, and there was no word. From time to time, I'd run into a judge or a lawyer who served on the task force. They didn't know anything, but they were always confident that nothing was going to happen on the new rules at any point before the next deadline.

So I kept my eye on the play clock . . .

2022

One of the things I anticipate in life with the greatest fervor is my high school class reunion.

Since we've first known each other, my wife has often heard me make the comment that "our class was the biggest bunch of losers who ever went through that place. The two success stories in our class are a standup comic and a Hollywood stunt man."

It's not true at all. All of us have done well in life, on many planes. There have been rewarding careers, solid marriages and successful offspring. It's just my conditioned response when my wife accuses me of being all hoity toity because I went to Dowling. See, my wife went to high school at *Roosevelt*. And if anyone is hoity toity it's the Rosies. There's some basis for that sentiment. As I always say, more famous people went to Roosevelt than all the other schools in Des Moines put together. Bill Bryson. Cloris Leachman. Lolo Jones. Congresswoman Patricia Schroeder. The fabulous Higgins brothers. To name just a few. Don't forget Bob Ray. The two stories of success I invoke in my schtick are stuntman Eddie Matthews, who has appeared in 243 major films, and Willie Farrell, who performs regularly in Vegas and Atlantic City and has had his own Showtime Comedy Special.

When I say things like that it's because I've heard it from others. Kids repeat what they hear, you know. They internalize things. The football team from my class went to the final game of the 1973 Iowa High School Football Championships and took second place to a Central Davenport team built around one-man wrecking crew Curtis Craig (Central beat Dowling a couple years later with Curtis' little brother Roger, who parlayed his success against the Maroons into a lucrative NFL career). Dowling also took second place in 1972 and in 1974. I don't remember why I was allowed to be in the room for it, but I managed to sit in on an interview with the coach after the 1974 game, six months after my graduation. *I was heartbroken when we lost the title in '72*, he confided. *I was heartbroken in '74. But making it to the final game in '73*, he boasted, *that was just good coaching.*

My class never got an iota of respect from anyone.

"Yeah," Pam responds invariably. "But you've got Quinlan. He's a *doctor*."

Steve Quinlan is a *urologist*. They couldn't pay me enough . . .

The crowning blow came at a pancake breakfast at my father-in-law's church in the mid-90s. Wayne bought tickets for every event at his church and distributed them to his children, his grandchildren, his siblings and their children and grandchildren, in a valiant effort to hold his family together after the death of his mother, the matriarch. At least a quarter century out of high school at that point, I stood in line in front of Father Tony Aiello. Father Aiello taught at Dowling, but never any class that I took. For a good ten minutes he stood stroking his chin (for him a trademark gesture) and eyeballing me.

"I know you from somewhere," he winced.

"I went to Dowling, but I never had you as a teacher."

"What class?"

"'74."

"1974? You guys were the *biggest bunch of losers who ever went through that place.*"

"See?" I snapped at Pam, who was stunned to hear a priest come out and say it, even if it *was* true.

But even if there was some validity to the label – even if we didn't go out and become multi-millionaires and bask in the glory of God to the same extent the other classes did, there was always one realm in which the class of '74 stood head and shoulders above the rest. Then *and* now.

We threw the best damned parties.

The crown jewel of our graduation weekend was a three-day all-day all-night kegger at a remote farm somewhere in northwest Polk County. I couldn't find it today. We came and went in the dark.

And our reunion weekends in the half century that followed have been legendary. Official events are scheduled on Friday nights, Saturday afternoons, Saturday nights, and sometimes Sunday mornings and afternoons. Usually, there's something on Thursday as well. Once they're underway, it's like no time has passed, even as we transition into our golden years.

I went solo to the five-year reunion, which for me worked out just fine. By the ten-year reunion, I was with Eleanor. We had been dating for about a year and a half and from all outward indications it was looking like serious business. But that came apart over the year that followed.

Two years before the 15-year reunion, I started dating Pam, and proposed to her on Christmas Eve 1988. I'd have that to bring with me to show and tell the following June.

I was a little giddy as reunion weekend approached. Like I say, I *really* look forward to them. So rather than going to a movie the preceding Saturday, Pam and I went out to dinner and then to Valley West Mall in search of the dress that would make the best impression on my classmates. I paid for the dress, which I thought was an excellent find.

For the Friday night event, the class had rented out the top floor of Jukebox Saturday Night, a hip night club that flourished for seven years just off Court Avenue on Third Street, and which I believe was managed and at least partially owned by Willie Farrell's brother, Tommy. Not wanting to miss a minute of the festivities, Pam and I arrived right at 7 p.m., the starting time.

As we reached the top of the stairs leading to the party room, I have to say I didn't recognize anyone who was in there already. Chalk it up to five years of the aging process. There was a guy at a podium with a list who greeted me with the *can I help you* vibe.

"I'm here for the reunion," I told him.

"I don't know about a reunion."

"Sure. It's the Dowling High School Class of 1974 fifteen-year reunion."

"I don't know anything about that."

"Well, maybe you should go find somebody who *does* know."

I mean, Jesus, there's like 400 of us. This guy doesn't even know about it. *Really*?

A different guy comes out.

"Dowling Class of '74 Reunion?" he asks.

"Thank you. Yes."

"That was last week."

There's a reason I tell this story.

It's that sinking feeling. The one you get when the rug is pulled out beneath you. The errant foul ball that hits you when you've stopped paying attention to the game, and it breaks your nose and your $93 Ray-Bans. Everything changes in an instant. All your plans – everything. It's that moment when it truly hits home that you have absolutely no control over the events in your life.

Acute nausea. Then despair. The stages of *your* grief.

Nothing will ever be the same. You missed your goddamn reunion.

I've had maybe four of those moments in my 67 years.

Hasty Revisions

Tuesday, February 1, 2022.

That was awful. But it wasn't one of the $93 Ray-Ban days. It wasn't one of those I-missed-my-high-school-reunion-because-I-was-out-at-the-same-moment-buying-a-dress days. But it was truly miserable. The $93 Ray-Ban moment would come soon enough.

I don't know what compelled me to go to the Iowa Supreme Court's website that morning, but I did. The proofs of my revised manual generally come to me on the first of February for my final review, although some years I've seen them a week or so later. There are usually about ten pages of new court cases to be worked into the manual. The publisher gives me two weeks to turn it around and send it back. Then I'm done. My copies of the finished product show up on my doorstep in April.

But today, I ventured onto the Supreme Court website. And what do I see?

On the previous day, Chief Justice Christensen had entered an order.

"In the Matter of Adopting Revised Chapter 2 Iowa Rules of Criminal Procedure (January 31, 2022)"

Oh, *shit*. Look at this. It's not a top to bottom rewrite of the original rules, but there are some serious changes, and enough of the rules were moved around and renumbered that I've got my work cut out for me. The chief justice says the rules go into effect on July 1.

I called my publisher. How far can we push back the release of the 2022 manual so that it's in the hands of the practitioners by July 1? Maybe we don't want it out sooner because in April, May and June the courts will still be operating off the old rules.

"We should get it out in April," she decides. "We can advise the practitioners to hold on to their 2021 volume until July."

"Okay. How late can I get my revisions in and still publish in April?"

"I can get you the proofs today. We'd still like them by February 18."

Seventeen days.

At this point, my career as a practicing attorney had now been over for 31 months. I was now a full-time singer/songwriter and author. People think that, because I'm no longer driving downtown every morning and whiling away my afternoons in the Courthouse and at the jail, it follows that I'm retired. I'm definitely *not* retired. I work full time, seven days a week, harder than I have at any point except perhaps when I was studying for the bar. And at the end of the day I still haven't accomplished everything I set out to do when I first rolled out of bed.

But on Tuesday, February 1, everything else in my life took a back seat. I dove headfirst into the manual, taking it line by line. Changing citations. Explaining to you working guys and gals the ways things would be done from now on. From now on starting on July 1. It's a slow, slow process. And it all had to be ready and on its way in seventeen days.

I dug in. To an email to Kinko's, I attached the Court's order, the new rules as they would look after the revisions, and the Court's summaries of the changes made to the existing rules and the changes made to the March 30, 2020 proposed rules. Print it all out for me, I instructed. That afternoon, and for the next three weeks, the entire surface of the kitchen table was covered with those pages and pages of materials, the volume containing the existing rules, and the 2021 volume of *4A Iowa Practice: Criminal Procedure*. And I went to work.

For every job like this, it takes about a day to develop a system. There was no easy, intuitive way of doing this. Starting on page one of the manual, I conducted a visual scan of its pages for all citations to the Rules. For each cite, I thumbed through the new rules to find the one corresponding to the old one. When that was completed I approached it from the opposite angle, leafing down the pages of the new rules to assure that each was incorporated into the manual.

At noon I made myself a sandwich and an apple. In the evenings on weekdays, I cooked dinner for my wife and myself. Twice a week I drove to the Edgewater Assisted Living Facility to visit my father, who had been there since about November. Friday evening we ate dinner at Christopher's Italian Restaurant, and on Saturday it was Ohana Steakhouse in West Des Moines. The following Saturday, we saw a movie and then returned to Ohana. Then on Monday, I took Pam to Texas Roadhouse for

Valentine's Day. She works until 8 p.m. and it was too late to go anywhere else. Every Thursday morning, I went grocery shopping at the Urbandale HyVee grocery store.

That was it. There were no musical gigs in the dead of winter. Every remaining minute was spent buried in the manual and the revisions.

There was some good stuff in the new rules. Again, I'll admit that I didn't pay as much attention as I should have paid to the proposed rules as they were revealed to us at the brown bag lunch two years earlier. And I hadn't really read through the public comments that followed their release. My concern was the final product. My concern, as the constitutional scholars would say, was content neutral. What would go into the manual? That's what mattered.

Holding the new rules up to the light of the public comments following the original 2020 proposals, it was extraordinary how responsive the Court and the task force were to the concerns expressed, especially to those put forth by the defense bar. Courts would not be required to put defendants under oath before taking their guilty pleas, but could do so at their own discretion. In its colloquy with the defendant during a guilty plea proceeding, the court would be required to inform the defendant of the collateral consequences of the plea, including the forfeiture of the right to vote and to possess firearms.

Under the new rules, the Iowa courts would now recognize the conditional guilty plea, allowing the defendant the opportunity to appeal an issue that was fully preserved and, if the appellate court rules favorably to the defendant, the conviction based on the plea could be vacated and the case remanded for a new trial. There was language in the new rule that "[w]hen a conditional guilty plea is approved by the court, this constitutes good cause for the defendant to appeal the ruling on the specified pretrial motion," addressing the Iowa Code § 814.6(1)(a)(3) prohibition of appeals of non-class A felony guilty pleas absent a showing of good cause. The court and defense counsel could question the defendant during the plea hearing, while the prosecutor could submit proposed questions but not question the defendant directly. The bill of particulars was returned to the tool kit, and the defendant's responsibility to notify the state of proposed defenses was limited to the defenses of "intoxication, entrapment, justification, necessity, duress, mistake, or prescription drugs." If both parties agreed, the defendant had the right to waive his or her presence during a discovery deposition. And the authority to grant a new trial *sua sponte* in the interests of justice was returned to the district court.

Other developments were an obvious response to the great pandemic which, contrary to all predictions, had continued to batter the judicial system to the same degree it plagued so many other societal institutions. Written waivers could be executed for many pretrial proceedings. Class D felons could now enter written sentencing agreements, a process limited previously to misdemeanor cases. Short of the actual jury trial, most hearings could now be conducted using video technology.

The bombshell of the January 30 rules was Rule of Criminal Procedure 2.15(3). Rule 2.15(3) established a procedure that allowed criminal defendants to apply to the court for subpoenas duces tecum for discovery purposes. Notice would be given to the state, which could file written objections. Any materials obtained through defense subpoenas must be disclosed to the state and timely notice must be provided if the defense intends to use them at trial.

A lion's share of the specific concerns raised by Nick Sarcone during the seminal meeting between the Iowa Association for Justice and Chief Justice Mark Cady were advanced in the response to the public comments. The process of incorporating the new rules into *4A Iowa Practice: Criminal Procedure* was tedious, and at the time the harsh deadline kept me from fully appreciating and internalizing them. But I relished the opportunity to be the harbinger of good news to the practitioners who had not closely followed their progress.

By Tuesday the 14th I was seeing the light at the end of the tunnel. It was doable. I *would* make my deadline.

This is where the $93 Ray-Bans get busted.

$93 Ray-Bans

I can try to describe the feeling in the pit of my stomach when I logged onto the Iowa Supreme Court website on Friday, February 18, 2022 and saw the chief justice's order, but I have neither the writing skills nor the vocabulary to do it justice. It was certainly a different set of circumstances from showing up at your high school reunion a week late and discovering that, on the evening the party was going on, you had been mall shopping for a dress for that very party. But that tsunami of emptiness, anger and self-loathing, that feeling that you've sustained an injury from which you're *never* likely to recover -- that flared up during both events. *This is the lowest it's ever going get for me.* That's the feeling.

At the outset, the 18th had promised to be a pleasant respite from the meat grinder through which I'd put myself over the previous two weeks. Mid-February in Iowa has the potential to be treacherous, bringing with it some of the real soul-crushing winter storms. You see a few signs of spring, then get hit with two feet of snow and wind chills in the mid-20s below zero.

Not today. A dry forty-three degrees under an azure sky. My dad, three months into his residency in the Edgewater assisted living facility, had asked me if I'd be able to drive him to an early afternoon visit with his lifelong friends, Chuck and Judy. It was great for me. On the date set by the publisher as my deadline, the manual revisions were complete. With a single keystroke on my Hewlett Packard laptop, I would submit them to the publisher and take the rest of the day off. My head was still spinning from the tortuous process of the previous two weeks.

My sister did most of the heavy lifting in this respect, but I think the day trip to Chuck and Judy's house may have been my father's final excursion away from Edgewater for any purpose besides medical appointments. There had been one Wednesday evening when they went to the Waterfront Restaurant for lobster night (in 58 years away from New England, my father never lost his taste for lobster). I heard that Chuck and Judy surprised my father by showing up there. I think that was before I drove him to their house. Either way, it was an opportunity to clear my head and just be the driver, as opposed to the whirling dervish I had been since the first of the month.

Just like the first of the month, I don't know what compelled me to sit down after breakfast and log onto the Iowa Supreme Court's website. The plan for the morning was to proofread the final revisions and get them off *tout de suite* to Thomson Reuters. I think I just wanted a final look at the January 31 order to make sure I got it down right in the author's notes.

Damn good thing I did that.

There was *another* order, signed two days earlier.

"In the Matter of Withdrawal of Revised Chapter 2 Iowa Rules of Criminal Procedure," read the caption. It wasn't a long one, unlike those of March 30, 2020 and January 31, 2022 that recounted the history of the task force, the objectives intended to be furthered by adoption of the new rules, and the valiant efforts made by the Court and the task force to accomplish them. This order was one sentence long.

> The Iowa Supreme Court withdraws the revised Chapter 2 Iowa Rules of Criminal Procedure submitted to Legislative Council, pursuant to Iowa Code Section 602.4202, on January 31, 2022.

Huh?

What the fuck? *What the **fuck**?*

John Burns saw red. John Burns was on the warpath.

Somebody tell me what happened here. Who knows what this is all about? I've got fifty-four pages of goddamned revisions sitting *here waiting to go out. Did they all of a sudden decide we're not going to revise the rules after all, so never mind? Do I have to go through all this shit again? I want it to be **over**.*

What the fuck is going on here?

There was a barrage of frantic telephone calls. People I know who were on the task force. People who work on the Supreme Court staff. Lawyers in the Appellate Defender's Office. Lawyers in the Attorney General's Office. Anyone I knew who might have a clue as to what the hell had changed during those two weeks.

They were all going to voice mail. Everybody must be taking Friday off. Or maybe they're together in a meeting somewhere.

I had to get an answer. *Today is my goddamn deadline.* I'm sitting on hundreds of revisions for a book coming out in two months. If I make the wrong decision, I'll be releasing a manual replete with inaccuracy. It will stay wrong until the next edition comes out in April 2023. Is this a temporary pause, or are the Rules kaput for *another* two years? And how do I get the last 18 days back? There's got to be somebody out there who can pick up the telephone and tell me what the hell is going on. All I'm getting is voice mail.

I don't need a lengthy detailed explanation. I just need to know if there are going to be new rules on July 1 or if we're sticking with the old ones. I just want *4A Iowa Practice*: *Criminal Procedure* to be accurate. Or at least not *inaccurate*.

My blood pressure is in the stratosphere. *Somebody **please** pick up the phone.*

As the morning progressed, people began responding to the messages I'd left on their voice mail. Some of the few who were aware that the Rules were not going into place in July were perturbed by what had happened but couldn't articulate for me what that was. One task force member who years earlier had been a coworker confided that she now wished she hadn't signed on with the task force.

Another, who I've known for years and whose political

views don't march in lockstep with mine, offered the best insight into what had transpired.

"We had prosecutors, judges and defense attorneys on the task force. Some of the prosecutors were very conservative, guys who take a hard line in their practices. Nobody got everything they wanted, but we hammered it out. In the end, everybody was on board. Then when the rules came out, some rural prosecutors who aren't on the task force ran crying to a few real conservative representatives and senators. That's when the hurdles went up."

In the year that followed, I would better understand the process my friend was describing. But the idea that these small-town prosecutors and extreme right-wing legislators could manage to wreak such havoc in my personal life was putting me in a foul mood.

At 9:59 a.m. on February 18, Supreme Court Communications Director Steve Davis forwarded to me the memo that had gone out a day earlier to members of the task force.

> As you know, the full court approved the revised criminal rules and submitted the rules to Legislative Council on January 31, 2022. Since then, some members of the general assembly have let us know that they have concerns about specific rules and the guilty plea form and that the rules would not be approved as submitted in the current form. The most significant concern relates to the rule change specifically allowing defense attorney investigative subpoenas, which requires notice to the prosecutor, an opportunity to object, and court approval before any subpoena can issue. Other concerns relate to the rule change allowing persons convicted of felonies who have had more than ten years pass since their release from confinement be eligible to sit on juries and the rule change allowing conditional guilty pleas.

The full court discussed the matter earlier this week and has decided that it would be best to withdraw the revised criminal rules and rework the problem areas rather than "hang the rules out to dry." Accordingly, the court will be filing an order withdrawing the submitted rules from Legislative Council later today. Once that occurs, with your help, the court plans to work on coming up with new rule language in the areas—and I believe they are not many—where the proposed rules take criminal procedure in a new direction that is not acceptable to the Legislature.

There's your answer, John. I called my editor, gave her the news, and informed her that my greatly abbreviated revisions would get to her by the end of the day.

Then I picked up my dad and drove him to Chuck and Judy's house. He knew I'd been going full stream since the first of the month to get the revisions ready. The full impact of what had gone on that morning was something that really only I could appreciate. I had him back to Edgewater at about three and spent the rest of the afternoon paring down my revisions from 54 pages to about the ten that involved recent appellate court decisions and not the new rules of criminal procedure.

And, once again, there was nothing for me to do but to sit back and wait for the bell for the next round.

I went back to my life. In April my wife and I returned to Waikiki for the first time since the pandemic. It had played out to our benefit that I'd made the fortuitous decision in 2020 to do Hawaii that year in January instead of April, when we usually visit. Had we followed the routine, there would have been no Hawaii trip in 2020.

A few weeks after Waikiki, I started playing music at farmers markets, coffee shops and other mostly outdoor events. Another outgrowth of the pandemic has been my annual hibernation from performing between late November and May.

The trips to Hawaii and getting back up in front of audiences are my perennial self-rewards for successful completion of a new annual edition of *4A Iowa Practice: Criminal Procedure*.

But this year it felt incomplete. I'd worked harder on the manual than I'd worked at any time other than when I wrote the first year's edition. And most of that work was for naught. Would I have to go through that again? Who knows what further changes would come? As before, even minor changes in rule numbering mean that I have to go through and modify each cite. The addition or removal of a single subsection in a rule has that ripple effect.

One week before it all fell apart on February 18, when I still anticipated putting the manual away for another eight months, I made the decision to go ahead and to self-publish some of my other books. At that point, I had four unpublished books. There was one in particular that I wanted to get out as soon as possible, but circumstances dictated that I hold off on that one for the time being.

So I set my sights on *Baby Pictures*, the story of my adventures in 1976 and 1977 on the road with Baby Lester and the Buggybumpers. I'd written the first draft in 1996 and had completed several drafts since then. Both of our drummers had died recently, so there were three of us left. Lester himself had been battling lymphoma, COPD and heart issues for the past decade. Wouldn't it be nice to get it out there while he was still with us? So I went to town on *Baby Pictures* and shipped it off to the company providing publishing services by the time we left for Hawaii. *Baby Pictures* was released in e-book format on June 17 and as a hardcover volume on August 19, the 45th anniversary of the day Lester called to tell me we were disbanding.

On June 16, I carried copies of *Baby Pictures* in hardcover format to Omaha to give to Lester and Donna, his erstwhile wife who had been our bass player on the road. Lester was elated. Three weeks later I was on a rare road trip playing shows in

Mesa, Arizona and Redlands, California when I got word from his daughter Natalie that Baby Lester had passed away. Before he did, he had taken the little money he had left and purchased copies of *Baby Pictures* for each of his grandchildren.

The year 2022 marked the fiftieth anniversary of the first song I ever wrote. In September, I rented out the xBk performance facility near Drake University for my "Golden Jubilee" concert. The sound in that room is perfect and the recording facilities are world class, so I was able to obtain a video of that show with audio and video qualities rivaling those found in productions shot on a network sound stage.

With *Baby Pictures* out, I went to work on *Dead Horses*, a collection of my stories that did not make it into *Baby Pictures*. I'd written the first draft of that one in 1999.

I did all these things with the knowledge that, at some point, I'd have to drop everything once more and immerse myself in the manual. If past events were any guide, such a moment could come on the eve of a major publishing deadline. No matter what else I did, *that* festered in the back of my mind.

On June 6, Chief Justice Christensen entered an order expanding the period for public comments to run until July 22, and scheduling an open public session on August 5 to allow any person or group to address the task force. In it, she explained that the rules were withdrawn in February when the Court "became aware that some legislators had concerns with a few of the revised rules. These concerns included the fact that the court had not allowed an opportunity for additional public input after making changes based on the original round of public comments as well as lessons learned from the COVID-19 pandemic." The Court held off in taking this action from February until after the legislative session adjourned in June. If the Legislature had concerns about what went into the rules, she reasoned, it might adopt legislation that would steer the Court in the right direction. In the absence of a legislative response, it was necessary to initiate another comment period culminating in the open session. She reviewed the history of the process followed by the task force and the Court that brought about the February 2022 version of the new rules.

"While not every task force member agreed with everything in the final draft," the chief justice reported, "the draft reflected the consensus of the task force."

The Empire Strikes Back

The extended review period elicited 24 comments in a 134-page document.

There are a few things I have to say before I go any further on the subject of the public comments regarding the February 2022 proposed rules of criminal procedure. I've come to this point in telling the story and have to try to visualize how I'm going to describe the public comments. I write a few words. Then I stop. And I put it down. I'll come back to it tomorrow and try to be more objective about it. I know what I want to write. But I also realize there are at least two sides to every issue, and just because you don't agree with me on some or all of them doesn't make you a bad person. Or stupid. I know that, believe it or not. I try not to vilify my adversaries. There is a song written by the most obscure songwriter in the midwestern United States that is entitled "How Can Everybody Know the Truth, and Still Disagree?" I understand that.

I still don't know if I can take the high road on this one.

I'm detecting in myself some symptoms of posttraumatic stress disorder from just reading what some of those rural prosecutors wrote in their comments. I don't like the person I become when I read them.

I spent 35 years doing nothing but criminal defense. Maybe that disqualifies me from passing harsh judgment on people doing a job I never had, to the same degree that some of those jackbooted thugs (*oops*)who pontificate with any aura of expertise about what I did for a living might want to heed the advice of our first Republican President that it's "[b]etter to remain silent and be thought a fool than to speak and to remove all doubt."

It's obvious, I guess, that a cooling-off period isn't about to hold me back from speaking my piece about rural prosecutors. It's not an unprovoked attack. They brought it on, didn't they, with their assaults on new rules intended to inject a modicum of fairness into the criminal trial process.

I have some history of making humorous (in my view) though not always complimentary public comments about prosecutors. I've told you the story about the September 2012 welcoming reception at the Iowa State Bar Association Building for the incoming United States District Court Judge, the first female to hold that position in the Southern District of Iowa and, at the time, the youngest federal district court judge in the United States. I was met in the parking lot by another attorney who gave me the heads up that the new judge had berated Assistant United States Attorney John Courter, a tough-as-nails prosecutor who had been a friend and adversary all the way back to our state court days (today John is the Clerk of Court for the Southern District of Iowa), for some disparaging comments about federal prosecutors that John had written a year earlier in a blog post. But John Courter didn't have a blog and, even if he did, why would he use it to attack federal prosecutors? I heeded my friend's cautionary advice, entered the Bar Association Building, took my place at the end of the line, and shook the new judge's hand.

"I'm John Burns," I introduced myself to her. "And I have a blog."

But see, I digress. I'm still dragging my feet. What *about* those prosecutors who filed second round objections to the January 31 proposed rules? The ones who ran to Republican legislators who threw up the roadblock to the rules' imposition? If the Legislature had concerns to address, the chief justice pointed out, they would have had between February 19 and the late April adjournment of the legislative session to pass a bill instructing the Court as to how they want the rules to be modified. But no bill came out of the General Assembly, so it was back to the drawing board with a new comment period followed by the August 5 public session.

They came out of the woodwork for that one.

I should digress again and make it clear that I don't think I've met most of the people who objected to the January 31 rules. In my 35 years, I considered myself privileged to appear across the aisle from attorneys from the Criminal Appeals Division of the Iowa Attorney General's Office, from the Polk County Attorney's Office and from the United States Attorney's Office from the Southern District of Iowa. The three offices were run professionally. I had good relationships with their attorneys and members of their staffs. A few are lifelong friends. All three offices were in a position to hire the cream of the crop, and their attorneys were reasonable and intelligent. Some of the best attorneys I ever met were career employees of those three offices.

So if it appears that I tend to generalize prosecutors as lazy, self-important hacks who cling to an air of privilege and are threatened by a system that offers a level playing field to all participants to the point that they cry like babies when a fair fight is even suggested, those are labels that apply to very few lawyers I've dealt with personally. If I actually knew the public-spirited ones who took the time to craft detailed comments for the sake of improving (in their minds) our system of justice, my guess is that I'd like and respect them.

Most of the objections were to proposed rules addressing concerns initially expressed by Nick Sarcone in his advocacy to the chief justice in favor of revamping the rules. Using dark, melodramatic rhetoric predicting the catastrophic harms that would befall mostly child witnesses in sexual abuse cases who inevitably would be further victimized by rampant abuses by the inherently unethical defense bar, the rural county attorneys complained about new rules that would allow defendants to take depositions of non-listed persons prior to indictment or information, rules that would authorize investigatory subpoenas, and a rule that would open the door to conditional guilty pleas.

The most vociferous focused on the availability of investigatory subpoenas. A representative sample appears in the first public comment submitted, five days before any of the others, by Monona County (home to 8751 residents) Attorney Ian McConeghey:

> Imagine you have been the victim of a violent crime. Someone has hurt you physically, financially, emotionally, and more profoundly than you ever could have imagined. It hurts exquisitely. It hurts every day; and it hurts every night as you lay awake trying to forget the horror of what you experienced at the hands of an evil man. Your family and friends will suffer with you through all of your tears, sleepless nights, emotional meltdowns, and years of medical and psychiatric appointments as you try in vain to put your former life back together. You replay in your mind what you did wrong, and what you could have done to stop this horrendous act from happening to you. Perhaps worst of all, you will never feel truly safe again.

> Now imagine that same evil man who victimized you can access your cell phone, computers, social media, bank records, medical records, and employment records. He can see everything about you, including all of your mistakes, vices, idle words, indiscretions, and embarrassing moments. He will comb through every detail of your life until he finds something that he can use to discredit and ruin you. You ask "how can he do this? I didn't do anything to deserve being a victim, and I certainly didn't do anything to deserve this! I thought the law was here to protect me!" All anyone can tell you is that it is his right. He victimized you, and therefore he has the right to know everything about you so he can try to avoid punishment for his crime.

Joni Mitchell, she says, has looked at clouds from

both sides now. In that sense, the best analysis of the merits of investigative subpoenas would probably come from a practitioner who has spent significant amounts of time working as both a prosecutor and a defense attorney. Having only ever functioned as a defense attorney, my view may be as completely myopic as that of the guy from Monona County.

The subject of my melodramatic scenario is not an evil man, because where I come from you attain that status only by being found guilty beyond reasonable doubt by a jury of your peers. In the meantime, the person accused of a criminal offense also suffers psychological harm. You stand to lose your freedom, your worldly possessions and your family. All of *your* "mistakes, vices, idle words, indiscretions, and embarrassing moments" are laid bare for the world to see. It's a process in which truth is found through an adversarial process in which both sides submit the evidence to the finder of fact and present arguments that the evidence supports your side of the case. But evidence, if it's out there, can be an elusive commodity. In my scenario, the government holds a vast advantage both in resources and access to witnesses and records. Some evidence requires the government to obtain a warrant, but a warrant can be obtained any time night or day if there's probable cause.

Defendants can't apply for a warrant. If the government has taken the initiative to obtain phone records, for example, they might be available to the defendant in discovery, especially if they are exculpatory. Otherwise, if there's something out there with the potential of turning the table of truth to the defendant's benefit, there is no mechanism available to obtain it. If the prosecutor is lazy or incompetent or has satisfied him- or herself that there's enough in the file to put away the person against whom charges have been lodged, the defendant is SOL.

Assistant Attorney General Andrew Prosser foresaw consequences of Biblical proportions if defendants were given access to investigative subpoenas:

> Every victim, witness, law enforcement officer,

law enforcement office and non-witnesses, individual and corporate, will be subject to investigation by subpoena by every criminal defendant in every criminal case. Open season is declared by the proposed rule for criminal defendants to obtain victim, witness and non-witness phone records, social media account records, bank records, business records, work records, school records, personal records, data of every variety stored either by third parties or in personal property such as cell phones, computers, cameras, and data storage devices, just to name a few of the unlimited possibilities. The rule limits the permissible objections to applications for such subpoenas to three essentially meaningless grounds. The rule does not mention, much less provide any protection, consideration or balancing of these egregious and costly invasions of privacy against any need or justification for the information sought. The proposed Rule will chill the essential role that victims and witnesses play in the administration of the criminal justice system by turning them into the targets of court authorized investigation by criminal defendants and their attorneys. It will discourage victims and witnesses from coming forward. It will slow the adjudicatory process and dramatically inflate its cost.

Prosser recognized that granting investigatory subpoena power in criminal cases would bring criminal practice in line with civil practice, where litigants have traditionally possessed access to this discovery tool. The disparity is justified, he argues, by the inherent difference between criminal practice and civil practice. Again from someone who has seen the clouds from the other side, I would think that the potential deprivation of liberty would militate in direction of providing more procedural protections to the criminal defendant than to the civil litigant.

If either side has the ability to subject others to

humiliation, harassment and intimidation, it's not the defense. Defense attorneys can't put people in jail. Defense attorneys can't take children away. Defense attorneys don't send people with badges and handguns to question their witnesses.

The proposed rule would require notification to the state and court approval for an investigative subpoena to be issued. All of the rampant ills perceived by Assistant A.G. Prosser would befall society only if prosecutors are drastically outgunned by defense attorneys in both skill and experience and if the judges and magistrates cannot be relied upon to prevent abuses.

The Iowa County Attorney's Association characterized defense investigatory subpoenas as a penalty on victims "for telling what happened in a case." Of course, if state law enforcement and its prosecutors are doing their truth-finding job, all of the phone records, employment records, school records, etc., that are relevant to the case are going to be subpoenaed anyway, by the state. At least in the jurisdictions in which prosecutors boast that defendants may rely upon them to gather the evidence, the documents will be turned over to the defense in discovery. And even prior to the process to revamp the rules of criminal procedure, defendants had access to subpoenas duces tecum requiring witnesses to appear with documents at trial, for depositions and for other hearings. Any increase in the "penalties" suffered by victims who receive investigative subpoenas duces tecum would, at most, be negligible.

Lyon County (pop. 12,011) Attorney Amy Oetken argued that investigative subpoenas are unnecessary.

"I have no interest in hiding anything from a defendant," she insisted. "If defense counsel comes to me with potential evidence, I am happy to acquire it so long as it isn't intrusive into someone's personal business and a way not allowed under the rules of evidence."

Such benevolence on her part nevertheless leaves the defendant at the mercy of the particular prosecutor handling the case. This one is willing to accommodate requests from the accused, but admits that she has certain standards to be met before she does. Others may not be so generous. And, in our system, the county attorney is not the final arbiter of what evidence is sufficiently intrusive into a witness's personal business and what evidence is not admissible under the rules to arise to the level that it is undiscoverable by the defense.

"[W]e have not seen any adverse consequences as a result of defendants not being allowed to serve investigative subpoenas," the Linn County (Iowa's second most populous) Attorney reported. "The rules of discovery and ethical responsibilities placed on prosecutors are and have always been a safeguard to ensuring the defendant has access to the information they may need to defend their case in court if they are actually charged."

It isn't clear who the "we" was to which the county attorney was referring, who had no complaints about the workings of the existing discovery scheme. And the theme of the heightened "ethical responsibilities placed on prosecutors" was a theme that resurfaced in several comments from state's attorneys. Those of us who have been corralled on the wrong side of the barbed wire are painfully aware of the adverse consequences of participating in a system in which the other side is visibly supplied with all the meaningful tools. And anyone who has gone to a prosecutor and suggested that it might be important to obtain surveillance videos from an adjacent business or the time records from a witness's employer may learn a different lesson about a prosecutor's "ethical responsibilities." *It's not my job to do your investigation for you.* I'll bet I'm not the only defense attorney who has heard that one.

There were, at times, some highly competent investigators working in the offices by which I was employed. And in the places and days in which we had access to subpoenas duces tecum for our investigations, it was far from uncommon to see my one guy uncover a plethora of evidence that the teams of law enforcement at the prosecutor's beck and call couldn't seem to locate. This was especially true for evidence we could obtain conventionally without the use of subpoenas. Some of what we found would have been damning to our cases had law enforcement been as zealous as our people were in excavating beneath the topsoil. It was always gratifying when the other side's investigators were less resourceful than ours. But the suggestion that we should rely upon the state's ethical responsibilities and neglect our own ethical duty to investigate our clients' cases strikes me as the punchline of a joke.

One often learns very early in a career as a defense attorney that the truth-finding function is not, in the eyes of some prosecutors, the prize feature of our adversarial system of justice. I've been present at gatherings in which defense attorneys are rated by them on the criteria of "client control." In other words, a competent defense attorney is one who can maneuver his or her client in the direction of a guilty plea as rapidly as possible, without wasting the time of the state's attorney, law enforcement and "my victim." Generous plea offers are extended on the condition that the defendants accept them immediately without taking discovery depositions or filing motions advancing potential constitutional issues. Are those prosecutors cognizant of the safeguards in place, as described by the Linn County Attorney, to ensure that my client has access to the information he or she needs? John Adams would be rolling over in his damn grave.

Several prosecutors objected to the rule recognizing conditional guilty pleas. A conviction based on a plea of guilty should be final. A few returned in their rhetoric to the plight of the victim, who now has to sit through the appeal and the retrial. The answer is that having a conditional guilty plea changes almost nothing besides making the process less expensive and time consuming for everyone concerned, and for the court. If there is no conditional guilty plea, the defendant can do a stipulated trial on the minutes. If that's not available, the parties can do a bench trial, during which the victim is more certainly traumatized by being summoned to appear than had the defendant been permitted to plead guilty. Nobody has to "sit through" an appeal. Unless victims and witnesses make concerted efforts to be apprised of the progress of an appeal it goes on almost unbeknownst to anyone besides appellate counsel and the appellate court. And only 12 percent of criminal cases that are appealed result in reversals of convictions. I would imagine that the preserved issues in a good number of appealed conditional pleas involve the constitutional admissibility of evidence, some of which is determinative of the outcome of the case. Consequently, a smaller proportion of cases return to a stage at which the victim might have to sit through a new trial.

Some of the commentators took issue with proposed Iowa R.Cr.P. 2.13(7) that would permit a person not yet charged with an offense to take depositions to preserve the favorable testimony of witnesses prior to indictment in the same manner as such depositions in civil cases. Rule of Criminal Procedure 2.13(1) previously allowed for the taking of depositions prior to the filing of an indictment or information if granted leave to do so by the court. That provision was retained in the proposed rules as Rule 2.13(1)(b).

"It is not difficult," a group of attorneys and staff of the Iowa Attorney General posited, "to imagine a criminal suspect directly undermining ongoing investigations, traumatizing victims, and harassing or dissuading witnesses from cooperating with law enforcement."

This litany of horrors may have been more persuasive accompanied by real world illustrations arising from application of a rule already in existence, than by a suggestion that they are "not difficult to imagine."

This group, among others, argued that the restoration of the right to serve on a criminal trial jury should not extend to persons still on probation or parole, required to register on the Iowa Sex Offender Registry, or serving an Iowa Code Chapter 903B special sentence of parole for a sex offense. One commentator who advanced a similar argument was the Guthrie County Attorney, who at the time was president-elect of the Iowa County Attorneys Association. She was elected Iowa

Attorney General in 2022.

Watching the Play Clock

So the prosecutors had their say. And once again I waited, with an eye on the play clock. My next deadline for revisions to the 2023 edition of *4A Iowa Practice: Criminal Procedure* was December 10. Would the new rules be revised and ready to go by then? Or, if not, would they be in place by late February, for the submission with the final revisions? In view of the prosecutors' objections, what would remain? Nick Sarcone had expressed profound disappointment in what had come out of the task force in 2020. But the January 2022 revisions were at least a modest reversal of fortune, giving him concessions in each of the areas he and the Iowa Association of Justice had marked for change. There would be slightly enhanced access to discovery depositions, the availability to the defense of investigatory subpoenas and the allowance of conditional guilty pleas.

But Iowa's prosecutors, clinging to their traditional birthright of holding all of the cards all the time, had screamed bloody murder. Buried in their prophesies of universal gloom and doom may have been some legitimate concerns. But the nostalgia for the *old days* clouded any instincts to at least appear to be conciliatory. Time would tell whether the Supreme Court was inclined to bite.

The last two weeks of October 2022 were dramatic ones for me. I had been invited several weeks earlier to play a show in the large performance area at the Edgewater Retirement Community on the evening of Thursday, October 13. Many of my contemporaries in the Des Moines music scene, due to their own ages and the fact that these gigs were increasingly attractive, were doing the retirement home tour. Edgewater is considered the Cadillac of retirement homes for local performers. My father had resided in their assisted living facility now for eleven months. I think the staff at Edgewater recognized that, if he was able to make it down the corridor to the large performance area, this would be the final time I would play for my father. He was able to make it, was showered with accolades from the other residents for having a rock star son (something that wasn't always a source of unmitigated pride) and, despite the fact that I don't think he could hear a note of what I played, viewed it as a memorable evening. Almost immediately after the 13th, my father began to decline rapidly. He passed away ten days later.

The order from Chief Justice Christensen came down the morning after the Edgewater concert.

The October Rules

There were two questions in my mind as I perused the October 14 version of the new rules. First and foremost, how much work is this going to be for me? Second, what's left of the advances that appeared in the January 31 version?

In terms of the impact of the October proposed rules on my lifestyle, it could have been a whole lot worse. Changes were made to four rules. Everything else was left intact. I could dig into the revisions I had intended for the 2022 version and simply make revisions to the revisions. What made it somewhat labor intensive was that I was now making revisions for the 2023 version. *4A Iowa Practice: Criminal Procedure* 2021 was 1140 pages long, and *4A Iowa Practice: Criminal Procedure* 2022 was 1159 pages long. Though the majority of the 40-some pages of revisions based on the new rules would for the most part be similar in both volumes, each and every 2023 revision would crop up on a different page and in a different paragraph from where it would have appeared in 2022. Still a lot less work than last year, but nevertheless I would have to drop everything until I'd plowed through it.

There were some October rollbacks on the advances made in January toward Nick Sarcone's three objectives but, as another lawyer/songwriter once wrote as he cowered on the deck of a ship moored off Baltimore Harbor, "the flag was still there."

The rule permitting conditional guilty pleas had not been

removed, although the language was stricken providing that "[w]hen a conditional guilty plea is approved by the court, this constitutes good cause for the defendant to appeal the ruling on the specified pretrial motion." I wondered when I saw this how the rule could have any teeth at all if approval of a conditional plea is not good cause to appeal, in view of the 2019 Iowa Code § 814.6(1)(a)(3) prohibition of non-class A felony appeals absent a showing of good cause. Several of the prosecutors who commented on the January proposed rules had objected to the allowance of conditional pleas as an end-run around § 814.6(1)(a)(3). Perhaps the Court removed the good cause language as a concession to them, with the understanding that it could make *ad hoc* determinations in each case, based upon the nature of the issues raised, that good cause did or did not exist to allow appeals to go forward. Certainly, the attorney general would argue in response that removal of the good cause language was an indication of the intent of the drafters of the rule that approval of a conditional plea does not cross the § 814.6(1)(a)(3) threshold. Messy days lay ahead but, as I say, the flag was still there.

Equally murky was the issue of depositions. Prior to any proposed revisions, the defendant had a right under Rule of Criminal Procedure 2.13(1) to take depositions of all witnesses listed to be called by the state. Under limited circumstances, Rule of Criminal Procedure 2.13(2)(a) authorized depositions of prospective witnesses who were not listed. The court had the authority under Rule 2.13(1) to permit depositions prior to the filing of an indictment or information. And under Rule of Criminal Procedure 2.13(5) a person expecting to be a party in a criminal case had the right to perpetuate favorable testimony to the same extent one would be permitted to do so under the civil rules.

The rules proposed on January 31, 2022 shuffled the provisions somewhat, but were not drastically different. Persons expecting to be parties in criminal cases could still perpetuate testimony under proposed Rule of Criminal

Procedure 2.13(7). Defendants charged by indictment could perpetuate testimony of potentially unavailable witnesses under proposed Rule of Criminal Procedure 2.13(6)(a). And, under proposed Rule of Criminal Procedure 2.13(1)(b), persons could still apply for leave of court to take the depositions prior to the filing of the indictment or information.

Notwithstanding the predictions of gloom and doom by the rural prosecutors, the only real change made to the deposition rules as they were proposed in October 2022 was removal of the phrase "before a case is filed" from the caption of proposed Rule 2.13(7), which still enabled persons not yet formally charged to perpetuate testimony that might be favorable to their cases. The change was made, the Court explained, to bring the language of the rule directly in line with how it read prior to the revisions. An entire section relating to protections for child witnesses during depositions was removed, as these procedures are set out in Iowa Code § 915.36A.

The procedural hoops through which a defendant would be required to leap to obtain investigative subpoenas became substantially more intense under the October proposed revisions. The flag was still there, but it was considerably battle worn. The burden would be on the defendant at the outset to list all of the good faith efforts he or she had undertaken to obtain the requested materials from other sources, to establish that the information sought would be exculpatory and would not include private information about the victim, to establish that evidence obtained through the subpoena would not be inadmissible under a court rule or statute, and to establish that the information could not be obtained through any other source. Before issuing a subpoena, the court would have to find that each of these factors have been proven by a preponderance of the evidence. There would be strict rules about getting notice to all interested parties and turning over to the state all materials obtained. As in the past, the defendant could request that materials be provided through subpoenas duces tecum for trial, hearings or depositions. Otherwise, the new Rule of

Criminal Procedure 2.15(3)(a) procedure would be the exclusive vehicle available to the defendant for obtaining a court order for the production of documents and other evidence.

Violating the provisions of proposed Rule 2.15(3)(a) could result in a finding of contempt of court and exclusion of any improperly obtained evidence.

The only other change in the October proposed rules involved the eligibility of convicted felons for service on a criminal jury. Credible evidence, including the testimony of the prospective juror, that his or her citizenship rights have been restored would be sufficient to remove the bar on jury duty, and there would no longer be a requisite ten-year wait after conviction or release from confinement, whichever comes later. Parties fearing anti-prosecutorial bias or other concerns would need to flesh them out in *voir dire*.

It appeared to me that the sausage produced by the meat grinder that was the task force and the Court was the endurable compromise. It probably fell short of what had been envisioned by Nick Sarcone and the Iowa Association for Justice when they first approached the chief in 2017. And it certainly didn't assuage the concerns of the rural county attorneys about the unsettling prospect of having to practice in a system in which there is a semblance of parity, a system in which opponents might actually put up a fight rather than accept their generous plea offers with the servient gratitude befitting their lofty position in the caste system that is the courthouse family.

Everybody'd had their day in court, so to speak, and it was safe to assume that what I was seeing was what would appear in the July 1, 2023 volume of the Iowa Rules of Court.

And in the 2023 version of *4A Iowa Practice: Criminal Procedure.*

This time around there was no great rush. The first round of revisions for the 2023 volume were due on December 10. I pulled out all the revisions I'd prepared in February for the 2022 volume, the revisions that I had to scrap at the very moment I was about to send them off to the publisher. As only a handful of changes had been made between the January proposed rules and the October proposed rules, I could relatively easily make new revisions to my earlier ones.

The challenge, once again, was that in February I was revising the 2021 manual and in October I was revising the 2022 manual. The latter had grown by 19 pages over the former. So while there weren't an inordinate number of new substantive changes to be made, I had to reposition all of the rule citations in the pages and paragraphs of the new manual.

I emailed my revisions to the publisher on Saturday, November 26. Rather than lump them altogether in one 74-page set, I split them up. There were about twenty-five pages of developments in the caselaw and changes in the Iowa Code. Three pages resulted from revisions to the Iowa Rules of Evidence. The remainder were the line-by-line revisions to the Rules of Criminal Procedure. I guess I was still a little gun shy.

"Primarily," I told my editor, "I was concerned about the imbroglio that arose this Spring, when the Court adopted the revised Rules of Criminal Procedure, then withdrew them after I'd invested over 100 hours in incorporating them into my book. One consequence of that is that there are a number of places in which there are revisions to the same paragraphs in the text coming from two different directions. As carefully as I could, I went through them all to make sure that there are no conflicts between them (i.e., making modifications based on new cases to text taken out as a result of rule revisions). All of the revisions I'm sending are to the text of the 2022 volume, and I'm not heaping one revision on top of another."

Admittedly, my head was spinning. Just doing it the one time back in February was, for me, a major undertaking. I did my best to update the references to the rules wherever they arose, to make my manual as accurate as it could be. But here, like I say, I was making changes to the changes. Ultimately, the time arrived to send them all in. They'd be back in February, and I'd get another look. But I got them off two weeks early, confident that I now had a manual that could be relied upon accurately in July 2023.

More Watching the Play Clock

It was a load off my shoulders. I could go back to being a full-time singer/songwriter which, since the beginning of the pandemic, meant being in hibernation through the winter. I did my livestream every Tuesday evening, wrote songs five days a week and stuck to a spartan regimen of rehearsing my expanding repertoire.

Baby Pictures had not propelled me to the top of the *New York Times* Best Seller List. I sold just under a hundred and gave away about half that many, but people who took the time to read it were very encouraging. Other books stored in the hard drive of my computer were pleading with me to be released. My father's passing was a reminder of the limits of my mortality. If I were to follow him out still waiting for some publisher to swoop in with an offer to publish all my works, they would remain forever entombed in that digital limbo.

The first draft of *Baby Pictures* had been written in 1996. Three years later, I worked up a first draft of *Dead Horses*, which was a collection of all my stories that didn't find their way into *Baby Pictures*. About two years ago, I dug out *Dead Horses* and added some tales about events that came after 1999. Once *Baby Pictures* was finished and out there in June 2022, I went to work revising and cleaning up *Dead Horses*. By the end of January, that one was ready to go.

I discovered Amazon Kindle Direct Publishing, a service that allows a writer to use its algorithms to format and publish a book, at no cost to the writer. The book is then released for print on demand and as an e-book. Consumers can purchase them directly from Amazon. The writer can order at wholesale prices as many print copies as he or she wishes in paperback or hard cover, to sell or to just give away. By the time I participated in my first book fair in late February 2023 I had two books to sell, in addition to *4A Iowa Practice*: *Criminal Procedure*.

And there were four more on the shelf. Two are relatively

finished products which, for different reasons, I have to hold off on releasing for the time being. Another is a fictional novel, a very rough first draft of which I had just completed when I made the command decision to go all guns on *Baby Pictures*.

I'd written the first draft of another, *El Mensajero*, in the spring of 2020, just as the pandemic was gathering steam. With *Dead Horses* out, I turned my attention to it.

Just When You Thought . . .

I was working on *El Mensajero* when the Iowa Supreme Court decided *Howsare v. Iowa District Court*.

You remember that *Howsare* is where this whole story begins. A boy and his dad arguing with some woman they don't think belongs at their business meeting find themselves charged with a simple misdemeanor assault. Picked up on a warrant, they spend a night in jail before being brought before a judge. This was wrong on several fronts, they complain to the Supreme Court. But their arguments fell on deaf ears.

I read the case two weeks after it came down, to condense its holdings into concise one-sentence summaries for the caselaw updates I present at continuing legal education seminars and ultimately to incorporate into the next edition of *4A Iowa Practice: Criminal Procedure*.

Howsare came down 364 days after February 18, 2022, the day the final revisions to the 2022 version of *4A Iowa Practice: Criminal Procedure* were due. The day I made the horrific discovery that fifty pages of them that I had compiled so frantically were for naught. Had the proofs for the 2023 edition been sent to me on schedule, and had I taken the time to read *Howsare* that day, 2023 would have been a carbon copy of the drama of 2022. But, as has happened occasionally in the past, the editors were behind schedule in getting the proofs to me.

The proofs arrived the following Monday, and I was given until March 7 to make my final revisions.

On March 1, I spotted the problem. In *Howsare*, Justice McDonald was citing the existing rule, with not even a footnote mentioning an impending rule change coming in four months. *Could it possibly be happening again*? Maybe I'm just paranoid, justifiably so after what I'd been put through last year.

Nope.

Once again, I was hurled back into limbo. Another pair of Ray-Bans.

Which was worse, you ask – 2022 or 2023? Well, these proofs came to me on February 21 with all the new rules incorporated throughout the book. I was *committed*. I spoke to my editor. There would be no sending out a volume that didn't incorporate the new rules. It was a book that would be obsolete before it was even published. I couldn't release it in its current form. Who knows how extensive the changes would be after the Legislature had its say?

Nobody had an answer for that one.

I was a hostage of the Iowa Legislature.

There was a bill. Two bills, actually. One in the House and one in the Senate.

Senate File 204 was introduced in the Senate on February 2 by Senator Dan Dawson, a 45-year-old Special Agent with the Iowa Division of Criminal Investigation, serving his second term in the Senate representing Pottawattamie County. SF 204 would create Iowa Code § 821A, dealing with defense subpoenas in criminal actions. Defense subpoenas would be permitted only on application to the court establishing by clear and convincing evidence a "compelling need" for the evidence sought, and that such evidence be "material, necessary, exculpatory, and admissible at trial."

The subpoenas could not be used to obtain private information, including information that the government would need a warrant to obtain. They would be the exclusive vehicle for obtaining items for which a subpoena is required unless provided for in a separate rule. They could not be requested or issued *ex parte* and the prosecutor would not be required to participate in executing them. A person subpoenaed under § 821A could not be compelled to sign a waiver, and would be entitled to appointed counsel, paid out of the indigent defense fund, to represent him or her in matters relating to the issued subpoena.

Within 24 hours of obtaining items through the § 821A process, the defendant would be required to disclose them to the state.

If the § 821A process is not followed, evidence obtained would not be admissible. Defense attorneys who do not comply may be charged with a simple misdemeanor. Defendants would be prohibited from making allegations of ineffective assistance of counsel in postconviction relief proceedings based on evidence obtained under § 821A.

Under the new Iowa Code § 701.13 a prospective defendant would have no right to depose witnesses prior to the filing of the indictment or information.

Conditional guilty pleas would be permitted under the new Iowa Code § 824.6(3) only with the consent of the prosecutor and the attorney general, and the appellate court would have jurisdiction to consider issues reserved by a conditional plea only where "adjudication of the reserved issue is in the interest of justice." This qualification would be a step up from the October rules, after removal of language making the reservation of an issue via a conditional guilty plea good cause for avoiding the prohibition of appeals from guilty pleas and leaving nothing in its place.

A convicted felon still under supervision, or who is required to register on the Iowa Code § 692 sex offender registry or who is serving the special sentence for sex offenders under Iowa Code § 903B would be disqualified from jury service under SF 204.

As this was going on Senator Nate Boulton, who gave me some guidance about the legislative process, cautioned me against placing too much reliance on the provisions of any bill until it is finally passed and sent to the governor. Changes were still being proposed.

The Senate subcommittee took up Senate File 204 on

February 23 and recommended its passage renumbered as Senate File 523. It was introduced and approved by the full committee on March 6, attached to House File 644 on March 23 and, on March 30, placed on the calendar as unfinished business. In the final version, the provision subjecting defense counsel to prosecution for a simple misdemeanor for failing to comply with Chapter 821B was amended to one under which defense counsel could be "sanctioned."

Conditional guilty pleas, which under SF 204 required consent of the prosecutor and the attorney general, under SF 523 now required consent of the prosecutor and either defense counsel or the defendant.

On April 25, SF 523 was withdrawn and substituted with House File 644.

The House version was introduced on February 13, as House Study Bill 156, by House Judiciary Chairman Steven Holt, a retired Marine Corps first sergeant and father of five who had represented House District 12 since 2015. HSB 156 appears to be virtually identical to SF 244. It passed through the subcommittee on February 15, and was approved as HF 644 on March 7. The renumbered version also replaced the simple misdemeanor provision with one permitting the court to sanction defense counsel for not following the statutory requirements for obtaining defense subpoenas. As in its Senate counterpart, conditional pleas under HF 644 now would require consent of the defendant or defense counsel, and not the attorney general.

On April 25, HF 644 was amended in the Senate to remove all language about defense subpoenas, and the bill was passed by a vote of 49-0. On May 1, a similar amendment was approved in the House, and HF 644 was passed there 94-0.

It was signed by Governor Reynolds on May 26.

And that was it. Just a legislative logjam in the stream of progress of amending the rules of criminal procedure. What did they get out of it? The defense may not depose witnesses prior to an indictment or information. It's a step back, perhaps, from the pre-task force era where there seemed to be an opening for a prospective criminal defendant to appeal to the discretion of the district court to depose a witness under certain circumstances. A convicted felon cannot serve on a jury if that person is still under supervision, on the sex offender registry or serving the special sentence. It's still better than the original proposed rule that required a waiting period of ten years following conviction or completion of confinement, whichever comes later. And there is a requirement that the Supreme Court's rules comply with statutory guidelines controlling depositions of child witnesses. In the end, the statute became the rule. The Court was required to bring its rules in line with all of these changes, but there wasn't much to change.

Five days later, the Court responded with new rules corresponding to the statutory mandate. The provision that "[b]efore indictment, depositions may be taken only with leave of court" was removed, along with the one that a "person expecting to be a party to a criminal prosecution may perpetuate testimony in the person's favor in the same manner and with like effect as may be done in expectation of a civil action." This one was a net loss for Nick Sarcone and the defense bar, as we came away with less than what we had before the revision process started.

The requirement that potential jurors no longer be on supervision, on the registry or serving a special sentence was advocated for by a number of the prosecutors in their public comments. But I doubt there was much dispute on our side of the aisle and, like I say, it's better than the ten-year waiting period in the initial proposed rules.

The May 31 rules did not include language from HF 644 that vests the appellate courts with jurisdiction to hear appeals of convictions based on guilty pleas "in the interests of justice." I was perplexed by the removal from the proposed rules of the provision that approval of a conditional plea is "good cause" for an appeal where an appeal is otherwise not permitted. The "interests of justice" standard would at least be a door through which defendants with meritorious claims could walk for appellate review. But it's in the statute, so that's probably sufficient.

July 1, 2023 has come and gone. Are the new rules in place?

What I learned from Caitlin Jarzin when she was guiding me through the process is that, when a court rule is adopted or modified by the Supreme Court it goes to the Iowa Legislative Council, which characterizes itself on its website as the "'steering committee' of the General Assembly during the interim." Before this ordeal began, I always believed that the Judicial Branch made its own rules. Now I know better. Historically, I guess it's rare for the Legislature to be involved in judicial rulemaking.

But we live in interesting times.

Once a new rule goes to the Legislative Council, the Council has two months to approve it or reject it. If the Council rejects it, the rule goes back to the Court, to decide whether it wishes to take another crack at resuscitating it. Sometimes the Legislature gives clear guidance, as it did here, for what it would find acceptable. It doesn't have to do that. The Court can keep formulating new rules, and the Legislature can keep batting them down for as long as both sides have the energy to keep the volley going. If the Council takes no action on a rule, which is most common, the rules go into effect after 90 days or the effective date stated in the proposed rule, whichever is later.

In her May 31 order adopting rules that comply with HF 644, Chief Justice Christensen noted that the Legislative Council took no action on the rules proposed in October 2022 and on some very minor revisions from November 2022. Scheduled to take effect on July 1, 2023, the Legislative Council review period had run. In her opinion, the October 2022 rules are now in place.

There were very minor changes to be made to *4A Iowa Practice: Criminal Procedure* based upon the May 31 revisions. It is impossible to believe they would be rejected, but regardless of what the Legislative Council did with them their substance appears in the Iowa Code. They're the law. All of it could now go into the book, leaving the citations to the May 31 rules out until August 1.

Adding one additional very thin layer of complexity was a June 30, 2023 order from the Court making two more changes to the rules. The first allows the clerk, rather than just the magistrate, to sign an arrest warrant after an indictment or information has been found. The second amends the procedure for taking the deposition of a complaining witness who is a minor, to remove the requirement of judicial approval before the deposition or interview may be conducted outside the presence of the defendant. To assert the right, the witness need only file notice with the court. This is another one that, unless it approved or rejected by the Legislative Council, will remain a temporary revision until August 30.

But as of July 1, the 2023 edition of *4A Iowa Practice: Criminal Procedure* was out on the tarmac, taxiing toward the runway and preparing for a long-delayed takeoff. The publisher sent me the proofs on Friday, July 21. I spent the day reviewing them and sent them back.

My copies of *4A Iowa Practice: Criminal Procedure* should be on my doorstep some day in August.

WHY THIS EVEN MATTERS

My affinity for our Class of '74 reunions every five years has diminished slightly over the past fifteen, for the same reason that family holiday dinners, office retreats and neighborhood block parties have lost some of their nostalgic charm. Like every cluster of individuals in the Venn diagram that 21st Century America has become, our graduating class is split right down the middle on politics. I have no trouble with that – at least I tell myself. I don't really believe that my views are the only views, or that I am necessarily right on every issue. I just don't want to be dragged into an eternal political debate at my high school reunion with people I grew up respecting and caring about. Nothing I say is going to change their minds. And they're not going to change mine. All that comes out of it, in this climate, are bad feelings. It gets so personal. Sixty-year-old men who'd played side by side on the offensive lines since preschool now belittle each other, then retire to opposite corners of the room for the remainder of the evening. There is no such thing as dignified political discourse in America, especially after 2016.

There is one classmate who I knew peripherally in high school. I have never run into him or had any other contact with him since high school outside of the reunions. He comes to all of them. And the only contact I have with him at the reunions is when he moseys over to my corner of the room just to start something.

The defining moment was the 35th reunion in 2009, ten weeks after the Iowa Supreme Court had announced its decision in *Varnum v. Brien* making us the third state in the United States to recognize the legitimacy of same-sex marriage. Gretsch, as I'll call him, wanted to talk about *Varnum*.

"Don't you think," he posed, endeavoring to come across as the thinking man's devil's advocate, "that this is something the voters should be able to decide, and not seven judges on a court?"

"Oh absolutely, Gretsch." I responded. "They should. And another thing. Remember last year when Barack Obama was elected President and the Democrats won all those elections? I think Congress should have immediately passed a bill that everyone who voted Republican in that election should be barred forever from voting again in the future."

Gretsch glazed over with that one. He just looked at me, scratched his head, joined me in a few moments of awkward silence, and wandered back into the safety of the herd.

The answer I was expecting, of course, was that *you can't do that. It's unconstitutional.* Yeah, but who enforces the Constitution? Who protects the minority from the majority when the minority lacks the power to do it?

It's something we would *never* think of doing in the real world. We just wouldn't. At least the Democrats wouldn't do something like that, as we are starting to find out. The Democrats aren't that devious. They aren't that diabolical. The Democrats are too naive and disorganized to undertake a strategy like that. Anyway, it's just downright wrong. But damn, we had the power. When you've got the power, don't you pull out all the stops to *keep* the power? It's worth it, isn't it?

The Democrats wouldn't do it. At least they couldn't. But you know who's good at things like that? We're finding out now.

On the national scale, look how quickly and decisively the ideological balance on the United States Supreme Court has shifted since just 2016, to a point from which we may never return. What they did when Justice Scalia died, and then what they did when Justice Ginsburg died, was pure genius. We must hold off until after the election to start the debate on Scalia's successor, just in case our guy wins. Then we should jump in and appoint Ruth Bader Ginsburg's successor before our guy is toppled by your guy. It seems seedy and unscrupulous but I hope to God that, if the shoe was on the other foot, we'd have gone down the same path. It's good politics. And all this talk about packing the Court – who do you think would benefit from *that*? There's always a way to turn the fortunes around, and those guys always find it.

I thought the hypothetical I posed to Gretsch was absurd enough to be apparent even to him. We would *never* sink to those levels, not in the United States of America. That would signal the unequivocal end of our two-and-a-half century experiment with democracy. Maybe Gretsch would chuckle a little and admit that I had a point.

But now look what's been going on in Des Moines.

"Preserving the Integrity"

The first line of attack is always going to be the laws that facilitate voting for your base while hindering the other guy's. We don't call it voter suppression, from what I hear. You want to "take measures to preserve the integrity of the system – to restore public trust." The perception at least is that voter identification requirements tend to discourage voters who favor progressive Democratic candidates. We saw action of that nature taken in 2017, along with a reduction in the early voting period from 40 days to 29, an apparent response to the observation that Democrats are more likely than Republicans to take advantage of early voting and absentee voting.

Then 2020 happened. Despite the fact that there has never been more than a statistically negligible smattering of voter misconduct cases in Iowa, and despite the fact that Donald Trump carried Iowa by a margin of 53.1 percent over Joe Biden's 44.9 percent, Governor Kim Reynolds joined the chorus touting the stolen election myth to crack down more strenuously on voters perceived to be aligned with the opposing party.

"The fact of the matter is," she explained in February

2021, "there are Americans across the state that have some concerns about what happened in this last election. And again, I think it's imperative that it's not just understood but they feel that there's integrity in the election process and they feel that it's fair and it's done in an equitable manner."

Sometimes you only feel there's "integrity in the process" when your guy gets more votes than the other guy. What can we do to make that happen?

Integrity was "restored" on March 8, 2021, when Governor Reynolds signed Senate File 413, which further pared the 29 days of early voting down to 20 and closed the voting booths an hour earlier on election day than they had been open previously. Absentee ballots, previously valid if placed in the mail by the day before Election Day, would now be counted only if received by the end of voting on Election Day or are clearly postmarked on the day before Election Day. Whether one's vote actually counts is now in the hands of a Postal Service which I hope is more reliable for the homebound voters than it has been for me. Election officials who do not follow the SF 413 restrictions could be subject to criminal penalties. The bill passed both houses on straight party lines.

As the 2020 election came at the height of the COVID-19 pandemic, the Iowa Secretary of State made the rather enlightened decision to mail applications for absentee ballots to all eligible voters. Under the bill, applications for absentee ballots may be sent out only at the voter's request. In the case of the declaration by the governor of a public health emergency, applications may be sent out to all registered voters if the Legislature directs the commissioner of voting to do so.

Did these measures bear any fruit? It's hard to gauge their effect since midterm elections naturally swing in the direction of the party that did not prevail in the previous general election. But the 2022 election certainly went well for the Republican Party in Iowa.

It's natural for those among us who are skeptical about the motives of our opponents to accuse the other side of putting redistricting to work to swing elections in their direction. We are told that our allegations are symptomatic of paranoia. Districting decisions, they tell us, are based primarily upon population along with other appropriate non-partisan factors. Factors that are not appropriate include those taking into account the geographic concentration of members of a particular political party, those that would tend to support an incumbent or another particular candidate, and those based on race or other demographic statuses. Iowa legislative districts are drawn up by the non-partisan Legislative Services Agency which submits its proposal to the Senate and the House. The Legislature does not draft the district maps, but instead may accept or reject the proposal and, if the plan is rejected, may articulate its reasons for doing so. The Legislative Services Agency then prepares a second plan, incorporating matters discussed by the Legislature in its reasons for rejection. If the second plan is rejected, the Legislative Services Agency prepares a third plan.

In this manner politics is kept out of voter districting in Iowa. So we are told.

But I just have to wonder. If everything's fair and square, how does it play out the way it does? Especially in 2022. You've got two parties. One has seven-tenths of one percent more registered voters than the other, yet that party wins commanding majorities in both houses of the State Legislature, re-elects its incumbent United States senator, wins every seat representing the state in the United States House of Representatives, and re-elects its incumbent governor along with all but one of the cabinet officials who are elected statewide.

Is it simply paranoid for me to suggest that these anomalies could be the product of voter districting that tends to favor the party in power, drawn and approved with an eye toward preserving that power balance *ad infinitum*? I know too little about the mechanics of legislative districting to really say. I will say that there are other people who are much smarter than

I am who take such concerns quite seriously, as illustrated by the United States Supreme Court's June 2023 opinion in *Allen v. Milligan*, 143 S.Ct. 1487 (2023), in which a majority of the Court upheld a lower court's injunction on an Alabama congressional districting plan that was likely to have the effect of violating the Voting Rights Act.   Then three weeks later, in *Moore v. Harper*, 143 S.Ct. 2065 (2023), the Court found that the North Carolina Legislature didn't have unfettered control over the conduct of federal elections in its state and its voter districting was subject to the supervision of state courts.

"My Auditor"

The only statewide elected official with a "D" beside his or her name who survived the 2022 midterm elections in Iowa was State Auditor Rob Sand, a 40-year-old graduate of Brown University and Iowa Law School who had spent seven years prosecuting public corruption cases in the Iowa attorney general's office.   According to its own website, the auditor "serves the citizens of Iowa as the 'taxpayers' watchdog.' We provide accurate and timely audits of the financial operations of Iowa's state and local governments to help ensure that government is open and accountable to its citizens."

As perhaps the only remaining check on the Republican-controlled executive and legislative branches of Iowa government, Sand had taken aim at Governor Kim Reynolds. Among the focuses of his investigations involved what he argued was the misuse of $152,585 of federal COVID relief benefit funds on media advertising that featured the governor advocating pandemic safety measures.   The ads, the auditor believed, violated a state law prohibiting the use of public funds by legislators and state-wide elected officials for personal promotion.

I will say that I'm not entirely on board with Rob Sand on this one.   It was a period of world-wide health crisis.   We lost a million Americans to COVID-19, including my brother-in-law. The spectacle of bodies being stored in refrigerated semi trailers in New York City was appearing on the evening news. One would think that it was one of those points in history during which politics would be cast aside. Americans, and citizens of the world, would line up to do their parts to battle this scourge.

But that, of course, just doesn't happen in this day and age. Everything today is a political issue. When the true *leaders* did what they could to stop the spread of disease by isolating it and, once available, through mass vaccinations, this large segment of the population screamed that their rights were being violated. Mostly Republicans. We had a character in the White House who mocked the vaccinations (although he submitted to them), mocked the efforts to stop the spread of the disease (although he himself was hospitalized with the disease), and mocked people who wore masks. The people who wore them did it not only for their own protection, but to do their part to protect others in their communities.

Kim Reynolds is not without blame. Her overall performance during the crisis was far from laudatory. In her 2020 re-election campaign, she touted her efforts to thwart every measure put in place to control the pandemic. She proudly "opened up the schools," exposing teachers and students to what, for some, might be a death sentence.

But when Kim Reynolds goes on television to use her bully pulpit to encourage Iowans to be sensible and wear masks, I'm not going to complain. That's a mark in her column, in my book. And if she's using COVID relief funds to do it, *c'est la vie*. The auditor thinks she's using public funds for self-promotion. I don't know if that's entirely true. It doesn't help much with her base, the types who to this day scream bloody murder at the suggestion that they should do their part to confront this national and global crisis.

At the same time, I'm not going to begrudge Rob Sand for raising the issue. It's his *job*, not mine, to sniff out malfeasance. He's hired by the voters, and not by the governor or the Legislature, to do it.

Then on November 15, 2021, Sand's office released a

report claiming that Reynolds had improperly used $448,448 of pandemic relief funds to pay the salaries and benefits for 21 of her staff members between March and June 2021. A year before that, the auditor determined that the governor had used $21 million in relief funds for implementation of a new computer software system. At that time, the governor returned the funds, and the Legislature passed a bill funding the conversion as part of the state's budget.

Several lawsuits were filed against Reynolds and the state by reporters and lawyers under Iowa's open records law for failing to comply with, or even to acknowledge, requests made in 2020 and 2021 for records relating to the state's handling of the pandemic. After the suits were initiated, the state released some of the records and then went into the Polk County District Court moving to dismiss one of them as being moot. Judge Joseph Seidlin denied the motion in May 2022, noting that if he accepted the state's position "there would be no enforceable obligation to turn over public records until the responsible party or entity is sued." The State of Iowa took the case up to the Supreme Court.

The decision, issued on April 14, 2023, was unanimous, and not favorable to the governor. Yes, the issue is moot once the state substantially complies with the request. But delay in responding can be paramount to a refusal. And the requesting party may still sue for their attorney's fees. The case went forward.

In June 2023 it was announced that a settlement had been reached in which a number of cases involving open records violations would be dismissed and a total of $175,000 would be paid out for attorney's fees. Publicly acknowledging the settlement, the governor's office tempered its rationalizations for the delay with a degree of contrition.

"The COVID-19 response put unprecedented demands on the governor's team to meet the immediate needs of Iowans," Deputy Communications Director Kollin Crompton explained in a public statement. "As a result, responses to requests were unintentionally delayed, which is not acceptable. Our office has assessed our internal processes and we continue to reevaluate the process to improve timeliness."

The settlement was approved by the Iowa Appeals Board. One board member, the state auditor, dissented.

Rob Sand objected to the use of taxpayer funds to compensate attorneys who challenge the transgressions of the Reynolds Administration.

"These insiders have no shame," he argued. "They abuse your rights and then want to use your money to pay for having abused you. I will not go along with this disgusting abuse of power."

Sand characterized the settlement as a "a brazen scam by those whose salaries are paid by taxpayers to skirt a law requiring their own personal responsibility for the fees and fines for hiding public records and using taxpayer funds instead."

It isn't the only time that Sand's was the voice of one crying in the wilderness calling out the executive for the expenditure of taxpayer revenue to pay for the misdeeds of state employees. Three months before authorizing the open records lawsuit settlement, the Iowa Appeals Board voted 2-1 that $2 million of a $4.175 million settlement of a lawsuit against the University of Iowa football program by a dozen former players who were African Americans alleging institutional mistreatment based on race would be paid out of state coffers. The remaining $2.175 million would be covered by the University's athletic department.

The board member who voted against using tax dollars for this purpose was the lone Democrat, State Auditor Rob Sand. Over the course of the seventeen years that Gary Barta was athletic director at the university, a total of $7 million had been paid out to resolve three prior racial discrimination cases. While the state is statutorily bound to pay one half of the settlements of malpractice claims filed against the University of Iowa Hospitals and Clinics, Sand reasoned, "show me a medical malpractice with the same doctor for a fourth time, and I'd be voting against that, too." A settlement of the players' claims against the university should include the removal of Barta as athletic director.

Sand's arguments did not sway the two Republicans on the Appeals Board. But two days later, on March 9, 2023, University of Iowa President Barbara Wilson announced that after "listening to the concerns of Iowans, and in consultation with the Board of Regents leadership," the University decided that the entire settlement would be paid by the athletic department. And with one year remaining on his contract, 59-year-old Gary Barta announced on Friday, May 26, 2023 that he would retire as Iowa's athletic director, walking away from an annual salary totaling $1 million.

During the midterm election campaign in the spring of 2022, Reynolds publicly articulated her desire to have her "own" attorney general and auditor "that's not trying to sue me every time they turn around." The voters granted half of her wish, ousting well-respected Attorney General Thomas Miller in favor of an unknown but vociferous small-town prosecutor whose television commercials promised Republican voters that she would "give [President Joe] Biden the Bird," a play on her last name, and who rode into office on the coattails of Governor Reynolds and 89-year-old Senator Charles Grassley.

But Iowa Republicans still have Rob Sand to contend with.

On May 11, 2023, the Legislature sent to the governor Senate File 478. The bill places limits on the authority of the state auditor to gather a total of eleven classes of information such as income tax returns, public health records, school records and police records of individuals under investigation. It bars the state auditor from suing other government officials, and requires all disputes to be settled through mediation before a three-member panel composed of one member selected by the audited agency, one member selected by the governor and one selected by the auditor. The board's decision is the final word.

The measure was necessary, the governor explained in a May 11 television appearance, to avoid the specter of "executive branch agencies competing against each other, taxpayers have to pay for it twice." When disagreements arise, she asserted, the people of Iowa expect the executive branch to "work things out." What is missing from the governor's logic was the recognition that most of the agencies have heads selected by the governor who serve at the governor's pleasure. As she is the chief executive of the State of Iowa, an action taken by one of her executive branch agencies is an action by the governor. In my view, at least, the elected state auditor answers to the voters and is independent of the governor. So what I see in an arbitration board with one member selected by the governor, one by the agency targeted by the auditor and one by the auditor is a panel in which the governor gets two votes and the auditor gets one.

Sand characterized Senate File 478 as the "greatest pro-corruption bill in state history." On March 8, after Senate File 478 was introduced, National Association of State Auditors President John Geragosian authored a letter articulating the costs inherent in clipping the wings of the state auditor.

"This bill will negatively impact Auditor Sand's ability to independently and sufficiently perform his audit work," he argued. "State auditors should have unfettered access to confidential records to ensure that state agencies are following their policies and procedures and state and federal law. This is also necessary to ensure that we prevent waste, fraud, and abuse of state programs and funds. State auditors also have the immense responsibility to guard against disclosure of any confidential information. It is a responsibility we take seriously."

Nevertheless, Senate File 478 passed in the House by a vote of 55 to 41 (with six Republicans voting nay) and in the Senate by a vote of 33 (all Republicans) to 16 (all Democrats).

The Press

The purge of all the checks on Republican legislative power in Iowa has not left unscathed what has been referred to as the Fourth Estate. Once considered a vital watchdog against abuse of governmental power in the United States, the news media found itself characterized regularly by the sitting President in 2017 through 2021 as the "Enemy of the People" and news reports that were unfavorable to the administration were labeled "fake news." The phrase "enemy of the people" can be traced back as far as the phrase *hostis publicus* employed by Emperor Nero in 68 A.D., but gained real traction during the French Revolution in the 1794 *Law of the 22 Prarial* which authorized the Revolutionary Tribunal to fire up the guillotine for "enemies of the people" for committing offenses that eerily included "spreading *false news* to divide or trouble the people" (emphasis supplied). The *loi de la Grande Terreur,* or "Law of the Great Terror," sparked thousands of executions before its ultimate repeal.

Following the Russian Revolution, lists of *vragi naroda* ("enemies of the state") were compiled to designate members of the erstwhile royal family and dozens of other groups damned to be prosecuted, deported and executed for holding the status. The brand was considered so derogatory and damaging that nearly 40 years later it was cast aside by Soviet Communist Party First Secretary Nikita Khrushchev, himself not known generally as a civil libertarian, as a designation that "automatically made it unnecessary that the ideological errors of a man or men engaged in a controversy be proven. It made possible the use of the cruelest repression, violating all norms of . . . legality, against anyone who in any way disagreed with Stalin, against those who were only suspected of hostile intent, against those who had bad reputations . . .The formula 'enemy of the people' was specifically introduced for the purpose of physically annihilating such individuals."

The term, however, was revived in that country in 2022 by a deputy secretary of Russia's security council to characterize Russians who opposed the invasion of Ukraine.

And by United States President Donald Trump as a label for media outlets who reported unfavorably about him.

The Iowa Senate was more subtle in its approach. Rather

than openly castigating the press as an enemy of the people, the Senate booted them out. For more than a century, journalists have been allowed on the floor of the Iowa Senate and the Iowa House of Representatives, sitting at tables facing members from the front of the room. They have functioned as the "eyes" and "ears" of the Iowa voting public on their elected representatives. Reporters and photographers have been permitted to observe legislators firsthand and to pose questions to them as they go about the people's business.

At the height of the COVID-19 pandemic reporters were removed from the floors of both houses as a safety measure. They were allowed to return to the Iowa House at the outset of the 2022 session.

But not to the Iowa Senate.

Beginning in 2022, reporters were relegated to observing the Senate from the gallery as spectators, with the rest of the general public. A spokesperson for the Senate Republicans rationalized the measure as a product of the changing nature of the media.

"As non-traditional media outlets proliferate," he explained in an email, "it creates an increasingly difficult scenario for the Senate, as a governmental entity, to define the criteria of a media outlet."

Apparently, the House of Representatives did not have the same difficulty ascertaining what constitutes a media outlet. Granted, the evolution of the internet as a source of information has changed radically the way Iowans receive their news. Still claiming on its masthead to be the "newspaper Iowa depends upon," news stories now surface on the *Des Moines Register* a day or two after they are first reported in online services such as the *Iowa Capital Dispatch*. The latter is now the home for journalistic pit bulls such as Clark Kauffman, an unrelentingly aggressive reporter in the field of Iowa politics, and other expatriates from the *Register* turned loose as the paper follows the evolutionary path toward extinction that has become inevitable for the print media. Perhaps the *Capital Dispatch* is one of those proliferating "non-traditional media outlets" the Republicans don't want roaming the floor of the Senate.

So what's left?

My Court?

My concern in all of this is that Governor Reynolds' professed desire to have her "own" attorney general and to have her "own" state auditor may not stop there. An unequivocal answer came on May 9, 2019, when she signed Senate File 658 which on its face was a general appropriations bill. Several segments of the bill had to do with control over the Supreme Court. One altered the process employed to select Iowa's appellate judges.

"I am proud to sign this compromise legislation reforming our process for selecting judges to give all Iowans a greater voice in the process," she boasted. "For the first time, a majority of the state nominating commission will be representing the people of Iowa instead of the bar and bench."

Prior to 2019, the eight members of the Judicial Nominating Commission were appointed by the governor, and eight were appointed by the Iowa Bar. The chairperson of the commission was the most senior member of the Iowa Supreme Court who was not the chief justice. Division XIII of SF 638 captioned "JUDICIAL NOMINATING COMMISSION MODERNIZATION" altered the makeup of the commission to allow the governor to select nine members, while the Bar would select eight. The commission would elect its own chairperson. While the governor's selections must be gender-balanced, both the governor's appointees and those submitted by the Bar must be selected "without reference to political affiliation,"

The notion that the 2019 modification gives "all Iowans a greater voice in the process" and that "the majority of the state nominating commission will be representing the people of Iowa instead of the bar and bench," is predicated on the assumption that putting majority control of the judicial selection process in the hands of Kim Reynolds gives "all Iowans" a voice in the process. It's essentially the same formula used for selection of the arbitration board set up to deal with Rob Sand.

And reducing the role of the "bar and bench" discounts the input of the professionals who have actual knowledge of how the system operates and transfers it to those with the greatest political influence. Despite the elimination of any "reference to political affiliation," the Iowa Senate was able to reject four of Governor Reynolds' subsequent appointments to the Commission on the ground that all of them were Republicans. The makeup of the Senate has now changed to a point at which such opposition would have no impact. There is no pressure on the governor to select a politically balanced Commission. That's the real point of the bill. And because the commissioners are selected to fill staggered terms, even if at some point Governor Reynolds is not re-elected her commissioners would still be in place for several years.

But it was another provision of SF658 that wreaked the most havoc.

Late in the evening of Friday, November 15, 2019, I was conversing in a pizza parlor in downtown Algona, Iowa with several people who, like me, had just attended a jazz concert in the auditorium of the local high school featuring several performers from Des Moines. One of them was Scott Buchanan, a prominent attorney in the Kossuth County seat of about 5,400 inhabitants. A more compelling connection between us is that Scott is also a musician. We had bumped into each other over the previous weekend, as we do each year, at Art on the Prairie, a two-day event in Perry, Iowa in which artists from all over Iowa show their work in rooms in the rejuvenated buildings on its town square. In each room is a musician or a small ensemble performing acoustically without any electronic amplification. More than a dozen performers converge on Perry for the weekend. One of the perennial favorites of those who attend, and a personal favorite of mine as well, is a trio calling itself Just Cause. Elaborate three-part harmonies with Scott on the guitar accompanying Mia, a clinical psychologist, and "the other guy" (as I refer to him. But I do know him as Todd, a local music teacher). The singer in the November 15 jazz concert in Algona and her husband were mutual friends of Scott and me. So, winding down in a pizzeria booth after the show, our discussions meandered between law and music.

Scott's attention was drawn away by a message that came in on his cell phone.

"I've got some news," he told me, in a now somber tone. "Chief Justice Cady died."

It didn't sink in immediately. Why would Justice Cady *die*? He was, from all appearances, a relatively young, active man. Was it foul play? Was it an accident?

"I don't know what happened," Scott admitted. "I just heard that he's gone."

"Damn," I muttered. "There was something I wanted to tell him the next time I saw him."

The *next time I saw him*? The chief justice of the Iowa Supreme Court?

"I just talked to him a few months back," I explained. To be honest, I'd had a grand total of two encounters with Chief Justice Cady outside the courtroom, that I could remember. Besides that, our paths had crossed very briefly when he was appointed to the Court of Appeals just as I was leaving the Appellate Defender.

A year earlier, he showed up at Woody's. Steve "Woody" Wasson, an old friend from Boy Scout Troop 202, now owned Woody's Smoke Shack, a very popular and successful barbeque shop in the Drake neighborhood. In 2009, the Smoke Shack was one of four finalists in a Good Morning America nationwide barbecue contest. As I arrived at the Iowa State Fairgrounds that August to play a show at the Fair, I fielded a message from Woody telling me he was thinking of putting music on his outdoor patio and inviting me to join the rotation. On Wednesdays over nine summers, I played five monthly three-hour sets at Woody's.

You never knew who would show up at Woody's. Some evenings it was just Rick and Linda Brundies, who pride themselves in attending as many of my shows, and those of other local musicians, as they can. On others, the lawn was crawling with large groups of my friends and coworkers. There was once a group of German and Austrian farmers in town for a John Deere convention of some sort.

Then one Wednesday I glanced out to the edge of the patio during a song and spotted *the chief justice of the Iowa Supreme Court* and his wife, enjoying Woody's cuisine. I don't know if he came for me, that he knew I was going to be there that evening, or that he even knew who I was. With the exception of the small handful with whom I've been acquainted personally over the years, I always wondered about all of them in that respect. The justices. When I'd bump into one of them in a restaurant or another location, they were always cordial and friendly (with the sole exception of the one justice who assaulted me from behind at the 2010 wake for the three justices voted out after *Varnum*). They were all cordial and friendly people. Even Chief Justice McGiverin who, I'd been told, once considered lodging a disciplinary complaint against me for my rhetoric in a rehearing petition, once threw me a very amiable "hello."

But there was always that blank up-in-the-clouds gaze that accompanied the friendly greeting. What were they thinking? Who *is* this guy? Maybe they don't read my book, or some of the juicier blog posts that enraged the assailant from the *Varnum* wake. Maybe I'm a legend in my own mind, and my stature in the legal community is negligible. Or maybe they *do* know who I am -- the proverbial mouse that roared. This loose cannon with an armada of opinions that don't pack a lot of weight at their level of play.

I made a few comments during that evening at Woody's about having the chief justice of the Iowa Supreme Court in my audience, all of which he acknowledged with a smile. As he and his wife walked past me on the way back to the car, the chief said hello and complimented my playing. But I don't know what he was thinking.

Then there was Friday, March 9, 2019, an overcast day which, parenthetically, would have been my mother's 90th birthday. I was invited that day to make the hour and a half drive to Fort Dodge to do the criminal caselaw update for the local bar in that town of 25,000. I was scheduled as the final speaker that afternoon but, as I often do, I attended the entire day's lectures to accumulate the credit hours needed to retain my license. The speaker just before lunch was Fort Dodge's favorite son, the chief justice of the Supreme Court.

Justice Cady approached me during the morning session, and we said a few words. He had some business in town after his presentation but hoped to make it back in time for mine. I was pretty sure he wouldn't be back. I've done my song and dance in front of scores of district court judges, an occasional Court of Appeals judge, and one or two former Supreme Court justices who had either retired or had been voted out during the purge. But sitting Supreme Court justices don't stick around for my caselaw updates, in which I comment and opine on their rulings. One of them even told me as much at the ballroom door during a seminar. He was going out while I was going in. I'd feel freer to air my criticism of the Court, he offered, if the justices weren't there to hear it.

It's funny, because over the past two decades I'd morphed into being more of a cheerleader for the Court than a critic, at least from the perspective of some of my colleagues in the criminal defense bar. Whatever it was, Justice Cady's business in Fort Dodge apparently had not concluded by 3 p.m., because he did not return to watch my presentation.

That was the last time I saw him in any capacity. But the chance meetings on a Wednesday evening in 2018 and a Friday morning in 2019 left me with the sense that our paths would soon cross again, because I had something interesting to tell him that I thought he'd want to hear.

But now, late on a Friday evening in November just eight months later, there would be no further crossing of paths with

Chief Justice Mark Cady.

So what was the big news I wanted him to hear?

Between those two dates fell Thursday, August 29, 2019.

That was the afternoon that I drove to the United States District Courthouse to handle the early afternoon initial appearances for two new clients just brought in by the federal marshals. As always, I first met with each of them individually in the holding cells of the courthouse. I gave them both the standard advice about not speaking about the case with anyone other than their attorneys, reviewed with them the initial complaints or, if the grand jury had convened in their case, the indictments, and assisted them in preparing the affidavits of indigency enabling them to apply for the services of court-appointed counsel. Within the next day or so specific attorneys would be assigned to handle their cases, who would be in touch to begin preparing their defenses. The one thing I could tell them with certainty was that it wouldn't be me.

I climbed the stairs to the magistrate's courtroom and handed the completed forms to the judicial assistant. Both clients were brought up and seated with me at counsel table, where the marshals removed their handcuffs. The clerk gaveled the proceeding to order, then Judge Celeste Bremer emerged from chambers and took her seat on the bench. She summarized the charge for each, repeated the advice about the right to remain silent, reviewed the hastily prepared financial affidavits, and appointed my office, the federal defender, to represent them. That was it. Two minutes at the most. As the marshal replaced their handcuffs and led them back through the passageway next to the judge's bench, I wished them both good luck.

Once the door slammed shut behind them, Judge Bremer came down off the bench and approached me with her right hand extended.

"Ask me what I do," I told her.

"What?"

"Ask me what I do."

"Okay. What do you do?"

"I'm a full-time singer songwriter."

I accepted Judge Bremer's handshake, took the elevator to our courthouse office space, dropped off the paperwork from the two initial appearances along with my keys to the courthouse and to the office space, walked out to the Dodge Grand Caravan parked on East Third Street, and rode off into the sunset, bringing to an end my thirty-five years as a practicing attorney.

My "retirement" from that profession. August 29, 2019.

It was something else that happened that day that I couldn't wait to discuss with Chief Justice Cady the next time I saw him. At the very same time I was making my final court appearance a funeral was getting underway at Saint Timothy's Episcopal Church in West Des Moines, two blocks from the house in which I grew up, for 89-year-old Mary Lou Imus. I can't say that I ever met Mary Lou, but I did know her husband, Harry, who'd passed away 31 years earlier. According to the obituary, Mary Lou had met Harry when they were both employed at Equitable of Iowa, a life insurance company founded in Des Moines in 1867 by 28-year-old Frederick Marion Hubbell. Hubbell's stately home, Terrace Hill, has served as the Iowa Governor's Mansion since 1976. Its first resident in that capacity was Bob Ray. Hubbell's great-great-grandson, Frederick Shelton Hubbell, a one-time president of Equitable of Iowa, lost a narrow race for Governor of Iowa in 2018, the first year Kim Reynolds had to run for the position she had inherited from Terry Branstad a year earlier.

My dad worked at Equitable for 27 years. It's the reason we moved to Iowa in 1964.

During all the years he worked at Equitable, my dad carpooled downtown from West Des Moines with various other Equitable employees. For several of those years, he carpooled with Harry Imus.

Perusing the obituary, I noted that Harry and Mary Lou had two daughters. One was Susan, currently living in Chicago. The other was listed as "Rebecca (Mark) Cady of Fort Dodge."

That's what I was so eager to tell Chief Justice Cady. My

dad used to carpool to work with *your father-in-law*. Small world.

But just eleven weeks passes and I'm sitting in a dark pizza place in Algona, and this lawyer is telling me that Justice Cady just *died*. How does that happen? Scott Buchanan didn't know.

We would soon learn that it was a heart attack. Sixty-six-year-old Chief Justice Mark Cady was out walking his dog, and it happened. Just like that. Men our age do die suddenly from heart attacks – men who are vital and active and have prime physical conditioning. Back in the years we were born, this was the average life expectancy for males in our country. Sometimes there's just not a good explanation.

Then sometimes there is.

I'm in absolutely no position to speculate as to what might have been going on in Mark Cady's life that would bring on a fatal heart attack. I met him those two times socially, both for only a few moments. I know there are people much closer to him who *do* have an opinion. All I can do is review the circumstances.

The circumstances tell me that 2019 hadn't been Chief Justice Cady's best year.

We've spoken about Senate File 638, the general appropriations bill signed by Governor Reynolds on May 9 that contained two major provisions unabashedly designed to rein in the Judicial Branch, to make it more subservient to the other two -- both at the time controlled tightly by the very right-wing Republican Party. The first swung majority control of the State Judicial Nominating Commission to the governor or, as she phrased it, to "the people."

The second was even more nefarious.

Once you have "my auditor" and "my attorney general" and now have the statutory wherewithal to assemble what you hope will be "my Supreme Court," how long does it take before you can acquire "my chief justice"? And ten years after *Varnum*, and eight years after three Supreme Court justices were swept out of office for the mere act of signing on to it, how do you exact an appropriate penance from the justice who *wrote the damn opinion*, with impunity, and has been out there boasting about it for a decade?

If those are the questions, the answer came in Section XIV of SF 638, captioned "CHIEF JUSTICE SELECTION." Prior to that, the term of the chief justice extended for the term of the justice who held the position. So, unless the chief justice retired, died or somehow left office, he or she served a term of eight years, until that justice went up for retention. If he or she survived retention, that justice was eligible for reappointment. Section XIV of the new bill provided that the chief justice would now stand for reelection or election every two years. The change would take effect on January 15, 2021 or sooner if the justices met earlier in January to select a chief justice.

Why would they do this? Why does the Legislature, or the governor, care about the term of service of the chief justice of the Supreme Court? What innocuous reason could there be for such a change?

Chief Justice Cady's current term began in 2017, when he won his retention election and was re-elected by the Court to remain chief justice. Under the pre-SF 638 scheme, he would remain at the helm until 2024. Under both old law and new law, he was eligible for reelection. But I don't imagine that anyone now envisioned the job going back to him in 2021. What would be the purpose of amending the process if the same result was to be attained?

No. Someone had an idea about how it was all going to play out. Deals were made. By whom? Who knows? I know absolutely nothing about it, so I don't even speculate. All I can do is look at what's out there.

Senate File 658 was challenged almost immediately in a lawsuit filed against Governor Reynolds by several prominent Democrats, including a number of Iowa legislators. They objected to the bill on the ground that the manner in which it was passed violated the "single subject" rule contained in article

III, section 29 of the Iowa Constitution. Senate File 638 on its face was an appropriations bill. Sections XIII and XIV were tacked on with no notice in the title of the bill that it included substantial changes in the selection of Iowa judges and the chief justice. The request for an injunction also alleged that the bill encroached on the separation of powers between the branches of government as set out in article III, section 1 of the state constitution.

The lawsuit was thrown out in the district court on the ground that the plaintiffs lacked standing. Only parties with a personal interest in the outcome of a case are entitled to participate in litigation. The legislators and other Democrats who filed the suit didn't have a personal interest, so the district court judge declined to rule on the suit's merits.

The Democrats filed their appeal on July 1 and, later that month, moved to have each of the justices recuse themselves from considering the appeal due to their potential personal interest in the outcome. There were concerns about communications between the justices and members of the Legislature during consideration of SF 638. Each of the justices responded individually to the recusal request.

On September 26, Justice Thomas Waterman signed an order transferring the case to the Court of Appeals. A motion to have the case heard *en banc* (by the entire Court of Appeals rather than by a five-judge panel) was denied on October 10, and the case was argued on November 6. The Court of Appeals' decision, ruling in favor of the governor, was announced on February 19, 2020. The Court affirmed the district court judge on the standing issue.

All of this drama was playing out in the final six months and two weeks of Chief Justice Cady's life. Amendment H-1321, that converted SF 638 from being a mere appropriations bill into an appropriations bill that gave the governor a majority share in the selection of appellate judges and lopped three to four years off the term of Chief Justice Mark Cady, was filed on April 26 and passed on April 27. The bill was passed and sent to the governor on May 2.

Could this legislative and gubernatorial incursion into the territory of the judiciary have that kind of impact on the chief justice's physical health? I don't know. I'm not a doctor and I didn't really know him. I know what the people who were close to him believe. I don't have an opinion.

There is a window into what was going on in the chief's mind during those months.

Of the seven justices on the Court, six declined to recuse themselves from considering the lawsuit in response to claims that they'd had communications with legislators during consideration of SF 638 that would raise questions about their impartiality. Justice David Wiggins declined to recuse himself on the ground that he "did not consult with, advocate with, and/or encourage any 1) defendant, 2) staff member of any defendant, or 3) member of the Iowa Legislature to support passage of Senate File 638." Justice Brent Appel "did not engage in any such communication." Justice Edward Mansfield responded that he planned to participate in the case. Justice Christopher McDonald and Chief Justice Christensen denied the motion without comment.

"Upon review of the appellants' motion for recusal and the appellees' response," Justice Thomas Waterman wrote, "after due consideration, I decline to recuse and will sit on this case. I will therefore exercise my duty under Rule 52:2.7 of our Judicial Code to hear this matter."

The one justice who did recuse himself, and who did so in a 14-page order filed on September 13, 2019, was Chief Justice Mark Cady. A judge who is asked to recuse himself, he started out, has two duties. First, he must disclose all the facts that might be relevant to a determination of whether he or she has a disqualifying interest in the pending case. Then the judge must determine whether, based on those facts, a reasonable person would question his or her impartiality. The process "involves an objective in-depth search of the conscience of each judge." If the answer is yes, recusal is mandatory.

The question posed in the motion to recuse was whether the Justices took any action to encourage passage of SF 638. Recusal, however, "should also address conduct in opposition to the bill." The judge must then determine whether "recusal is needed to protect public trust and confidence in the judicial system."

Early in the 2019 session, the chief justice recalled, he started getting word that the governor and the Legislature had their eye on modifying the process of judicial selection in Iowa. Prior to the session he was not contacted by any legislator or staff person on either side of the aisle and, as far as he knew, no other justices had contact of that nature. The Court, he decided, would remain out of the fray, and would leave the matter to "the legislative process and public discourse." From his discussions with his colleagues, he believed this to be the consensus of the Court. It was important to him to respect the constitutional separation of powers among the branches of government and to maintain the appearance of impartiality in ruling on the challenges to legislation that come before the Court. It was a regular practice for the chief to set aside office hours each Monday for legislators who had questions or concerns about judicial administration in the state and to meet legislative leaders in their offices several times each year to discuss court administration. Legislators would contact the Court's attorneys with questions about the judicial selection process. Others communicated their opposition to the changes to Chief Justice Cady. Generally, however, he strove to avoid commenting on the merits of the legislation.

On February 4, the chief justice was presented for the first time with a draft of the bill that would not only alter the judicial selection process but would also limit the chief justice's term to two years. Once more, he declined to discuss its merits. He did not, however, maintain complete silence about them.

"On one occasion in March 2019," the chief justice admits, "at the conclusion of a meeting with a representative on the Judicial Branch budget, I did express my disappointment to him that the Legislature was seeking to eliminate my current term as Chief Justice as a part of the Merit Selection Reform Bill. I inquired into the rationale for that portion of the bill and if I might have done something to warrant such a provision in the bill."

The chief instructed his staff to keep an eye on the progress of the bill and its progress in the Legislature and the media. In the early stages, it did not appear to have sufficient support to pass in the House of Representatives as the end of the 2019 session was approaching. All of the reports he received were passed on to other members of the Court, as late as April 23.

At an April 25 meeting of the National Association of State Courts, an organization in which Chief Justice Cady was a member of the board, he was apprised over the telephone by a staff member that the measure was still unlikely to pass. On the following day, he was contacted by a legislator concerned about the effect that limiting the chief justice's term to two years would have upon Iowa's role in the Conference of Chief Justices. He answered all her questions and articulated concerns that would arise from such a change, but once again expressed an intent to remain neutral and to leave the matter to the Legislature. It was apparent from the nature of her questions, however, that the legislator was rethinking her opposition to the bill. He then spoke to another legislator who had previously opposed the bill but was now changing his position.

Later that day, Justice Cady learned from an attorney acquaintance that the first legislator with whom the chief had spoken informed the attorney "that current Justices on the Supreme Court are telling legislators that they think the bill is good policy and should vote for it." After the call, he spoke with his assistant who informed him that the report was consistent with what she had been hearing from other sources in the Capitol Building. He then called another justice on the Court, who indicated that the report was accurate.

Before hearing these things, the chief justice had

considered abandoning his neutrality and publicly opposing the bill, to illuminate the negative impact the change would have upon the administration and the authority of the Court. In view of these revelations, however, it seemed better advised to take no position, as "any further involvement by me in the legislative process would be seen as political and would only expose a fractured Supreme Court and risk inflicting greater damage on the court as an independent institution of government." From that point on, there were no further discussions with members of the Legislature.

As part of his job, the chief justice had meetings with Governor Kim Reynolds and her staff, but at no time did they discuss any proposed changes in judicial administration.

In his meetings with members of the bar, many would express their opposition to the proposals. But Justice Cady made it clear to everyone that the Supreme Court was taking no position on decisions that were within the province of the legislative branch.

Based upon all these disclosures, Chief Justice Cady concluded that he had done nothing that would disqualify him from hearing the appeal of the lawsuit challenging SF 639. For reasons not raised in the motion to recuse, however, he felt compelled to remove himself from the case. He had a personal stake in the outcome. Under the current law, he stood to remain as chief justice until 2024. The bill would shorten his term by three years.

"[T]his portion of the new law at the center of this appeal," he explained, "took away a right given to me by a legal process to serve an eight-year term . . . [A] reasonable person could conclude that I have a personal interest and a financial interest in the outcome of this portion of the appeal and cannot fairly and impartially decide any matter concerning the disposition of the claims raised on appeal that affect the term of the Chief Justice."

That was September 13, 2019 – two months and two days before 66-year-old Chief Justice Mark Cady took the dog for a walk. All things considered, I can't imagine it was a pleasant two months.

Based upon a *Des Moines Register* article that identified him as one of the justices who had collaborated with legislators including the bill's floor manager, Representative Steven Holt, on September 24 the plaintiffs in the lawsuit filed a second motion to recuse Justice Thomas Waterman from the case. The plaintiffs did not question whether Justice Waterman could be fair and impartial, nor did they argue that he was biased. The issue under these circumstances was "whether a reasonable person could question this justice's fairness and impartiality." If Justice Waterman was not inclined to recuse himself, the motion argued, he should "make a public record disclosing all relevant facts and circumstances relating to the claim of disqualification," as Chief Justice Cady had done. Justice Waterman denied the motion, tersely reiterating that "I said or did nothing requiring my recusal or further comment."

Again, I have absolutely no knowledge of what went down in 2019 beyond what can be gleaned from reading the Court documents. So I don't have an opinion. I don't know what vision the justices who collaborated with the Legislature had in mind for the future of the Iowa Judicial Branch or, specifically, the Supreme Court. It is worthy of note that the chief justice who succeeded Mark Cady (after a brief stint as acting chief by Justice Wiggins) was not one of the two identified as being in contact with the Legislature during consideration of SF 638.

The opinion that I do have is that Mark Cady will be remembered along with Marsha Ternus, Michael Streit and David Baker as being jurists of undeniable integrity and foresight who, along with many others, carried on a long proud tradition that stretches back to the first case ever decided by the Iowa Territorial Supreme Court.

With the enhanced control over the selection of justices and hopefully with a more cooperative chief justice, the next step in the Republican power grab was to seize control over the Court's jurisdiction. Under both the Constitution and the Iowa Code, the Legislature admittedly has some say in matters relating to the judicial branch. Article V of the Iowa Constitution provides the framework for the court system in the state. Section 14 of Article V reads that it is "the duty of the general assembly to provide for the carrying into effect of this article, and to provide for a general system of practice in all the courts of this state." It doesn't specify how much detail comprises "a general system of practice."

On the other side of the coin, Iowa Code § 602.4201 vests the Supreme Court with the authority to "prescribe all rules of pleading, practice, evidence, and procedure, and the forms of process, writs, and notices, for all proceedings in all courts of this state." Rules of court devised by the Supreme Court are subject under Iowa Code § 602.4202 to approval by the Legislature. Any changes made by the Legislature supersede the rules submitted by the Court.

In 2019, the same year the changes were made in the judicial selection process, the Legislature adopted a slew of rather significant provisions altering the types of cases the Iowa courts may hear, the types of issues that may be presented, and who is entitled to present them. The ones I discuss relate to criminal procedure, because that's my field of battle. I couldn't tell you if the Legislature was as intrusive in other areas of practice.

Some of the 2019 changes are not entirely unjustified, as they address issues that have weighed on the court system for as long as I've been acquainted with it. But they're issues of which the Supreme Court is fully aware and has acted incrementally over the years to forge policies that are workable and equitable, in contrast with the one-fell-swoop approach of the Legislature.

An example of what I'm talking about has to do with the filing of *pro se* documents by defendants represented by counsel. I mention that one because I think I had something to do with the evolution of the law in that area.

I had a client in 1986, when I will still a novice appellate defender, who was appealing his conviction and his mandatory life sentence for a class A felony. From the outset, there was tension between us over the issues we would present to the Supreme Court in his case. In the course of representing a client there are decisions that are, from an ethical standpoint, for the client to make. Whether to plead guilty or go to trial is an example of a choice that must be made exclusively by the client, with the advice of counsel. Whether to testify at trial is another. Then there are decisions made ultimately by the attorney. As the attorney is the expert on the law, he or she is allowed the final selection of issues of law to present on appeal. The attorney must discuss the case fully with the client, must make certain that the client has been shown all the relevant portions of the file and must fully apprise the client as to the applicable law.

There is one school of thought that you raise your strongest issues on appeal to give your client the best chance for success. You try not to dilute them with ones you know will not succeed. Not every appellate lawyer agrees, but generally that was my theory as an appellate attorney. However, when a client insisted on raising a particular issue, I did what I could to accommodate those wishes. It is, after all, the client's life, not mine.

An attorney, however, may not ethically raise an issue he or she knows to be frivolous, lacking any arguable basis in the law or the facts.

My client in the 1986 appeal was articulate, intelligent and, other than the fact that we butted heads from the get-go, someone with whom I may have been close friends under other circumstances. On the outside, he had been a traveling musician. He wasn't about to place the remainder of his natural life in the hands of a young, relatively inexperienced stranger from Des Moines appointed by the court and paid by the state, who refused to raise the issues he wanted to raise. We went around and around. He sent me long excoriating letters. I visited him several times at the State Penitentiary. He was reasonable, non-threatening, and almost pedagogical in his approach to me. But he didn't change my mind and I didn't change his.

He wrote long letters to the Court, asking that I be taken off his case. The Court receives a large volume of mail from defendants with court-appointed attorneys and, at least in those days, wasn't likely to accede to his request. If he can't get along with me, they reason, he won't get along with the next guy, either.

This was my first "difficult" client, as some lawyers refer to people like him. For months, it affected my sleep. How do I build some kind of a bridge with this guy? In a sense, I really liked him. In other sense, I didn't.

I felt trapped in the middle. The client had a right to go *pro se*, to represent himself. He was smart enough not to do that. The old proverb says that a man who represents himself has a fool for a client and an idiot for an attorney. He didn't want to go it alone. He just wanted an attorney who would raise his issues.

And you can't do both. You can't have hybrid representation, where you have a court-appointed lawyer and represent yourself at the same time.

Then it started to dawn on me. Why not let the guy file a supplemental brief? I can file the brief that raises what in my opinion are the non-frivolous issues. And he can raise the ones he considers meritorious. I filed a motion with the Court which, after the barrage of letters they'd received from this client, saw it as an acceptable compromise.

Since 1986, the Iowa appellate courts have considered *pro se* filings from criminal defendants represented by attorneys. And I have to say there were more than a couple times that, after reading through a client's *pro se* supplemental brief, *I* was convinced and I amended my brief to include the client's issue. I think I may have actually won a case once with one of those issues. There weren't that many wins in those days.

My first "difficult" client became my friend, and we remained in contact with each other for several years after that.

The Legislature stepped in and halted that progress abruptly in 2019. Iowa Code § 814.6A now decreed that "[a] defendant who is currently represented by counsel shall not file any pro se document, including a brief, reply brief, or motion, in any Iowa court. The court shall not consider, and opposing counsel shall not respond to, such pro se filings." The sole exception was that a "defendant currently represented by counsel may file a pro se motion seeking disqualification of the counsel, which a court may grant upon a showing of good cause."

Problems with Section 814.6A cropped up instantly. In a number of cases, appointed trial attorneys considered their jobs done at sentencing. Yet some of the clients wanted to appeal. Whether or not a possible appeal has merits, it is always the duty of appointed counsel to initiate an appeal at the request of the client. Knowing that they would be barred from appealing their convictions and sentences if their notices of appeal weren't filed within strict time deadlines, many defendants were filing their own notices *pro se*. But because the trial attorneys had not withdrawn from representation, their appeals were now being dismissed under the new § 814.6A prohibition against pro se filings.

In a number of cases decided in 2022, the Supreme Court slapped a Band-Aid on the problem by finding there was good cause to consider the merits of appeals filed after deadlines had passed, where defendants had showed unequivocal interest in pursuing this essential right by filing timely notices on their own accord. The lone dissent from one of these, in *State v. Davis*, 969 N.W.2d 783 (Iowa 2022), came from Justice McDermott, whom I've regarded as being generally one of the more progressive on issues relating to criminal trial rights. The appeal deadline, he stressed, is "mandatory and jurisdictional" and the Court *cannot* consider the case once the notice of appeal deadline has passed. Under § 814.6A, the defendant's *pro se* notice is the equivalent of *no* notice.

In fairness to Justice McDermott, the ultimate conclusion of his opinion was more favorable to Davis than that of the majority. The majority found good cause to consider the merits, then rejected Davis' claim on the merits. Justice McDermott would require judges to inform represented defendants during sentencing hearings that, if they wish to appeal, their notices must be filed by their attorneys to be valid. Since that wasn't done in Davis' case, he would have remanded the case back to the district court for resentencing, at which time the proper advice could be given.

The Legislature did respond to this issue in 2022 by creating an exception to § 814.6A permitting represented defendants to file *pro se* notices of appeal. An additional exception allowed defendants to respond to motions by appellate attorneys to withdraw from their appeals on the ground that the appeals are frivolous. The grant by the Supreme Court of such a motion to withdraw may also result in dismissal of the appeal.

Also in 2019, as I've mentioned earlier, the Legislature clamped down on the right to appeal a conviction obtained by guilty plea. Under Iowa Code § 814.6(a)(3) there is no right to appeal the final judgment in such a case except "a guilty plea for a class 'A' felony or in a case where the defendant establishes good cause." Additionally, the new Iowa Code § 814.29 provided that a conviction following a plea of guilty "shall not be vacated unless the defendant demonstrates that the defendant more likely than not would not have pled guilty if the defect had not occurred. The burden applies whether the challenge is made through a motion in arrest of judgment or on appeal. Any provision in the Iowa rules of criminal procedure that are inconsistent with this section shall have no legal effect."

There is sound logic underlying both changes. It is axiomatic that by entering a guilty plea, at least one that is not a conditional plea, the defendant surrenders all defenses and challenges he or she may have mustered with respect to the charges. There are, nevertheless, defendants who experience buyers' remorse after a plea and insist on appealing their convictions notwithstanding their admissions of culpability. A lot of time is taken up by the Court, by the attorney general and by appellate defenders (both appointed and retained) going through the motions of a guilty plea appeal. Most are frivolous.

But the more accurate characterization is that most guilty plea appeals are frivolous, *except the ones that are not*. There are occasional reversals by the appellate courts based on valid grounds argued on appeal. But § 814.6(a)(3) slams the door shut on them.

Except where there is "good cause."

So what is good cause? That's something the Court will have to decide over time. At the outset, the Court has found good cause to consider on appeal most challenges to sentencing proceedings and the sentences imposed during them. The notion that the defendant surrenders all rights and challenges with the plea doesn't hold as much water when applied to proceedings that follow its entry. The Court's wings are clipped even further by § 824.29 – even if there is good cause to appeal and even if there is some valid claim of a defect in the plea, the conviction will not be vacated absent a finding that but for the defect the defendant would not have pled guilty in the first place. This is true regardless of what is written in the court rules.

The final major volte-face by the Legislature in 2019 was Iowa Code § 814.7. Ineffective assistance of counsel. I've discussed it before. Steeped in the Sixth Amendment right to counsel, an allegation of ineffective assistance can mean one of two things. Or both. There can be a general claim that one's attorney, especially an attorney appointed by the court, is so blatantly incompetent that the defendant essentially didn't receive counsel at the level guaranteed by the Bill of Rights.

More commonly, ineffective assistance is a device to raise an issue on appeal that otherwise would be waived. The issues were there but the lawyer didn't object, or didn't object sufficiently to preserve them for consideration by the appellate courts. The argument goes that (1) one of my constitutional trial rights was violated by the admission at trial of certain evidence or by the context of the proceedings, (2) my attorney did not object at trial, (3) there was no valid strategic reason my attorney did not object, (4) a competent attorney would have objected, and (5) the outcome of my case would have been different had my attorney objected.

Ineffective assistance is a very, very common argument to be advanced in criminal appeals. As an erstwhile appellate attorney, I brought claims of ineffective assistance against nearly all of the criminal defense bar practicing at the time. And I've had several raised against me. It is a necessary tool for error preservation.

As difficult as it is generally to secure the reversal of a criminal conviction on appeal, it is substantially more difficult to prevail on a claim of ineffective assistance. Most lack merit, and many are downright frivolous. But like everything else, ineffective assistance claims are weak grounds for appeal *except when they are not*. And when you find one that does have merit, and you manage to obtain relief for a client whose conviction is the product of an attorney's mistake, then justice is done.

How to approach ineffective assistance claims has been the subject of constant evolution over the years. When a defendant's appeal is concluded and final, the next possible avenue for relief is to file a petition for postconviction relief under Iowa Code Chapter 822. An action for postconviction relief is the Iowa equivalent of a request for a writ of habeas corpus mentioned in article I, section 9 of the United States Constitution. It is a lawsuit against the State of Iowa arguing that the petitioner is being held illegally in custody. It is a collateral attack on one's conviction, on grounds that do not appear in the record and thus can't be advanced on direct appeal.

Whether a claim of ineffective assistance belongs in the Supreme Court on direct appeal or in a petition for postconviction relief in the district court has been the funny bone of the criminal review process. In the majority of cases, there are aspects to the claim that must be proven by facts outside the record of trial. Did the trial attorney have some valid strategic ground for neglecting to object? That's the big one, for which the trial attorney must be put on the witness stand to answer the question. But there are some failures that are justifiable by no valid strategy. Had counsel not been asleep at the wheel the defendant would not be serving a massive prison sentence. Everything the Supreme Court needs to know is in the trial record. A Supreme Court appeal can last about a year. A postconviction relief proceeding can go on for two or more years, followed by another year on appeal. The defendant with the winning lottery ticket would prefer to cash it out as quickly as possible, rather than sitting on it on a bunk in Fort Madison for three or four years.

The appellate courts went back and forth over the years on how to address ineffective assistance claims in a manner that would further judicial economy while protecting litigants with colorable claims. Postconviction relief has always been the preferred remedy but, as I say, there are exceptions. There was a period of time prior to 2004 during which the Court made itself the gatekeeper. If there was a potential argument of ineffective assistance, even one provable only with facts outside the trial record, the defendant was expected to mention it in the direct appeal and ask that it be preserved for postconviction relief. That defendant might be precluded from raising ineffective assistance claims in a postconviction action if they were not preserved on direct appeal. A major risk in this scheme was that the Court might, and occasionally did, find the record sufficient to resolve the issue on appeal and might render a final decision on an issue that needed to be fleshed out in more detail. The issue would then be considered fully litigated and could not be re-asserted in postconviction relief, where it could have been more sufficiently proven out.

And in some cases there is absolutely nothing in the trial record to even suggest an error by counsel. Such an issue may not even come to light until after the appeal process is concluded, yet the defendant might be penalized for not preserving it in the direct appeal.

In 2004, the Legislature stepped in with, what to me at least, was a workable solution. Under Iowa Code § 814.7, a defendant could raise an ineffective assistance claim for the first time by filing a petition for postconviction relief and was not required to do so on appeal. Or the defendant could take the position that there is enough in the record to raise the issue on direct appeal and take that route. If so, it was for the Court to decide if the question was ripe for review at that point, or whether to preserve it for postconviction review.

All of that went out the window in 2019 when § 814.7 was amended to remove all its provisions except that ineffective assistance may be raised in a petition for postconviction relief. The "claim shall not be decided on direct appeal from the criminal proceedings." Regardless of guilt or innocence, a defendant convicted in a constitutionally defective proceeding whose attorney failed to object, solely out of incompetence and without any strategic justification, must now sit in prison for two or three years or more to await his or her day in court.

All these 2019 limitations on the jurisdiction and the authority of the Court came in Senate File 589. I don't know much about the history of the bill, which was jam-packed with other developments in Iowa criminal law and procedure. As I say, there is some logic in each of them, and each addresses lingering issues with which the Court has wrestled over the years. But the solutions consist of very sweeping and absolute restrictions on judicial authority. It very well may have been the attorney general, who at the time was Democrat Thomas Miller, who walked the proposals over to the Legislature. Even then, it was not uncommon for the attorney general to lobby for statutory changes. I don't know if Chief Justice Cady or the Court had any position on them. References to the rules of criminal procedure as having no effect where they are inconsistent with the new statutes are, to me, an indication that they didn't come from the Court. Perhaps the justices who spoke approvingly to legislative leaders about modifying the process for the selection of the chief justice had other ideas that went into the drafting of SF 589.

All I can say about them is that they were passed in 2019

by the same Legislature, and signed by the same governor, that approved the new plan for the selection of justices and of the chief justice.

By any measure, it didn't end in 2019.

The War Rages On

Another strategy employed by the Legislature to block the Supreme Court from functioning as a check on its activities came to light in the 2023 session during consideration of Senate File 542, relating to the employment of minors. Among other things, the bill allows minors between the ages of 14 and 17 to work in fields in which they previously were not able to do so, including manufacturing, roofing and demolition. The bill was the subject of intense debate that continued throughout the night until its passage just before 5 a.m. on April 18, on a vote that closely followed party lines. Democrats in the Senate attempted to mitigate the potential dangers presented by broadening the access to child labor with a series of unsuccessful amendments that would do such things as increasing workers compensation for minors injured in perilous jobs and removing a provision that would allow minors over the age of 16 with parental permission to serve alcohol in bars and restaurants.

During the debate, Democratic Senator Bill Dotzler, Jr. attempted to pose questions to the bill's floor manager, Republican Senator Adrian Dickey, to determine its scope. The floor manager refused to yield the floor for the question, and Senate Majority Leader Matt Whitver joined the refusal. Senator Dotzler, a veteran of the United States Army Security Agency now in his 20th year in the Senate, could recall no time during his service in that body that a bill's sponsors refused to entertain questions during debate.

Though unprecedented, the Senate File 542 tactic was not isolated. On the following day, Senator Ken Roozeboom, sponsor of a bill to limit students' access to certain books and to gender-affirming care, refused to answer questions about penalties to which schoolteachers might be exposed by violating its terms.

The Republican leadership did not deny employing the tactic, and did not deny that Republican senators had been instructed not to answer questions during debate or to provide any indication of the intent behind the sweeping legislation that was being passed. Candidly, it was admitted that the purpose of the scheme was to evade judicial review of the bills by the Supreme Court.

The reason was the March 23, 2023 decision of the Supreme Court in *LS Power Midcontinent, LLC v State*, 988 N.W.2d 316 (Iowa 2023).

LS Power Midcontinent involved Iowa Code § 478.16, that gave "incumbent" energy producers the right of first refusal in the market for electric energy over other prospective bidders. Challenges to the legality of § 478.16 were denied in the district court on the ground that the otherwise qualified non-incumbent bidders did not have standing to sue, and projects by the incumbent providers were allowed to proceed. In a unanimous decision of the four justices who participated in the ruling, Justice Thomas Waterman granted a temporary injunction allowing the plaintiffs to proceed with their challenge.

What drew the ire of the Republican leadership in the Senate was language in Justice Waterman's opinion that was highly critical about the manner in which § 478.16 was enacted by the Senate. At 1:30 a.m. on the final day of the 2020 legislative session, the right of first refusal provision was tacked onto a general appropriations bill that was over fifty pages in length and contained 34 divisions. The addition was spotted by several Democratic senators, who questioned the Republican floor leader about its history, which in fact was non-existent. The floor manager responded with several vague and inaccurate claims that it had passed through the subcommittee, the committee and the Senate. Additionally, he attempted to explain the bill away with the dubious assertion that the right of first refusal means that the incumbent supplier must be willing to provide the service at the rate proposed by a lower-bidder, or else lose the project to the latter. Justice Waterman characterized the process as "logrolling."

One month after the *LS Power Midcontinent* opinion was announced, the Republican leadership was not going to let that happen again. The majority leader, a former wide receiver for the Iowa State Cyclones and former assistant coach for the Iowa Barnstormers, has a law degree from Drake University. One of the factors used by appellate courts to interpret and gauge the validity of legislation is the intent of the Legislature in passing it. The majority leader's position (which is not inconsistent with that of many prominent appellate jurists) is that the clearest statement of the Legislature in passing a bill is the language of the bill itself, and not remarks made during debate on the floor. Senate Republicans, therefore, would no longer discuss the intent of their legislation "until that question is resolved." In effect, bills would now be introduced and passed without debate, for no other reason than to cut the prospect of Supreme Court review out of the process.

A possible alternative, of course, might be to base legislative decisions on proper, high-minded motives rather than sinister ones and to strive, as much as possible, for honesty in their debates. For now, however, the Supreme Court would have no evidence upon which to rely in exercising its judicial review of the Legislature.

Sometimes when the Supreme Court does its job and reviews the validity of a statute or a government activity under the bright light of the Iowa Constitution, the Legislature endeavors to step in and to overrule statutorily the Court's decision. Remember *State v. Wright*, 961 N.W.2d 396 (Iowa 2021), in which our Court determined that under article I, section 8 of the Iowa Constitution it would not follow the Fourth Amendment holding of the United States Supreme Court in *California v. Greenwood*, 486 U.S. 35 (1988) that a person has no expectation of privacy in trash left out for pickup? Under our Constitution, the seizure and search of trash without a warrant is not valid.

In 2022, the Legislature responded to *Wright* with Iowa Code § 808.16, captioned "Exception to search warrant requirement - garbage searches." It's public policy in Iowa under the bill that there is no expectation of privacy in garbage left out for collection in a publicly accessible area. Any local health ordinance restricting trash collection "shall not be construed by a person to create a reasonable expectation of privacy in garbage placed outside of the person's residence for waste collection in a publicly accessible area." Garbage left outside the house is "deemed abandoned property and shall not be considered to be constitutionally protected papers or effects of the person." Law enforcement, consequently, "may conduct a search and may seize garbage placed outside of a person's residence for waste collection in a publicly accessible area without making an application for a search warrant."

To the extent that it's not fully able to hogtie the Judicial Branch and to populate the courts with judges who share its extreme political philosophy, the Legislature believes that it is within its province to fashion a statutory exception to the constitutionally mandated search warrant requirement, to usurp the judicial function of defining a subject's reasonable expectations of privacy under the constitution, and to construe local health ordinances. The latter, admittedly, is not outside the province of the legislative branch. There is a notion under Iowa's home rule scheme of what's referred to as conflict preemption. The cities, towns and other municipalities may make their own laws but, to the extent that a local law conflicts with one passed by the Legislature, the statewide law wins out. But, as far as I now, no species of preemption authorizes the Legislature to overrule a Supreme Court interpretation of the state constitution.

Any feeling that the war is over between the Executive and the Legislature, on one side, and the Judiciary on the other, dissipated with what happened on June 16, 2023 in *Planned Parenthood v. Reynolds*, the fetal heartbeat bill case. Back in

2018 Governor Reynolds got her bill that prohibited health care providers from performing abortions on fetuses that displayed a fetal heartbeat, usually at about six weeks. To anyone aware of the status of the law at that time, the fetal heartbeat bill was dead on arrival. *Roe v. Wade* was still in place, and the Iowa Supreme Court had previously found that, as in *Roe*, the right to an abortion was fundamental under the Iowa Constitution. A state district court judge granted a permanent injunction in 2019 barring enforcement of the bill. Four years later, the Iowa Supreme Court backtracked a little and found that choice wasn't a fundamental right under the state constitution but that under *Planned Parenthood v.Casey* restrictions were invalid if they placed an undue burden on the recipient. Then *Dobbs v. Jackson Women's Health Organization* came down in 2022, and the governor went back into court to undo the injunction. The district court balked, so she took it to "her" Supreme Court.

She didn't get the result she wanted. Actually, she didn't get *any* result, on the grand scale of things. The Court split 3-3. The injunction remained in effect. But the governor and the Legislature were free to go back in and enact something that was equally, or perhaps *more*, draconian.

The written opinions, in a case where written opinions were not required, fascinated me, along with the split in the justices on the case. On one hand, Justice Waterman authored the opinion that would uphold Judge Gogerty's continuation of the enforcement of the 2019 injunction, and her reasoning. He was joined by Justice Mansfield and Chief Justice Christensen. Justice McDonald and Justice McDermott both wrote opinions finding essentially that, with *Dobbs*, the fetal heartbeat bill is no longer invalid, and could now be enforced. Justice May came down on that side. It's dangerous to use these votes to evidence assumptions that Justices McDermott, McDonald and May support restrictions on abortion, and that Justice Waterman and those who joined him do not, because the issues are more complex than that and there may have been more at play than what meets the eye.

Notwithstanding the constant unpredictability of all of the members of the Court since 2010 (with the possible exception of Justice May, on whom the jury is still out), I still have a tendency to want to put them in boxes. This one is our guy. This one is theirs. I form those judgments based upon my reading of their opinions. But the opinions I read are almost exclusively in criminal cases. So a justice who comes across as progressive for my purposes may not be so liberal for others.

I personally suspect, as I've said, that Governor Reynolds is doing everything she can do to assemble "her" Court, a gift that will keep giving even long after she is gone. Of the seven justices, she has selected five – Justice McDonald, Justice McDermott, Justice Oxley, Justice May and Chief Justice Christensen. Governor Branstad appointed Justices Mansfield and Waterman. From the outset, Justices McDermott and Oxley seemed to be ones most likely to fall my way in a case. I was gravely concerned about Justice McDonald at first, then pleasantly surprised by some of huge steps he has taken in cases that followed. Chief Justice Christensen is a very reasonable swing vote. Although they've "helped out" in some criminal cases, Justices Mansfield and Waterman are most predictably conservative.

That's my perspective, based upon my interests. The public perception is that they're *all* conservatives, because they were all appointed by Republican governors. The perception of at least a segment of the public is that the Republicans have taken advantage of the opportunity to "stack the Court." But what I see, based on the cases I read, is a better Court *for me* than what we had 30 years ago, when I last played that venue.

I have a suspicion that some Presidents and governors (Kim Reynolds included) don't care a whole lot about where their judicial appointees come down on criminal procedural issues. The bread and butter of judicial selection is *abortion*. There's always been this block of voters who will go your way for no other reason than how you come down on abortion. I've heard supporters of Donald Trump refer to him as our greatest pro-life President, a God-fearing Christian man who espouses all our best values. *Give me a fucking break.* What Donald Trump did was to throw out three names that shifted the ideological balance of the Court from where it was in *Roe* to where it was in *Dobbs*. It was all about holding that block of voters. Nothing more.

Is there a litmus test with Governor Reynolds? Does the question come up in her interviews for open seats on the Court? Who knows?

But how did she fare in the 2023 *Planned Parenthood Case*? Of her five appointments, two were women. Neither voted to restrict abortion. One simply did not vote. The other three did. Of those three, two were justices I would most likely expect to see in my corner in a criminal case that has constitutional overtones. On the other hand, two of the three who voted to preserve the right to an abortion were, in my eyes, the most conservative voices on the Court. They were appointed by Governor Branstad, a lawyer himself. The third was a woman.

What really struck me about the *Planned Parenthood* case was the content of Justice Waterman's opinion. The word is that he and Justice Mansfield were the two who crossed the road in 2019 to collaborate with the Legislature in restructuring Iowa's judicial selection process, and its process for selecting the chief justice. But his opinion, onto which Justice Mansfield signed, was a trembling broadside blow to the Legislature and the governor. We generally don't write opinions in these cases, he notes, but it is necessary to articulate our position in response to opinions written by Justices McDonald and McDermott. The governor didn't appeal the injunction in 2019. The Legislature passed the fetal heartbeat bill knowing it wouldn't be allowed to go into effect. It was, as Justice Waterman put it, a "hypothetical law." An amendment to the Iowa Constitution declaring that there is no right to an abortion was passed in 2021, but the second vote necessary to get it on the 2024 ballot did not occur in 2023. The Legislature had time after Judge Gogerty declined to dissolve the injunction to once again pass a fetal heartbeat bill, but did not do so. An amicus brief was filed in the appeal of her ruling that was signed by a number of Iowa legislators, but not enough to pass the bill if it was brought up for a vote. The undue burden standard remains the law in Iowa regardless of *Dobbs*. We (the Court) are being asked to do the Legislature's job.

Justice Waterman's opinion goes on to address the merits of the issue that remains unresolved in the case because of the 3-3 tie. He reminded readers that he dissented from the majority in *State v. Wright*, dealing with the warrantless seizure of garbage left on the curb of a private residence.

"It would be ironic and troubling," he posits, "for our court to become the first state supreme court in the nation to hold that trash set out in a garbage can for collection is entitled to more constitutional protection than a woman's interest in autonomy and dominion over her own body."

In view of the recent history of the governor, the Legislature and the Court, how likely is it that such behavior will go unpunished? Does voting with Justice Waterman in this case generate a likelihood of opposition in an upcoming judicial retention election? How much does it matter to these three? Setting aside factors like gender and by which governor each justice was appointed, it just so happens that Justices Waterman and Mansfield and Chief Justice Christensen are the oldest members of the Court. All three are slated for retention elections in 2028. With the exception of Chief Justice Christensen, each faces mandatory retirement within three years of retention. The wrong result in a retention election would wreak less havoc on their lives than it would upon those of a 48-year-old (in 2023) Justice Christopher McDonald or a 45-year old Matthew McDermott.

What else might they stoop to? It's beyond the limits of *my* imagination.

That sounds pretty melodramatic, doesn't it? And more than a little paranoid.

But maybe not. Get this. Just hours after I wrote out the "what else might they stoop to" language above about the potential blowback from the *Planned Parenthood* decision (or, more aptly, the *non*-decision) that was announced two days earlier, what comes out over the Associated Press but Bob Vander Plaats going after Justices Waterman and Mansfield and Chief Justice Christensen.

"These three dissenters," he tells us, "have shown blatant disrespect for the Constitution, the people's representatives, and we the people. They should resign, be impeached or be ousted."

In the first place, the three justices weren't dissenters. It was a 3-3 affirmance by operation of law. There is no governing majority opinion and therefore no dissent. And if there was an opinion that would be considered the majority opinion (or at least the plurality) it would be Justice Waterman's, because it's consistent with the result. When Bob Vander Plaats talks about disrespect for "we the people," he doesn't take into account the fact that the majority of Iowans don't share his vision of morality on this issue.

The glaring irony of these circumstances is that two of the three justices he now wants to run out of office are the remaining replacements following the purge he initiated in 2010. The circumstances bear a striking resemblance to those we've seen in third-world countries such as North Korea, Iraq under Saddam Hussein, and Rwanda (or here during the Trump Administration) where the fair-haired boys find themselves catapulted into positions of authority, only to vanish from public view when they are perceived as no longer toeing the party line. Perhaps Bob Vander Plaats could learn to see this as evidence that there may be other, more accurate, interpretations of the constitution than just his.

It may be that the only way Bob Vander Plaats would ever get the results he wanted would be if we had a Supreme Court populated exclusively by evangelical pastors.

But once again I digress, don't I?

Why This All Matters

Having said all of the above, this is a book about revisions to the Iowa Rules of Criminal Procedure. After convening a blue-ribbon task force to review them and to revise them extensively, the Iowa Supreme Court produced a set of rules more in tune with our changing times and designed to level the playing field somewhat for all participants. As the day approached that they were to take effect, the author of *4A Iowa Practice*: *Criminal Procedure* worked feverishly to bring his treatise in line with the impending changes. Then out of the blue, on the eve of publication, the Iowa Legislature stepped in and flipped on the red light. Twice.

So, all of what's gone on with the new rules, and with me especially, since February 2022 -- who really cares?

I care, obviously, because of all the time I've had to invest in putting together an up-to-date, accurate manual that will help guide practitioners through the changes. Maintenance of the manual is the final vestige of my law career, and there have been times during this recent ordeal that's it's been my full-time job. I have no complaints about that. What aggrieves me are the multiple times I've stood at the precipice of publication, then found myself having to chuck the hours and hours of work I've sunk into revisions that now once again are damned to be superseded.

Yes, I care. My publisher cares. They need to put out a book. The practitioners care — the criminal attorneys on both sides of the courtroom, and some on the bench, who rely on *4A Iowa Practice: Criminal Procedure* as a starting point in maneuvering through the turbulent rapids of our field of practice. How is life going to change for them after the final manifestation of the rules emerges through the mist of battle?

Other than that, I realize, the rest of the world is oblivious. Unaffected. I'm the little guy in the thatched roof hut whose home is knocked off its foundation during the siege.

You may not worry about me. But you should worry

about the siege. My tongue-in-cheek hypothetical in response to Gretsch's question about *Varnum* at the 35-year reunion. Think about that.

Why *don't* we let the voters decide whether gay people have the right under our Constitution to marry each other?

Okay. Then why don't we disenfranchise all the voters who went for Republican candidates in 2008? The votes may have been there for that at the time. Maybe it's not a joke. Maybe it can be done.

Well, let's first decide who gets to vote. Let's modify the voting districts and voter qualifications to ensure that as many as possible of the people who cast their ballots are people who think and vote like I do. We can do it under the pretense of combatting the voter fraud we suspect, though were unable to prove, occurred in prior elections. But only in the elections we lost.

Once we've got our guy living in Terrace Hill and we've commandeered a sizable majority in both houses in the Legislature, let's ram as many of our extremist policies down the throats of our populace as we can manage. In doing that we can tighten our grip even more firmly on the wheel of power.

Let's hogtie the state auditor, the only remaining elected official with the power and motivation to reach for the brakes.

And then finally, when it comes down to any meaningful review of this power grab in the courts, let's do what we can do to hogtie the courts. Let's appoint ourselves the *guardian ad litem* of the Supreme Court and keep a watchful eye on their every move.

What happened to me was a small peripheral symptom of all of that. But it happened. And there's no end in sight.

It's not just Iowa. It's happening all over the United States. These tactics aren't something Governor Reynolds and her Legislature just came up with. She's following a well-scripted, oft-utilized game plan developed in other states. And she's not just a follower. Governor Reynolds and what she's done to our state are held up by her like-minded allies as a shining example of how it could be in theirs. Especially as the Iowa Caucuses remain the first defining battle in the year-long war for the Republican Presidential nomination, I've been pandered to in political commercials by candidates declaring *I want to run America the way Governor Kim Reynolds has run Iowa.*

And that's why this all matters.

THE MUSIC OF B. JOHN BURNS

John's 2022 album *Garbage Day* is available for downloading and streaming on Apple Music, iTunes, Spotify, Amazon Music Unlimited, YouTube Music, Deezer, and many other services.

Other Available Albums:

A Mile Off Shore (2021)

Badass Storm 2020

My May Day Songbook (2020)
Form Letter from a Retired Prostitute (2019)
Ample Waves of Gray (2018)
The Creator (2017)
Hit From Behind (2016)
Forty Years Ago Today (2015)
Mutants That I'll Never Understand (2014)
Undefeated (2013)
Ridiculously High (2012)
Year of the Jumping Flea (2011)

Up Here on the 19th Floor (2010)
High Adventure on the Road (2009)
Let Me Play (2008)
The Holiday Album (not really) (2007)
Lillian Asplund (2006)
West Highland White (2005)
Long Talk on a Windy Day (2004)
The Dunk Tank (2003)
Some of my Friends (2002)
Report of the Chairman (2000)
The A.S.P.C.M. (1999, 2001)

B. JOHN BURNS III

Three Sonatas for Piano (1982, 1983, 1984)
Twenty Two (1978, 1979)

ABOUT THE AUTHOR

B. John Burns

B. John Burns is an obscure Johnston, Iowa songwriter celebrating his Golden Jubilee in 2022. Since writing "Last Airport Home" in September 1972, John has written approximately 5,000 songs in nearly every genre of music. He has appeared in 25 states, and continues to perform his tunes for mostly small, intimate audiences on piano, guitar and ukulele.

To put food on the table, John has worked as a busboy, a stereo salesman, a bank messenger, a criminal defense attorney, a grill cook, a Pinkerton guard, a political organizer, a bank bookkeeper, a published author, a paid actor, and a martial arts instructor. Through it all, he has continued to write music on nearly a daily basis.

www.bjohnburnswriter.com

BOOKS BY THIS AUTHOR

Baby Pictures: My Year On The Road With Baby Lester And The Buggybumpers

Dead Horses: A Random Collection Of Longwinded But Entirerly True Stories About My Favorite Subject

El Mensajero

4A Iowa Practice: Criminal Procedure